First World War
and Army of Occupation
War Diary
France, Belgium and Germany

7 INDIAN (MEERUT) DIVISION
20 (Garhwal) Indian Infantry Brigade
39 Garhwal Rifles
9 August 1914 - 26 November 1915

WO95/3945/2

The Naval & Military Press Ltd
www.nmarchive.com
Published in association with The National Archives

Published by

The Naval & Military Press Ltd

Unit 10 Ridgewood Industrial Park,
Uckfield, East Sussex,
TN22 5QE England
Tel: +44 (0) 1825 749494

www.naval-military-press.com

www.nmarchive.com

This diary has been reprinted in facsimile from the original. Any imperfections are inevitably reproduced and the quality may fall short of modern type and cartographic standards.

© **Crown Copyright**
Images reproduced by permission of The National Archives, London, England, 2015.

Contents

Document type	Place/Title	Date From	Date To
Heading	WO95/3945/3/39 Garhwal Rgt		
Heading	Meerut Division Garhwal Brigade		
Heading	Meerut Division Aug-Dec 1914 2/39th Garhwal Rifles		
Diagram etc	Diagram		
Heading	Garhwal Rifles Form 21/8/14 To 31/12/14 Volume I Pp 1 To 50 Volume II Pp 1 To 15		
War Diary	Dogadda	21/08/1914	21/08/1914
War Diary	Kotdwara	22/08/1914	30/08/1914
War Diary	Lahore	31/08/1914	31/08/1914
War Diary	Samasata	01/09/1914	01/09/1914
War Diary	Karachi	02/09/1914	15/09/1914
War Diary	S.S.Coconada Kiamari Docks	16/09/1914	20/10/1914
War Diary	S.S.Coconada at Sea	21/09/1914	02/10/1914
War Diary	S.S.Coconada Suez	03/10/1914	03/10/1914
War Diary	S.S.Coconada Port Said	04/10/1914	11/10/1914
War Diary	S.S.Coconada at Sea	06/10/1914	11/10/1914
War Diary	S.S.Coconada and Maeseilles	12/10/1914	13/10/1914
War Diary	Camp La Valentine Marseilles	14/10/1914	18/10/1914
War Diary	In The Train	19/10/1914	20/10/1914
War Diary	In The Train And Camp Les Grouves Orleans	21/10/1914	21/10/1914
War Diary	Camp Les Groues Orleans	22/10/1914	26/10/1914
War Diary	In The Train	27/10/1914	27/10/1914
War Diary	In The Train And Calonnes	28/10/1914	28/10/1914
War Diary	Billets Calonnes And In The Trenches 1st Day	29/10/1914	29/10/1914
War Diary	In The Trenches 2nd Day	30/10/1914	30/10/1914
Miscellaneous	In The Trenches 3rd Day	31/10/1914	31/10/1914
War Diary	In The Trenches 4th Day	01/11/1914	01/11/1914
War Diary	In The Trenches 5th Day	02/11/1914	02/11/1914
War Diary	In The Trenches 6th Day	03/11/1914	03/11/1914
War Diary	In The Trenches 7th Day	04/11/1914	04/11/1914
War Diary	In The Trenches 8th Day	05/11/1914	05/11/1914
War Diary	In The Trenches 9th Day	06/11/1914	06/11/1914
War Diary	In The Trenches 10th Day	07/11/1914	07/11/1914
Miscellaneous	P.A. 2/39 Garhwal Diary		
Miscellaneous	Broad Park House		
Miscellaneous	From The Brigade Major Garhwal Brigade		
War Diary	In The Trenches 11th Day	08/11/1914	08/11/1914
War Diary	In The Trenches 12th Day	09/11/1914	09/11/1914
War Diary	In The Trenches 13th Day	10/11/1914	10/11/1914
War Diary	In The Trenches 14th Day	11/11/1914	11/11/1914
War Diary	In The Trenches 15th Day	12/11/1914	12/11/1914
War Diary	In The Trenches 16th Day	13/11/1914	13/11/1914
War Diary	In The Trenches 17th Day	14/11/1914	14/11/1914
War Diary	In The Trenches 18th Day	15/11/1914	15/11/1914
War Diary	In The Trenches 19th Day	16/11/1914	16/11/1914
War Diary	In The Trenches 20th Day	17/11/1914	17/11/1914
War Diary	In Billets La Touret	18/11/1914	18/11/1914
War Diary	In Billets La Touret And Rue De Bois	19/11/1914	19/11/1914
War Diary	Billets Rue De Bois	20/11/1914	22/11/1914
War Diary	Billets La Couture	23/11/1914	24/11/1914

War Diary	Billets La Couture And In The Trenches Festybert	25/11/1914	25/11/1914
War Diary	In The Trenches Festubert	26/11/1914	28/11/1914
War Diary	Billets La Couture	29/11/1914	01/12/1914
War Diary	Billets La Couture And In The Trenches Riche Bourg	02/12/1914	02/12/1914
War Diary	In The Trenches	05/12/1914	24/12/1914
War Diary	In The Trenches Christmas Day	25/12/1914	25/12/1914
War Diary	In The Trenches	26/12/1914	26/12/1914
War Diary	In The Trenches And Billets Lacouture	27/12/1914	27/12/1914
War Diary	Billets Paradis	28/12/1914	28/12/1914
War Diary	Billets Robecq	29/12/1914	29/12/1914
War Diary	Billets	30/12/1914	30/12/1914
War Diary	Billets Hurionville	30/12/1914	30/12/1914
War Diary	Hurionville	31/12/1914	31/12/1914
Heading	War Diary of 2/39th Garhwal Rifles From 1st January 1915 To 31st January 1915		
War Diary	Hurionville	01/01/1915	20/01/1915
War Diary	Calonne	21/01/1915	21/01/1915
War Diary	Vieille Chapelle	22/01/1915	22/01/1915
War Diary	Richeborg St Vaast	23/01/1915	25/01/1915
War Diary	Trenches Rue De Bois	26/01/1915	29/01/1915
War Diary	Billets Vieille Chapelle	30/01/1915	31/01/1915
Heading	War Diary of 2/39th Garhwal Rifles From 1st February 1915 To 28th February 1915		
War Diary	Billets Vieille Chappele	01/02/1915	03/02/1915
War Diary	Billets Richebourg St Vaast	04/02/1915	07/02/1915
War Diary	Trenches Rue De Bois	08/02/1915	11/02/1915
War Diary	Billets Vieille Chapelle	12/02/1915	20/02/1915
War Diary	Trenches Rue De L'Epinette	21/02/1915	26/02/1915
War Diary	Rue De L'Epinette	27/02/1915	28/02/1915
Heading	War Diary With Appendices Of 2nd Battalion 39th Garhwal Rifles From 1st March 1915 To 31st March 1915		
War Diary	Billets Zelobes	01/03/1915	07/03/1915
War Diary	Zelobes and Richebourg St Vaast	08/03/1915	08/03/1915
War Diary	Richebourg St Vaast	09/03/1915	09/03/1915
War Diary	Neuve Chapelle And Vicinity	10/03/1915	10/03/1915
War Diary	Trenches	11/03/1915	11/03/1915
War Diary	La Couture And Croix Marmeuse And Richebourg St Vaast	12/03/1915	12/03/1915
War Diary	Richebourg St Vaast And Zelobes	13/03/1915	13/03/1915
War Diary	Zelobes	14/03/1915	28/03/1915
War Diary	Calonne	29/03/1915	31/03/1915
Miscellaneous	The Officer Commanding	16/03/1915	16/03/1915
Heading	7 Meerut Div 20 Garhwal Bde Garhwal Rifles Late 1/39 2/39 Garhwal Rifles 1914 Aug-1915 Nov		
Heading	War Diary 1/39th Garhwalls From 9.8.14 To 29/8/14 Volume I		
Heading	Meerut Division 1/39th Lahore Rifles 1914 Aug-1915 Mar		
Diagram etc	Diagram		
War Diary	Lansdowne	09/08/1914	20/08/1914
War Diary	Dogadda	21/08/1914	21/08/1914
War Diary	Kotdwara	22/08/1914	29/08/1914
Heading	1/39 Garhwal Rifles 30/8/14-1/10/14		
War Diary		30/08/1914	01/09/1914
War Diary	Karachi	02/09/1914	02/09/1914

War Diary	H.T. Ekma	03/09/1914	03/10/1914
War Diary	Port Said	04/10/1914	14/10/1914
War Diary	Camp La Valentine	15/10/1914	16/10/1914
Miscellaneous	Extract From Routine Orders By Lieut General C.A. Anderson C.B. Commanding Meerut Divn. At Sea.	07/10/1914	07/10/1914
War Diary		16/10/1914	18/10/1914
War Diary	In The Train	18/10/1914	18/10/1914
War Diary	Trenches To Orleans	19/10/1914	20/10/1914
War Diary	Orleans	21/10/1914	27/10/1914
War Diary	Calonne	28/10/1914	28/10/1914
War Diary	Richebourg Vicinity	28/10/1914	28/10/1914
War Diary	Les Glatigmes	29/10/1914	29/10/1914
War Diary	Richebourg	29/10/1914	31/10/1914
Miscellaneous	On His Majesty's Service.		
War Diary	Richebourg L'Avoue	31/10/1914	19/11/1914
War Diary	Richebourg L'Avoue Letouret	20/11/1914	23/11/1914
War Diary	La Couture	23/11/1914	23/11/1914
Miscellaneous	Office Commanding		
Diagram etc	Diagram		
Heading	39th Garhwal Rifles 9th Dec-29th Dec 14		
Miscellaneous	On His Majesty's Service.		
War Diary	Richebourg L'Avoue	09/12/1914	27/12/1914
War Diary	Paradis	28/12/1914	29/12/1914
War Diary	Appx I		
Miscellaneous	The Adjutant 1/39th G. Appx II		
Miscellaneous	Report On German Trenches	25/12/1914	25/12/1914
Diagram etc	Diagram		
Heading	39th Garhwal Rifles 30/12/14-31/1/15		
Miscellaneous	On His Majesty's Service.		
Miscellaneous		31/01/1915	31/01/1915
War Diary	Fosse No3 De Ferfay	30/12/1914	20/01/1915
War Diary	Calonne	21/01/1915	22/01/1915
War Diary	Vielle Chapelle	22/01/1915	22/01/1915
War Diary	Rue De Berceau	23/01/1915	23/01/1915
War Diary	Rue De Bois	24/01/1915	25/01/1915
War Diary	Richebourg St Vaast	26/01/1915	29/01/1915
War Diary	Vielle Chapelle	30/01/1915	31/01/1915
Heading	War Diary With Appendices Of 1/39th Garhwal Rifles From 1st February 1915 To 29th March 1915		
War Diary	Vieille Chapelle	01/02/1915	04/02/1915
War Diary	Richebourg L'Avoue	05/02/1915	08/02/1915
War Diary	Richebourg St.Vaast	09/02/1915	11/02/1915
War Diary	Lacouture Vielle Chapelle	12/02/1915	21/02/1915
War Diary	Rue De L'Epinette	25/02/1915	28/02/1915
War Diary	Locon	01/03/1915	08/03/1915
War Diary	Vieille Chapelle	09/03/1915	09/03/1915
War Diary	L'epinette (Lestrem Area)	14/02/1915	14/02/1915
War Diary	L'epinette	15/03/1915	23/03/1915
War Diary	Epinette	24/03/1915	24/03/1915
War Diary	Vielle Chapelle	25/03/1915	28/03/1915
War Diary	Vielle Chapelle And Calonne	29/03/1915	29/03/1915
Miscellaneous	Appx XVII	09/03/1915	09/03/1915
Operation(al) Order(s)	Operation Order No 25 By Brigadier General C.G. Blackader D.S.O. Commanding Garhwal Bde	09/03/1915	09/03/1915
Miscellaneous	Distribution of Attacking lists		
Miscellaneous	Table 4	09/03/1915	09/03/1915

Miscellaneous	Battle of Neuve Chapelle		
Miscellaneous	Report Of Operation From 10 March To 8 am 11 March 1915	11/03/1915	11/03/1915
Miscellaneous	Report Of Operation From 8 am 11th March To 8 pm 12 March		
Heading	Meerut Division Garhwal Brigade Garhwal Rifles April-Nov 1915		
Heading	War Diary of Garhwal Rifles From 1st April 1915 To 30th April 1915		
War Diary	Calonne	01/04/1915	09/04/1915
War Diary	Vielle Chapelle	10/04/1915	12/04/1915
War Diary	La Couture	13/04/1915	22/04/1915
War Diary	La Couture Calonne	23/04/1915	23/04/1915
War Diary	La Couture	23/04/1915	27/04/1915
War Diary	Trenches Neuve Chapelle	28/04/1915	30/04/1915
Heading	War Diary of Garhwal Rifles From 1st May To 31st May 1915		
War Diary	Trenches Neuve Chapelle	01/05/1915	05/05/1915
War Diary	Billets Loretto Road	06/05/1915	08/05/1915
War Diary	Trenches	08/05/1915	15/05/1915
War Diary	Trenches B2 Rue De Bois	16/05/1915	16/05/1915
War Diary	Croix Barbee	17/05/1915	17/05/1915
War Diary	Billets Croix Barbee	18/05/1915	25/05/1915
War Diary	Trenches Rue Du Bois	26/05/1915	26/05/1915
War Diary	Trenches Rue Du Bois Richebourg L'avoue	27/05/1915	28/05/1915
War Diary	Trenches Rue Du Bois	29/05/1915	30/05/1915
War Diary	Trenches Rue Du Bois Richebourg L'avoue	31/05/1915	31/05/1915
Heading	War Diary of Garhwal Rifles From 1st June 1915 To 30th June 1915		
War Diary	Billets Vielle Chapelle	01/06/1915	01/06/1915
War Diary	Billets Rue Marsy Vielle Chapelle	02/06/1915	07/06/1915
War Diary	Bivouac Trenches Near Rue Des Berceaux	08/06/1915	18/06/1915
War Diary	Trenches C.Sub-Section	19/06/1915	19/06/1915
War Diary	Trenches	20/06/1915	23/06/1915
War Diary	Trenches Rue Du Bois	24/06/1915	24/06/1915
War Diary	Trenches	25/06/1915	30/06/1915
War Diary	War Diary of Garhwal Rifles From 1st July 1915 To 31st July 1915		
War Diary	Trenches	01/07/1915	04/07/1915
War Diary	Vielle Chapelle	05/07/1915	09/07/1915
War Diary	Haverskerque	10/07/1915	20/07/1915
War Diary	Billets Haverskerque	21/07/1915	21/07/1915
War Diary	Billets Near Laventie	22/07/1915	22/07/1915
War Diary	Trenches Near N Of Neuve Chapelle	23/07/1915	31/07/1915
Heading	War Diary of The Garhwal Rifles From 1st August 1915 To 31st August 1915		
War Diary	Trenches N. Of Neuve Chapelle	01/08/1915	01/08/1915
War Diary	Billets Pont Du Hem	02/08/1915	08/08/1915
War Diary	Billets Near Riez Bailleul	09/08/1915	15/08/1915
War Diary	Billets, Near Riez Baileul And Trenches Fauquissart	16/08/1915	16/08/1915
War Diary	Trenches Fauquissart	17/08/1915	26/08/1915
War Diary	Billets Near La Gorgue	27/08/1915	28/08/1915
War Diary	Trenches Neuve Chapelle	29/08/1915	31/08/1915
Heading	War Diary of Garhwal Rifles From 1st September 1915 To 30th September 1915		
War Diary	Trenches Neuve Chapelle	01/09/1915	01/09/1915

War Diary	Billets Near La Gorgue	02/09/1915	12/09/1915
War Diary	Trenches Mauquissart	13/09/1915	18/09/1915
War Diary	Billets Near La Gorgue	19/09/1915	22/09/1915
War Diary	Bivouac Bout De Ville	23/09/1915	24/09/1915
War Diary	Trenches	25/09/1915	26/09/1915
War Diary	Billets Harrow Road	27/09/1915	30/09/1915
Heading	War Diary of Garhwal Rifles From 1st October 1915 To 31st October 1915		
War Diary	Billets Regnier L'eclerq	01/10/1915	01/10/1915
War Diary	Billets Mesplaux	03/10/1915	07/10/1915
War Diary	Billets Near Essars	08/10/1915	10/10/1915
War Diary	Trenches Givenchy	11/10/1915	18/10/1915
War Diary	Billets Locon	19/10/1915	19/10/1915
War Diary	Trenches Rue Du Bois	20/10/1915	28/10/1915
War Diary	Billets King's Road	28/10/1915	31/10/1915
Miscellaneous	The Officer Commanding		
War Diary	Billets King's Road	01/11/1915	01/11/1915
War Diary	Billets Paradis	02/11/1915	02/11/1915
War Diary	Billets Pecqueur	03/11/1915	07/11/1915
War Diary	Enroute Marseilles	08/11/1915	09/11/1915
War Diary	Marseilles	10/11/1915	10/11/1915
War Diary	En-Route Egypt S.S Aronda	11/11/1915	15/11/1915
War Diary	Port Said	16/11/1915	18/11/1915
War Diary	Port Said Canal Defences 3rd Section	19/11/1915	26/11/1915

WO/45/3945/3

39 Garhwal Rifles

Meerut Division
Garhwal Brigade

1/39th & 2/39th Garhwal Rifles amalgamated in March 1915 and thenceforth known as Garhwals.

Meerut Division Aug-Dec 1914

2/39th Garhwal Rifles.

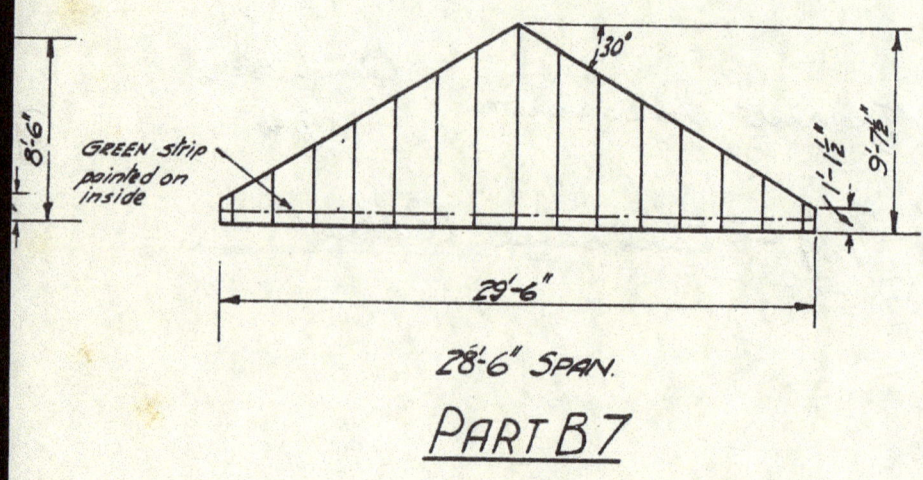

28'-6" SPAN.

PART B7

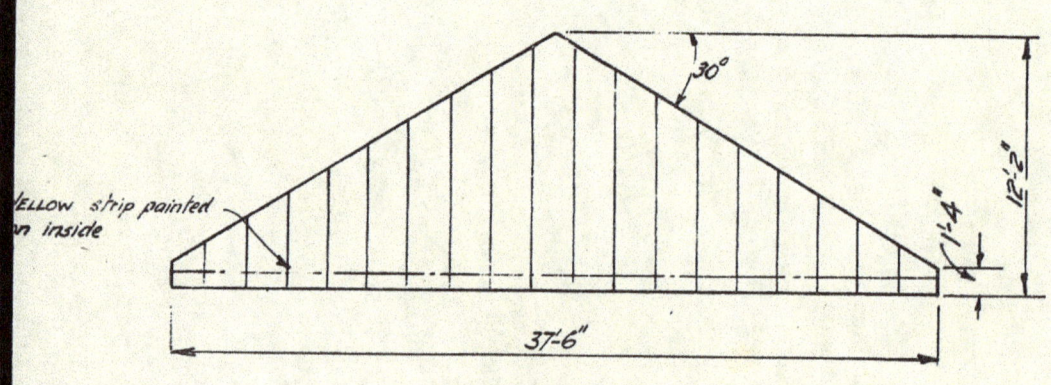

36'-6" SPAN

PART B8

SETS OF EXTERNAL GABLE SHEETING

WHEN FIXED

fixed they conform to the dimensions shown.
be clearly marked by means of a 6" coloured
indicated
× 24 gauge, & to be laid with single side laps.

AMENDED 19-10-38.

SHEETS.   DRAWING No. H. 356/37

Artillery Rifles
from 21/8/14
To 30/12/14

121/4046

Volume I
pp 1 to 50

Volume II
pp 1 to 15.

Army Form C. 2118.

2nd Bn. 39th Garhwal Rifles
Garhwal Bde.
Meerut Division

WAR DIARY

INTELLIGENCE SUMMARY.

(Erase heading not required.)

Instructions regarding War Diaries and Intelligence Summaries are contained in F.S. Regs., Part II, and the Staff Manual respectively. Title pages will be prepared in manuscript.

Hour, Date, Place.	Summary of Events and Information.	Remarks and references to Appendices.
DOGADDA. 21-8-14.	The Battalion marched out of LANSDOWNE as part of the 20th Infantry Brigade, VII War Division, Indian Expeditionary force at 10 a.m. marching out strength as per margin. A damp misty day. Reached DOGADDA 3 p.m. when it commenced to rain heavily. Five Companies D - H were accomodated in some tents lent by O.C.2/8th G.R. but A.B.C.Coys., had to remain in the open, as it was quite impossible to pitch tents or bivouacs owing the camping ground being flooded. The Rain ceased about 6 p.m. and the C.O. decided to send on A.B. & C.Coys., atonce to Kotdwara, where the tents of the Battalion had been sent on some days before., about 6.30 p.m. orders were received from the G.O.C. at Lansdowne to halt the night 22nd-23rd at Dogadda, but the C.O. replied that owing to the impossible state of the camping ground and the fact that our tents were at Kotdwara., he proposed marching there on 22nd. It rained heavily again during the night.	STRENGTH. 8 British Officers. 17 Garhwali Officers. 14 Buglers. 734 Rank & File. Lt.Col.D.H.Drake Brockman Commandant. Major H.M.MacTier. Major J.H.K.Stewart. Major G.H.Taylor. Capt.A.W.Robertson-Glasgo Capt.E.R.P.Berryman. Lieut.A.E.Clarke. Major J.Woods.I.M.S. (attached).
KOTDWARA. 22-8-14.	The transport left Dogadda at 12 noon, arriving Kotdwara at 3.30 p.m. to find the transport already in and tents pitched by A.B. & C.Coys., who had arrived the previous night. Rather a hot, stuffy march, but no rain, Road good, and not broken anywhere. On arrival received orders to entrain for KARACHI at 6 p.m on 23rd, but these were cancelled by wire later in the evening, the Battalion being ordered to stand past till further orders. Battalion camped on regular camping ground, which was in good condition. Weather close and very hot, but no rain,. Captain Bunbury, 13th Rajputs, attached to the Battalion for Active Service, joined the Battalion here.	

Army Form C. 2118.

WAR DIARY
or
INTELLIGENCE SUMMARY.
(Erase heading not required.)

Instructions regarding War Diaries and Intelligence Summaries are contained in F. S. Regs., Part II, and the Staff Manual respectively. Title pages will be prepared in manuscript.

Hour, Date, Place.	Summary of Events and Information.	Remarks and references to Appendices.
KOTDWARA. 23-8-14.	A fine, hot day opportunity taken for drying Kits and cleaning up accoutrements, and issuing boots and equipment that had arrived at KOTDWARA but had not arrived at LANSDOWNE in time to issue before the Battalion marched. At 3.30 p.m. 62 N.C.O's and men, including 40 Reservists arrived from Lansdowne, this bringing the Battalion up to full War strength i.e. 827 Indian Ranks, including 75 men in excess of War Establishment, this being the 1st 10% reinforcement ordered to be taken by Infantry Units. No rain during the day.	
KOTDWARA. 24-8-14.	A cloudy muggy day, but no rain till the night. Kits, accutrements etc., seen to. 5 grains quinine per man issued in the evening on the recommendation of the Medical Officer.	
KOTDWARA. 25-8-14.	A hot muggy day, but no rain. No events of importance to record during the day.	
KOTDWARA. 26-8-14.	The Battalion paraded at 7 a.m. and went for a short route march, 6 miles, to give the men some exercise, and get them used to their new boots. Weather fine and hot, and some rain in the evening. 5 grains of quinine per man issued in the evening on the recommendation of the Medical Officer.	

Army Form C. 2118.

WAR DIARY
INTELLIGENCE SUMMARY.
(Erase heading not required.)

Instructions regarding War Diaries and Intelligence Summaries are contained in F. S. Regs., Part II, and the Staff Manual respectively. Title pages will be prepared in manuscript.

Hour, Date, Place.	Summary of Events and Information.	Remarks and references to Appendices.
26-8-14. (continued).	1 Naik and 2 Riflemen joined Headquarters from the Depot to-day, and 3 Riflemen were returned to the Depot. This makes the strength of the Battalion at Headquarters 17 G.O's, 40 Havaldars 43 Naiks,14 Buglers,713 Rank and File, total Indian Ranks 827.	
KOTDWARA. 27-8-14.	The Battalion paraded at 6.30 a.m. for a short route march, 6 miles, as for yesterday. A fine hot day, but about 6-30 p.m. heavy rain fell, and it rained intermittently throughout the night.	
KOTDWARA 28-8-14.	Hot day and fine, giving all tents, which had got thoroughly went during the previous night, a chance to dry. 1 Rifleman(a Reservist in E.Coy.) was this day transferred to the Civil dispensary, Kotdwara, with pneumonia, thus making the Battalion one rifleman under strength. 5 grains of quinine per man issued in the evening on the recommendation of the Medical Officer. Received orders at 9 p.m. to entrain for KARACHI at 6.15 p.m. on 30-8-1914.	

KOTDWARA.
29 - 8 - 14.

Hot day and fine Right ½ Batt. went for a short route march, 6 miles; left half Batt. one hour's physical drill.
No rain during the day.

KOTDWARA.
30 - 8 - 14.

A fine day. All kits were packed ready by 11 a.m. and tents struck shortly afterwards; all baggage, tents etc., was carried down to the goods platform, and loading commenced at 2 p.m. being finished at 3.45 p.m.
The battalion marched to the Station at 5 p.m. entrained in two trains, the first leaving KOTDWARA at 6.15 p.m. the second at 6.50 p.m. on arrival at NAJIBABAD these two trains were joined up and proceeded the remainder of the journey as one train.

LAHORE.
31-8-14.

A cool journey all the night of 30/31 August. Original routes to KARACHI was via BHATINDA, but this was altered, and the train proceeded via LAHORE. Just before reaching LAHORE CANTT.. station the engine jumped the rails, ploughed up the permanent way for about 50 yards, followed by the first 3 carriages (1 brake van and 2 3rd class bogies) which also left the rails, and finally fell through a small culvert. No one was hurt, as the train was fortunately going dead slow at the time. This derailment caused some delay, but fresh engines and carriages were procured from LAHORE. A four hours halt was made here and the men cooked. A hot day.

SAMASATA.
1 - 9 - 14.

Left LAHORE at 4.45 p.m. travelled all night, cool journey, reached SAMASATA (½ hour behind time) at 7.45. a.m. The men cooked a meal here, and after a two hours halt proceeded again at 7.45 a.m. fairly hot journey all day, but cool nights.

KARACHI.
2 - 9 - 14.

Proceeded to KOTRI on 2-9-14, reached the place at 8-45 a.m. and halted till 11.45 a.m. The men cooked a meal.

Reached KARACHI 6 p.m. and proceded to troop siding near rest camp. The battalion was accomodated in tents (pitched ready) in the rest camp to await orders to Embark.

The train journey from LANSDOWNE to KARACHI had been performed without any accidents, excepting the derailment at LAHORE referred to above. The whole Battalion was fit and well and animals all well on arrival at KARACHI. There were one or two cases of mild fever on the way, and one man arrived at KARACHI with fever, but otherwise there was no sickness of any kind.

Fairly cool at KARACHI, with a nice breeze blowing. Rest camp very dusty.

No orders regarding Embarkation received.

KARACHI.
3-9-1914.

A guard of 2 N.C.O's and 40 men proceeded at 6 a.m. to KIAMARI docks to relive a guard of 1/39th G. who embarked to-day.

Warm clothing (F.S. free issue) issued to all ranks and followers.

Warm day, but nice breeze blowing.

| Hour, Date, Place. | Summary of Events and Information. | Remarks and references to Appendices. |

KARACHI.
4-9-1914.

Weather fine and warm, cool breeze.
The S.S.COCONADA in which the Battalion is to sail arrived in KIAMARI docks to day, and commenced coaling and getting rations on board.

KARACHI.
5-9-1914.

Weather fine and warm, cool breeze.
Guard of 2 N.C.O's and 40 men at KIAMARI docks relieved by guard from troops already on board in docks.
1 man was transferred to 127th Baluchies Hospital suffering from dysentry. Health of regiment otherwise good, except for about 25 cases of mild fever, evidently due to the weeks halt at KOTDWARA.

KARACHI.
6-9-1914.

Weather fine and warm cool breeze.
Companies marched to the sea shore about 2 miles off and bathed in the sea, 6.30 a.m.

KARACHI.
7-9-1914.

Weather fine and warm, cool breeze, but camp getting rather dusty.
Companies paraded for physical drill for an hour in the morning.
Orders were received to embark on 8-9-1914 at 2 p.m. but these were cancelled later in the day, all units being ordered to stand fast till further orders.
A few more cases of fever, but general health of of regiment good.

15-9-1914.
(continued)

orders to proceeded to depot, and Captain Burton received orders to join the Battalion, and Captain Bunbury (attached) to rejoin his unit (13th Rajputs).

S.S.COCONADA
KIAMARI DOCKS.
16-9-1914.

A fine warm day.
Entrained at Rest Camp siding at 10-25 a.m. and left for docks at 10-45 a.m. arriving there at 11-15 a.m.
Commenced embarking at once, and all on board by 12 noon.
Horses and mules were embarked at 7 a.m. previous to the arrival of the Battalion.
Accomodation on the S.S.COCONADA good, though men were a bit close together but quite roomy and comfortable on the whole. ½ Batt.2/3rd Q.A.O.,G.R. and some Ordnance and Supply details also embarked on the same ship.
1 N.C.O. and 8 men of the Signalling Unit detached and embarked on S.S.BRAUNFELS.
Rather hot on board, especially on lower decks. Remained along side wharf for night of 16th/17th September.

S.S.COCONADA.
KIAMARI DOCKS.
17-9-1914.

Rather a hot day.
Day spent in generally settling down for the night voyage.
Captain Burton joined the Battalion to day from Lansdowne, Major Holland having rejoined from leave and taken over the depot. Captain Bunbury,13th Rajputs, rejoined his unit.
No orders received re sailing, but the ship's Captain received order to stand fast till further orders.

Hour, Date, Place.	Summary of Events and Information.	Remarks and references to Appendices.
S.S.COCONADA. KIAMARI DOCKS. 18-9-1914.	Rather a cooler day, ship remained along side wharf, and no further orders received. Col.Fuller, Embarkation Commandant, and Staff visted the ship, and asked if all was correct. Arrangements made to alter position of hospital on board. Men fit and well, except for some cases of mild fever.	
S.S.COCONADA. KIAMARI DOCKS. 19-9-1914.	Weather considerably cooler, ship remained along side wharf, and no further orders received. Arrangements made to communicate with H M.S. DARTMOUTH from 9-10 p.m. by lamp, for practice. Companies ashore for an hour in the morning for walking and running exercise. Mules and Officers Chargers exercised on board in the morning.	
S.S.COCONADA. KIAMARI DOCKS. 20-9-1914.	Weather cooler, as yesterday, and cool breeze blowing. Ship moved out of harbour at 8.30 a.m. and anchored outside. A slight swell on, and a strongish wind which made the weather nice and cool. The transport convay took up its positions preparatory to sailing next day. All ships lights out by order at 10 p.m.	
S.S.COCONADA. at Sea. 21-9-1914.	The convay commenced getting into position about 8 a.m., proceeding in three lines of ships, line ahead, 12 transports in all, escorted by H.M.S.DARTMOUTH,	

21-9-1914.
(continued)

R.I.M.S.HARDINGE AND MINTO. Sailed 9 a.m.
Moderate swell, and ship pitching a bit, a good many men sea sick-strong head-wind, and weather cool in consequence. Fever cases less than previously.

S.S.COCONADA.
At Sea.
22-9-1914.

Cool day with strong head wind. Weather fine and sea calmer than previous day, and men less sea sick in consequence.

S.S.COCONADA.
At Sea.
23-9-1914.

Cool day with strong head wind. Weather fine, sea calm, and sea-sickness considerably less. Still a good many fever cases.
About midday the transport convoy from BOMBAY was sighted, and the two convoys joined up and proceeded on their way, H.M.S.SWIFTSURE and H.M.S.FOX joining as escort with the Bombay convoy, the total number of ships in the two convoys combined being now over 40.

S.S.COCONADA.
At Sea.
24-9-1914.

Cool day, strong head wind. Weather fine, sea calm, and about the same amount of sea-sickness. Transport DILWARA proceded ahead of remainder of convoy to ADEN, escorted by R.I.M.S.HARDINGE. H.M.S.DARTMOUTH and H.M.S.FOX left convoy on 23rd, and proceded South.

S.S.COCONADA.
At Sea.
25-9-1914.

Cool day, strong head wind; sea calm, but rather rougher towards evening; weather fine. A good many fever cases still, and 3 cases of entric amongst 2/3rd Q.A.O. G.R.

S.S.COCONADA.
At Sea.
26-9-1914.

Rather a hot day, and wind considerably less; sea quite calm. One man of 2/3rd (Q.A.O.)G.R. died today and was buried at Sea, (supposed to be entric fever).

S.S.COCONADA.
At Sea.
27-9-1914.

Hot day, but a fair breeze blowing. Sea calm. About midday the convoy adopted a fresh formation, sailing in 3 lines abrest, preparatory to entering the Red Sea. The convoy was abrest of ADEN at 10 p.m. Here H.M.S. SWIFTSURE left the convoy, H.M.S. BLACK PRINCE coming in her place.

S.S.COCONADA.
At Sea.
28-9-1914.

Hot day, and very little breeze. Sea calm.
Passed PERIM at 8 a.m.

S.S.COCONADA.
At Sea.
29-9-1914.

Hot day, and very little breeze. Sea calm.
6 Coys.(4 of 2/3rd Q.A.O.G.R. and 2 of 2/39th G.) did physical exercise, doubling etc. on boat deck for 1 hour in the morning; this arrangement, 6 Coys. per day on alternate days, to hold good throughout the voyage.

S.S.COCONADA.
At Sea.
30-9-1914.

Not so hot and a good breeze blowing all day Sea calm. Several transport left the convoy and went on ahead to SUEZ.

S.S.COCONADA.
At Sea.
1-10-1914.

Strong head wind all day, and sea a little rougher than yesterday; weather fairly cool in consequence. Several more ships left the convoy during the day proceeding ahead to SUEZ. Passed Duedalus shoal and light house 4 p.m.

S.S.COCONADA.
At Sea.
2-10-1914.

Cool day with strong head wind; sea moderately calm, as yesterday, Sea-sickness amongst men considerably less. Entered GULF of SUEZ shortly after noon.

S.S.COCONADA.
SUEZ.
3-10-1914.

Arrived SUEZ at 3 a.m. and anchored. Weather cool, and light breeze blowing. Several ships of the convoy entered the canal during the day. Five sick men of 2/3rd (Q.A.O.) G.R. landed here to be transferred to hospitals. Captain Reed joined the Battalion here.

S.S.COCONADA.
PORT SAID
4-10-1914.

Entered Canal at 12.30 a.m. Weather fine and warm. Proceded slowley up canal, reaching PORT SAID at 3 p.m. and anchored. Took on coal, water and provisions. Captains. Blair, Lyell, and Wilcox, joined the regiment here, having been re-

4-10-1914.
(Continued)

recalled from furlo' in England, and awaited the arrival of the Battalion in EGYPT.

S.S.COCONADA.
PORT SAID.
5-10-1914.

Weather fine and warm, Steamed out of PORT SAID, at 9.45 a.m. and anchored outside together with 18 other ships of the CONVOY, preparatory to sailing at 4 p.m. on 6th.

S.S.COCONADA.
At Sea.
6-10-1914.

Weather fine, cool day, at 2 p.m. the convoy (18 transports in all) got into formation, 3 lines of ships 6 in each line, preparatory to sailing. Weighed anchor shortly after 4 p.m. and left at 4.45. p.m. for MARSEILLES and proceded on the voyage, escorted by the French battle ship JAURE GUIBERRY. Received order to send on disembarkation at Marseilles 1 B.O., 1 G.O., and 1 N.C.O. with similar detachments from other units to the Concentraction area to arrange billets for the force.

S.S.COCONADA.
At Sea.
7-10-1914.

Weather fine and cool. Sea quite calm. Fever cases less than previously.

S.S.COCONADA.
At Sea.
8-10-1914.

Weather fine, and colder. Sea began to get rough during the night, and was very rough all day and the ship rolled and pitched considerably, and a good deal of Sea-sickness in consequence among the men.

Hour, Date, Place.	Summary of Events and Information.	Remarks and references to Appendices.

S.S.COCONADA.
At Sea.
9-10-1914.

Weather cloudy and cold. Sea not so rough as yesterday, but ship still rolling and pitching a little. One or two squalls and showers of rain during the day.

S.S.COCONADA.
At Sea.
10-10-1914.

Weather fine and cool. Sea calm. Passed MALTA at 7 a.m. Passed CAPE BON 9 p.m.

S.S.COCONADA.
At Sea.
11-10-1914.

Weather fine and cold. Sharp squall of rain about 9 a.m. Passed SARDINIA about 10 a.m. The French battle ship left the head of the convoy at midday and dropped astern, and several ships of the convoy steamed ahead, and the COCONADA also increased her speed during the day on receipt of orders from the Flagship to proceed on to Marseilles.

S.S.COCONADA.
and MARSEILLES.
12-10-1914.

Weather fine and cold. Reached MARSEILLES and anchored 1 p.m. Received orders to be ready to disembark on morning of 14th, 9 a.m. and to find a fatigue of 500 men to unload other transport in harbour. (These orders cancelled at 12.30 a.m. on 13-10-14). Also received orders to change rifles for latest pattern, also all ammunition, and Machine Guns at 7 a.m. on 13th.

S.S.COCONADA
and MARSEILLES.

Received orders 12.30 a.m. to be ready to disembark 9 a.m. on 13th. So all previous orders cancelled. Actually went alongside at 12.30 P.M. and commenced disembarking

13-10-14.
(continued).

immediately. Battalion formed up in one of the sheds on wharf; and unloading of ship commenced, this being done by dock labourers. Orders received to find working parties to unload ships holds (4 N.C.O's and 44 men, with reliefs) and to load medical stores on a train (1 G.O. and 60 men with reliefs) at 5.45 p.m., to work from 6 p.m. to 7 a.m. on 14th. A, B, C, and ½ D.Coy. detailed for this duty. These Companies remained night of 13/14 on wharf. Meanwhile all rifles, ammunition, and the machine Guns were exchanged for latest patterns. All Kit loaded up as it was unloaded from ship on 10 large two horsed lorries. These were full by 6 p.m. and proceeded to CAMP LA VALENTINE under Capt. Blair and ½ D.Coy. as escort. Owing to the ship having been loaded by coolie labour at Karachi, the hold was in a great state of confusion, rations and kit being all mixed up, consequently a good deal of kit was taken out of the ship after the lorries had started; all this however was brought on by the Coys. remaining at the wharf next day. E, F, G, H, Coys., with machine guns left the wharf at 8.15 p.m. en route for Camp LA VELENTINE. Route lay through Marseilles town, over rough cobbled streets, and uphill all the way. The march through the streets caused a certain amount of enthusiasm among the inhabitants.

Camp reached at 12 midnight after some difficulty the Battalion camping ground was located, and the kit roughly sorted out. Tents were pitched, and the best arrangements made as possible in the darkness. No men fall out on the march. The Battalion settled down to sleep at about 2.30. a.m.

Weather fine and mild, but during the march it looked threatening, and there was a good deal of lightning.

CAMP LA VALENTINE
MARSEILLES.
14-10-14.

Commenced raining at 5.30 a.m. and the camp, which was situated in meadows, rather marshy in places, soon became muddy. Rain accompanied by cold east wind but men seemed fairly comfortable, thanks to the tents having been pitched before the rain commenced. Major General Kerry. C.B.
D.S.O.

14-10-1914.

visited the camp during the day. Major Taylor and remainder of Battalion arrived at 3 p.m. having been detained at the docks till 10 a.m. went and miserable all day, and very little sign of weather clearing.

**CAMP LA VALENTINE
MARSEILLES.
15-10-1914.**

Rain continued all night, but seemed to clear somewhat towards morning. A cold damp day, with intermittent dorizzle. The G.O.C.15th French Army Corps and the Governor of Marseilles had intended to visit the camp but postponed their visit. Lieut. General Sir James Wilcocks K.C.B., K.C.S.I., K.C.M.G., D.S.O., Commanding the Indian Army Corps visited camp at about 1.30 p.m., but no parade etc., was held. Less rain towards evening, but weather still misty and cold. Two French interpreters attached to the Battalion reported themselves for duty.

**CAMP LA VALENTINE.
MARSEILLES.
16-10-1914.**

A damp cold day, but not so much rain. The 9 Signallers who embarked on board S.S.BRAUNFELS at KARACHI arrived today, having disembarked the previous night. Very heavy rain accompanied by thunder and lightning at 7 p.m. which continued nearly all night. Camp in a very bad state with mud. Five men had been transferred sick to No.129, I.F.A. during our stay in camp.

**CAMP LA VALENTINE.
MARSEILLES.
17-10-1914.**

A fine warm day with plenty of sun up to midday, when it clouded over. But opportunity taken to dry kits while the sun was out, and general state of camp much improved. Coys. packed up spare kit which is to be left at the base. The 19th Indian Infantry Brigade left camp today for for place of assembly. Rifn. Kunwar Sing Negi joined A.G's office at the base to-day.

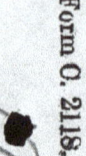

WAR DIARY or INTELLIGENCE SUMMARY.

(Erase heading not required.)

Instructions regarding War Diaries and Intelligence Summaries are contained in F.S. Regs., Part II, and the Staff Manual respectively. Title pages will be prepared in manuscript.

Army Form C. 2118.

Hour, Date, Place.	Summary of Events and Information.	Remarks and references to Appendices.

CAMP LA VALENTINE.
MARSEILLES.
18-10-1914.

A cloudy dull morning. Received orders to entrain at at the GARE d'ARENC at 2.5 a.m. on 19th. Captain Wilcox, was sent to MARSEILLES to obtain transport to convey baggage to the station; he arrived back at 2 p.m. with some of the carts, which were loaded up immediately. The 20th and 21st Brigades both moved off to-day, and there was a great deal of muddle over the transport, as no defunite times had been laid down for each regiments transport to load up and move off. Meantime at about 2 p.m. very heavy rain fell, and once more the camp was flooded out; the rain continued for about 2 hours, and the camp because a perfect quagmire. After some difficulty in obtaining carts, owing to so many regiments moving off at once, and the auful state of the camping ground, the transport finally left at 6 p.m. The Regiment marched off at 8.30 p.m. reaching the station at 12.30.p.m. Two French Interpreters, M. Bree and M. Richand of the 10th Heavy Artillery (Toulon) met the regiment en route and conducted us to the station, where the 3rd interpreter, 2nd Lieut. Watney, joined. These three interpreters had already reported themselves for duty when the regiment disembarked, but had not been in camp with the regiment, though they had paid daily visits and proved useful in many ways. Nine A.T. carts and 34 mules for first line transport were taken taken over to-day.

The train was dreun up at about 2 a.m. and loading commenced at once, E. and F. Coys. supply the loading parties. Accomodation for British and Indian Officers was 1st Class carriages, for the rank and file cattle wagons fitted with seats. The trained steamed out at 6 a.m. on moving of the 19th.

In the train.
19-10-1914.

Travelled all day via CETTE to BEZIERE, arriving there at 4 p.m. Here the men cooked and fed, entraining again at 6.15 p.m. and moving on again at 6.30 p.m. Officers had dinner at the hotel.

Left at Base, Marseilles, as 1st 10 %
reinforcement.
    Subr. Shib Sing Negi.
       3 N.C.O!s.
      60 Riflemen.

WAR DIARY or INTELLIGENCE SUMMARY.

(Erase heading not required.)

Army Form C. 2118.

Hour, Date, Place.	Summary of Events and Information.	Remarks and references to Appendices.
In the train. 20-10-1914.	Travelled all night of 19th/20th, reaching CAHORS at 8.30 a.m. on 20th. Here men cooked and fed. Entrained again at 11.45.a.m. and moved off at 12 noon. Short halt at LIMOGES at 11 p.m.	
In the train, and Camp LES GROUVES ORLEANS. 21-10-1914.	Reach VIERZON at 6 a.m. and halted for 1 hour arrived at LES AUBRAIS station, orleans, at 10.30.a.m. detrained immediately G.& H.Coys.remained to unload train and load baggage on motor lorries; remainder of Batt. marched off at 10.15 a.m. reaching Camp LES GROUVES at 11.30 a.m. camping ground rather muddy, but clean, though rather cut up by horses and wheeled traffic. Weather cold and cloudy. Transport arrived shortly after the regiment and tents were pitched at once. Throughout the train journey the inhabitants had been very enthusiastic, cheering the troops, and giving them cigarettes etc., at all the halts. The French Railway and military officials also had been extremely polite and obliging, and ample supplies of wood and water were available at the halte-re'pas (cooking stations) on the way. All kit in excess of scale α laid down to be taken in the field was packed in bundles and left at the base with the 1st 10 % reinforcement. In lieu of the hold all each man took 1 pair socks, and cleaning material. Each man carried a blanket on his back, wrapped up with his greatcoat. Officers were allowed field kits as follows C.O.50 lbs. others 35 lbs.	Per man. 1 Water Proof Sheet. 1 Blanket. 1 Logline. 1 pair socks. 1 Towel. 1 Balaclava Cap. 1 Hold all Per Follower. 1 Water Proof Sheet. 1 Blanket. 1 Set Cooking pots. Indian Officers. 10 lbs in addition to above.

CAMP LES GROUES ORLEANS.
22-10-1914.

Weather cold morning and evening, otherwise mild. Cloudy but no rain. More warm clothing for men drawn from ordnance,(1 Shirt,1 Vest,1 pair Drawers) but of these only the drawers were taken, as the men already had sufficient warm kit. Nine bicycles also received. Machine Guns and mountings returned to ordnance for fitting with new mountings.

CAMP LES GROUES ORLEANS.
23-10-1914.

Weather mild and cloudy. Lieut.General Sir James Wilcox, Commanding Indian Army Corps, paid an informal visit to camp in the morning. Six G.S.Wagons, 2 water Carts and 1 Cook Cart, of the train, with 18 draught horses, received during the day.

Weather fine and warm, and mud in camp dried up considerably. Captain Blair, Jemadar Lachham Sing Rawat and 4 N.C.O's left by train at 5.20 a.m. for an unknown destination to make billeting arrangements.
The Meerut Division practised route marching to-day. The 20th Brigade followed the 19th, the leading regiment of the Brigade (2nd Leicesters) passing the starting point at 11.40 a.m. This Battalion being the rear Battalion of the Brigade, passed starting point at 12.15 p.m. Returned to camp at 2.45 p.m. after a pleasant march through the country of about 6 miles. Officers and men in full F.S.Order men carrying 100 rounds ammunition, all transport, 1st line and train, loaded up as for service with the exception of the supply wagons. Men seemed fresh and not very tired after the march, only 5 fell out.

CAMP LES GROUES ORLEANS
25-10-1914.

Weather cloudy and colder than yesterday. D.C's went for route march under D.C.arrangements during the

25.10.1914.
(Continued)

morning. Remounts, 8 in number, received for officers who had no chargers, and the 3 Interpreters. Received orders during the evening to entrain at on 26th; the whole division being moved up to the front on that date.

26.10.14.
CAMP LES GROUES
ORLEANS.

Weather cloudy and cold. Orders to entrain at 11.55.P.M. Tents struck and handed over to Ordnance Department at 4 p.m. being left on the camping ground. Paraded 10.30.p.m. transport being sent on ahead. Reached HUPLINS station 11.30 and commenced loading at once all G.S. wagons put on trucks loaded; men in wagons with straw. Also took with us one wagon of 1/39th G. and 40 men who had got left behind. Train loaded by 12.30 p.m. Some difficulty being experienced in loading the G.S. wagons. Started at 1.35 a.m.

27.10.1914.
In the train.

A cold journey in the train 2 days cooked ration carried in the train, and one days ration in the supply wagons. Reached MANTES 10.45.a.m. and halted for an hour. Proceeded via ROUEN to ABBEVILLE, reaching latter place at 12 midnight, and halted for ¾ hour. Train early two hours late arriving at Abbeville.

28.10.1914.
In the train
and CALONNES.

Reached Calais at 10.30 a.m. though due at 4.30 a.m/ a.m. 6 hours late, after a short halt, proceeded by S OMER, HAZEBROUK to LILLERS, reaching latter place at 2 p.m. detrained immediately, No. III D.C. being left behind to un-

WAR DIARY or INTELLIGENCE SUMMARY.

(Erase heading not required.)

Hour, Date, Place.	Summary of Events and Information.	Remarks and references to Appendices.
26-10-1914. (continued)	load and escort baggage, marched to CALONNES, about 7 miles where regiment was billetted for the night arriving 7.15. p.m. Weather cold, men billetted in barns and houses, and very comfortable. Sound of guns audible here. One or two aeroplanes seen during the day, men had to set to work and cook rations on arrival and so did not get to rest till very late nearly 1. a.m. finally early start ordered next morning.	

Hour, Date, Place.	Summary of Events and Information.	Remarks and references to Appendices.

WAR DIARY or INTELLIGENCE SUMMARY.
(*Erase heading not required.*)

Army Form C. 2118.

29-10-1914.
Billets CALONNES
and in the trenches
1st day.

Paraded at 7.10.a.m. to march to LES GLATIGNES Brigade marched in following order 2/Leicester Regiment 1/39th G., 2/3rd G.R., 2/39th G. 1st line transport with regiments train in order of march in rear marched along good roads to LOCON, reaching the place at 11 a.m. sound of heavy firing heard all along. Halted at LOCON in some fields; artillery and musketry fire going on not far ahead, and aeroplanes busy in vicinity. The day was cloudy and cold.

At 2 p.m. C.O's and Adjutants were summoned to G.O.C's headquarters, in a farm home about 2 miles from where regiment was halted. Here orders were received that the Brigade was to relieve the 14th Brigade 5th Division British Expeditionary Force, consisting of the Worcestershires, the East Surreys, K.O.S.B's, and K.O.V.L.I. the regiment being detailed to relieve the latter in the trenches.

The regiment was called up, and arrived at 7 p.m. at a road called RUE de L'EPINETTE, where a halt was made. Here ammunition was issued to complete to 200 rounds a man extra entrenching tools taken over from the Brigade, and preparations made for our portion of the trenches, as all 1st line transport was sent back from the point, and the train, (baggage and supply wagons) was left packed well in rear, and did not come up at all.

At about 7.30.p.m. the sound of very heavy firing was heard ahead, and continued for about ½ an hour. At 8.p.m. C.O's interviewed the G.O.C. and afterwards the C.O. and Adjutant accompanied a representative of the K.O.V.L.I. to the trenches, the regiment meantime halting at RUE de L'EPINETTE.

After being taken round the trenches by the C.O. of K.O.V.L.I. and having had the general situation explained and all available information given, the G.C. sent for the Battalion to come up, and at 12 midnight they arrived and commenced taking over the xxxxxx a trenches. While the trenches were being taken over, heavy firing broke out, and lasted about ½ hour, during which 5 men were wounded Intermittent firing continued all night.

Battalion headquarters were located in a ruined barn in the centre of the position. the position occupied

28-10-1914.
(continued)

by the Battalion was on the extreme left of the Brigade, and one to which the enemy had been paying particular attention of late. The left of the position linked up with the Seaforth Highlanders (the R.flank Battalion of the 19th Indian Infantry Brigade) and on our right were the 1/39th G. The trenches as taken over from the K.O.Y.L.I. were not very good, and required to be much deeper to make them safe under shrapnel fire, and better traversed and loopholes. The majority of such work could only be done at night, owing to the proximity of the enemy's trenches and the persistency of his snipers. For this purpose he evidently had picked marksmen at vantage points, with field glasses, who kept a constant look out on our trenches, and fired at any movement they saw. Several casualties were due to there marksmen, and they were a source of constant worry throughout. Several of them were shot by us, but this had little effect as they were constantly firing at loopholes etc., on one dead german, found by our scouts, close up to the enemy's entrenchments, a magnificent pair of Goerz Binoculars was found, evidently supplied by the german government. hence the accuracy and persistency of this form of shooting.

Rations and water could only be brought up at night and distributed in the trenches, as the road up from RUE de L'EPINETTE was unsafe to traverse by day, except for single men or small parties, and even these were invariably 'sniped', and several casualties occurred in this way.

All evacuation of sick and wounded, burial of dead, and reliefs of companies in the firing line from the support companies had to be carried out by night, as some of the enemy's trenches were only 50 yards away from ours, and his main position was only 350 - 400 away.

For the general line of trenches, see map of position taken up, attached.

Rations arrived in time to be issued before dawn; and meantime work started on improving the trenches, work which it may be said never really ceased till the Battalion was relieved on the night of 19th/20th November. But it was absolutely necessary, and tremendous improvements were made, the trenches being hardly recognisable as the same

29-10-1914.
(continued).

as originally taken over by the Battalion, and every one who came round the trenches (Staff Officers, Officers from other parts of the line etc.) remarked on the excellence of the trenches, which, considering the work was nearly all done at night and in such close proximity to the enemy, was very satisfactory. There is no doubt that the casualties from shell fire were much reduced by the depth and skilful traversing of this trenches.

Casualties. Indian Ranks 9 wounded.

30-10-1914.
In the trenches(.
(2nd day)

Intermittent rifle fire all the morning, chiefly from snipers. Enemy also shelled the trenches, and 2 men were killed during the morning.

3 Coys. 1/39th G. were shelled out of their trenches during the morning and some of their men took refuge in E. and F. Coys. trenches till the 1/39th G. trenches were occupied again.

Some casualties occurred in the M.G. section, 1 man being killed and 2 wounded, but improvement in the epanlment were made and very few casualties occurred in future.

Shelling ceased at dusk, and at 9 p.m. the enemy opened fire from their trenches. It seemed as if they were making an attack, but it was very hard to say. Heavy firing continued till 9.30 p.m. and then died down. Intermittent firing all night, and heavy bursts at 11, 12-45. a.m. and 4.p.m. the last again appearing to precede an attack, but this was driven off.

Cold and damp nights, but weather fine in general.

Casualties. Indian Ranks 2 Killed 10 wounded
Total to date 3 Killed 19 wounded.

WAR DIARY or INTELLIGENCE SUMMARY.

(Erase heading not required.)

Army Form C. 2118.

Hour, Date, Place.	Summary of Events and Information.	Remarks and references to Appendices.

31-10-1914.
In the trenches
(3rd day)

A quiet day., usual sniping, and 2 or 3 of their snipers were accounted for. During the day heave sharpnel and howitzer bombardment, which fortunately did little damage, an german aeroplane was conspicuous during the day flying over the lines and in rear of them, dropping smoke bombs, indicating targets for their artillery, a few rounds of shrafnel and howitzer was the result.

A quiet night with little firing. Both water carts broke down on the way, owing to their faking into the enormous shell holes made in the road by the german howitzers. They paid particular attention to roads, and the explosion of one of their howitzer shells in the middle of an ordinary road was sufficient to wreck it so as to make it impassable for wheeled traffic.

Relived the Coys. in the fire trenches by those from support C.O. received Message to go in and see G.O.C. left 4.a.m. with Quartermaster in 1st November. 1914.

<u>Casualties</u>. Indian Ranks 17 wounded. 1 killed.
Total to date. Indian Ranks 3 killed 36 wounded

1-11-1914.
In the trenches.
(4th day).

Warm and sunny morning a quiet day on the whole, about 3 p.m. some shrapnel and howitzer fire commenced, some shells falling very close round Battalion Headquarters.

Trenches widened and improved during the day as far as possible without exposing the men to fire.

C.O. returned from visit to G.O.C. at 10.a.m. and sniped at along the road back, slight attack during the night.

<u>Casualties</u>. Indian Ranks 2 wounded.
Total to date Indian Ranks 3 killed 38 wounded.

2-11-1914.
In the trenches.
(5th day)

A quiet day; usual sniping, and a brief, but accurate howitzer bombardment during the forenoon. A detailed sketch of the line of entrenchment occupied by the Battalion was submitted to the Brigade, shewing approximate position of the enemy's trenches, and recommending artillery fire to be directed on certain portions. A quiet night, very little firing.

There appeared to be good reason to suppose that spies were frequenting the buildings etc., in rear of the line, and signalling by means of lights etc., to the enemy. Measures were therefore taken to search the houses, but nothing suspicious was found., patrol being sent to patrol the main road and search all houses in rear of our section of the defence.

<u>Casualties</u> Indian officers wounded 1 Indian Ranks wounded 1.

```
Total        K.   W.
  I.O's.-    -    1
  R.& F.     3   39
             3   40
```

3-11-1914.
In the trenches.
(6th day)

Nothing very much of importance happened to day. Heavy firing on our right in the direction of 1/39th G. in the evening, but nothing occurred in our portion of the line. Allies and german aeroplanes busy in the morning. Usual sniping all day, and some shell fire on the trenches. Fine day.

<u>Casualties</u>. Indian Ranks Killed 1 wounded 1.

```
Total to date         K.   W.
  I.O's    ...        -    1
  R.& F.   ...        4   40     4.K.41.W.
```

4-11-1914.
In the trenches.
(7th day)

A very misty morning. About 10 a.m. maxims suddenly opened to our front and left front. Then shrapnel and howitzer fire opened, especially on the seaforth's trenches on our left, and A Company who were occupying our left trenches.

4-11-1914.
(continued)

Several shells fell in the trenches, but the men sat still and remained steady. Then musketry fire broke out and was directed chiefly on the Seaforth's, who at 12-15 sent over and asked for reinforcements B.Company under Captain Reed went over, and ½ F.Company was sent up to take B.Coy's place in the firing line. E Company having been detached today to form a brigade reserve, this left only 2 sections in Regimental reserve. Enemy managed to establish a machine gun in a trench W.of the LA BASSEE road about 350 from our trenches. The attack on the Seaforth w was not pressed home.

Heavy howitzer and shrapnel fire all day, several big howitzer shells falling very near Battalion headquarters and wrecking portions of the farm where they were located.

The night was quiet, except for usual sniping.

B.Company remained with the seaforths all night, as they (the Seaforths) had suffered severely from shrapnel fire, and they needed reinforcements.

Casualties. Indian Ranks Killed 3 wounded 6.
Total to date.   K.   W.
  II.O's.   ...   -   1
  R.& F.   ...   7   46
                    7   47.

5-11-1914
In the trenches
(8th day)

Fine warm morning. Shrapnel opened on our left and on Seaforths, continuing intermittently till 2 p.m. but not much damage done.

Howitzer shells fell round Battalion headquarters necessitating their temporary evacuation.

Our own and german aeroplanes very busy in the afternoon.

During the shelling of the Battalion Headquarters the shells fell actually in the farm buildings wrecking them, and knocking down garden walls. All buildings had to be evacuated, and the Lce.Nk. commanding the Head-

5-11-1914.
(continued)

quarters guard was killed while taking orders regarding the evacuation of the guard-room, which was in an out house near Battalion Headquarters.

Sappers and miners came after dark to put up barbed wire, but a good deal more is required to make the trenches more secure.

After dark the C.O. went over to the Seaforths, and interviewed their right flank Coy., Commander concerning the blunting of the salient held by the Seaforths on the right of their line, and which is a source of weakness to the line, and the chief object of the enemy's attacks. If the Seaforths draw back their line, it will necessitate the withdrawal of our left flank trenches also; a full report was submitted to the Brigade on this point.

Casualties. Indian Ranks Killed 1 wounded 7.
Total to date

	K.	W.
I.O's. ...	-	1
R.& F. ...	8	53
	8	54

6-11-1914.
In the trenches.
(9th day)

A quiet morning, except for a few howitzer shells. One of these unfortunately struck the house on the main road where a guard of the Regiment was situated, killing the sentry, but the rest of the guard escaped. In consequence of this the guard was removed by day, and only posted at night, as it has been observed that the germans do little or no firing at night.

A misty day, and very little firing during the day.

About 5.30.p.m. a brisk fire opened on our right trenches, but it died away again after about 25 minutes.

Casualties. Indian Ranks 1 killed 3 wounded.
Total to date.

	K.	W.
I.O's. ...	-	1
R.& F. ...	9	56
	9	57

7-11-1914.
In the trenches.
(10th day)

Very heavy shelling of buildings in vicinity of Battalion Headquarters took place, commencing about 8.30 a.m. and continuing for about 1¾ hours.

Howitzers and shrapnel also opened on the left flank trenches, there being broken in several places.

The enemy then proceded to attack out left trench and the Seaforths, the attack on the latter being pushed right up to the trenches. During this attack, very heavy shrapnel fire was kept up on very left flank trench, and this continued till the enemy were right up to the Seaforth trenches, and many of their own men must have suffered from this fire. However our left flank trenches managed to help the Seaforths by enfilade fire.

About 6 p.m. heavy fire was again opened on our left, and it seemed as if the germans were making another attack, but nothing came of it.

Again at 11.40 p.m. a furious furillade began, but resulted in nothing.

During the night a patrol of our scouts reconnoitred the enemy's nearer trenches and found them unoccupied. On their return journey they saw a cart with an escort of (according to them) 50 men ahead and 50 men behind, going along a road. The patrol leader line up his men (10 in number) and opened rapid fire on the rear party who scattered and returned the fire, but in the wrong direction. The enemy must have suffered some loss, but the patrol returned intact.

A working party from the Brigade reserve came at 5.30 p.m. to commence digging the trenches necessary in rear of our left flank with a view to blunting the salient held by the R.flank Coy. of the Seaforths.

C.O. went in to see G.O.C. during the day.

Casualties. Indian Ranks Killed 1 wounded 21.
Total to date   K.   W.
    I.O's.   ...   -   1
    R.& F.   ...   10   77
                          10   78

pa. 2/pg Gerhard
diary.

put copy as the
correspondence is.

Vol V corrigenda
_____

Broad Park House
Ilfracombe
Devon
28. July 28

Dear Edmonds

Your H/3 of 19th inst.

I enclose a certified copy by Drake Brockman of the order to make the raid of 9/10th Nov 1914 and hope it is what you require.

Yours ever,

Hoatt

From the Brigade Major Garhwal Brigade.
To The Officer Commanding 2nd Bn. 39th Garhwal Rifles.

No. B.M.194 dated 9th November 1914. 9.50. a.m.

Officer Comdg 1/39th G. reports enemy have occupied a trench 50 yards in front of your right flank. This trench seems to threaten to enfilade 1/39th G. left trench. I consider enemy should be driven out of this close proximity. Please concert measures in conjunction with O.C.1/39th G. to make combined attack on this trench rendering it ineffective for enemy's further occupation. No Sappers available to mine it being withdrawn by Division. Repeated to O.C.1/39th.G.

TRUE COPY.

D.H.Drake Brockman

Br.General. late Lt.Col.Comdt.2nd Batt.39th Garhwal Rifles.

8-11-1914.
In the trenches.
(11th day)

A quiet day; nothing of note to report our artillery shelled NEUVE CHAPELLE, and the enemy fired a few rounds of shrapnel and howitzer shells at our trenches, without doing any damage.

At 9.45 p.m. a sapper with party and material for laying miner came up, but as the moon was up it was decided to postpone any attempt to mine the enemy's nearer trenches till a more favourable opportunity. Sounds of a terrific bottle going on up North.

Casualties. NIL.
Total to date.   10 killed 78 wounded.

9.11.1914.
In the trenches
(12th day)

Misty day though fine. Heavy shelling of the Seaforths trenches began about 8.30.a.m. also on our left flank, for nearly two hours shrapnel burst continually in rear of there trenches, those coming from a N-W direction being suspiciously like our own guns, others came from a N-E direction, and must have been from an enemy's battery enfilading our line. Right flank and support trenches were also subjected to heavy shrapnel and howitzer fire.

On the left flank the enemy had sapped up unpleasantly close, and with a view to the posibilities of a local counter attack, two Coys. from the Brigade reserve were sent up. These however only arrived by dark, and were not employed for making a counter attack, as the ground was unfamiliar to them, and acquaintance with the ground was essential to success.

Meantime preparations had been made for rushing one of the enemy's trenches 50x from our R.flank trenches 25 men from 2/39th G.assisted by 25 men from 1/39th G. the whole under Major G.H.Taylor were detailed to carry out an assault on this trench, but later on this party was increased to 100 men. The assault was termed for 6 p.m. but owing to unforeseen delay did not take place

WAR DIARY
or
INTELLIGENCE SUMMARY.
(Erase heading not required.)

Army Form C. 2118.

WAR DIARY or INTELLIGENCE SUMMARY.

(Erase heading not required.)

Hour, Date, Place.

9-11-1914.
(continued)

Summary of Events and Information.

till somewhat later.
The whole party were lined up in the ditch just in front of the R.flank trenches, and the order to advance given. For some reason the 1/39th G., party lost touch, and the 2/39th G. arrived as the parapet of the enemy's trench alone, and quite unknown to the enemy who would be heard talking in the trench.

Major Taylor then fired his revolver in to the trench, and the whole party rushed over the parapet. The occupant of the trench fired a few rounds and bolted. Three prisoners were made in the trench, 3 more being rounded up shortly afterwards.

When the 2/39th G. charged, the 1/39th G. also charged, and firing and shouting was heard from their direction.

Some of the party had brought spade and picks with them with a view to filling in the trench, but it was found to be 7 or 8 feet deep, revetted, and provided with head cover, so the task was considered impossible.

Meanwhile a terrific fusilade had broken out from the enemys trenches in rear, about 400 away, so Major Taylor deemed it advisable to retire to our own trenches.

The prisoners were relieved of all papers, documents etc., taken to Battalion Headquarter and from there despatched to Brigade Headquarter.

Only 4 men were wounded during this operation.
Major Taylor brought the following to notice for good work during the operation.
Jem. Kushal Sing Danu.
Hav. Ranjor Sing Pundir.
Hav. Dewan Sing Padhiyar.

It is known that 2 of the enemy were killed, but then other casualties could not be discovered.

The operation was extremely well carried out by Major Taylor whom the C.O. brought to the G.O.C's favourable notice.

Early this morning a patrol of scouts sent out, and one of them No.1191 Rifn.Betal Sing Rana was mortally wounded. It was getting light, and the patrol leader L.Nk.Diwan Sing Bhandari and No.1342 Rifn.Ganeshu Sing Surjwan assisted him back to the trenches under the enemy's fire. The latter having done best has been re-

9-11-1914.
(continued)

commended for the order of merit.
Casualties during the day. I.O. wounded 1 (Jm. Indar S. Negi)
Indian Ranks wounded 3 Killed 1.
Total to day.   K.   W.
I.O's.   ....   -   2
R.& F.   ...   11   81   11.K.83.W.

10-11-1914.
In the trenches.
(13th day)

A quiet day, except for usual sniping and some shell fire, and rather misty.
Our guns shelled the trenches E of the LA BASSEE road, making excellent practice.
Digging of trenches for new alignment continued, a company from the reserve being employed for this purpose.
Received a consignment of caps and comforters from General Evatt for Officers.
29 Rank and File, of the 1st 10% reinforcement originally left at the Base joined today.
Casualties. Indian Ranks Killed 3 wounded 14.
Total to date.   K.   W.
I.O's.   ...   -   2
R.& F.   ...   14   95
                    14   97

11-11-1914.
In the trenches
(14th day)

Sniping as usual all day, and some shell fire, a cold day with wind and rain.
Work on new line of entrenchments continued at dusk. Sappers laid out wire entanglement in front of this line.
Our artillery shelled enemy's entrenchments heavily at midnight for 1 hour. extremely cold wet night. Casualties. Indian Ranks Killed 2 wounded 1.
Total to date. I.O's. W.2. R.& F. K.16. W.96.

12-11-1914.
In the trenches.
(15th day)

A quiet day, except that the new line of trenches was persistently shelled, also our left flank trenches.

The enemy's trenches appeared to be strongly held today, and there is a machine gun in the nearer trenches opposite the L.flank.

3 men went in to LOCON in the morning to be inspected by Field Marshal Earl Roberts.V.C.Commander-in-chief of the Indian Army Corps.

Casualties. Indian Ranks Killed 2 wounded 2.
Total to date.

	K.	W.
I.O's. ...	-	2
R.&F.	18	98
	18	100

13-11-1914.
In the trenches.
(16th day)

A quiet day, and sniping as presistent and accurate as ever. C.O. went in to see G.O.C. and discuss arrangements for second assault on enemy's near trench.

A windy rainy day, and the trenches in consequence a regular quagmire.

At 9 p.m. another assault was delivered on the same trench of the enemy's that had been assaulted on the 9th. The assaulting party consisted of 250 men of the 2/3rd G.R. and 50 men (under Major Taylor) of 2/39th G.

On the first gun firing previous to the advance (the artillery having been ordered to cooperate) the whole detachment advanced. A very short time after the advance began a cheer was heard on the right, where the 2/3rd were, which was immediately followed by heavy firing on the enemy's part.

It appears that on the firing breaking out heavy casualties occurred among the assaulting party, and though some managed to reach the trench, the majority retired to the ditch from where they had started.

Several wounded men returned to the trenches, but had no news to give, as to what was happening in front. Meanwhile Col. Brackspear, Commanding the 2/3rd Detachment,

13-11-1914.
(continued)

returned from the enemy's trenches for more men, as only a very few had got in, and there were several wounded there, including two British Officers.

Nothing was known as to what had happened on the left where Major Taylor and his party were. Meanwhile the enemy's search-light began to play all along the line of trenches shewing up the place like day light.

On the situation being explained to Col. Omasby, 2/3rd G.R., (who was in command of the Brigade reserve from whom the assaulting party had been detailed) he determined to make another advance to try and reach the enemy's trench and bring in the wounded, and he asked the C.O. to send another party in the left with a similar object.

Meanwhile the enemy were keeping up a very heavy musketry fire from their rear trenches, about 350 - 400 away.

Captain A.W. Robertson-Glasgow was then despatched with 22 men to try and reach the trench and ascertain what had happened to Major Taylor and his party on the left. The searchlight playing along the line of trenches made advancing very difficult, and as soon as a man appeared above the edge of the ditch to advance a hail of bullets came at him. Under there circumstances it was extremely difficult to get men to advance, and several more casualties occurred here.

The trenches were now getting full of wounded men, and there were sent back as quick as possible to be dressed and sent to the aid post.

Scouts were now sent out to see if they could ascertain what had happened to either Major Taylor's or Captain Robertson-Glasgow's parties, but they could not get any distance owing to the searchlight and the intensity of the fire.

A double company of the 1/9th G.R. had been sent up in support but had not arrived, and finally the O.C. 1/9th G.R. himself arrived to see the situation. Captain Forster, Staff Captain, Garhwal Brigade, now arrived in the trenches to see the situation.

After many attempts had been made to advance,

13-11-1914.
(continued)

the conclusion was arrived at that it was useless to try and advance any more in face of the searchlight. It was decided to leave the wounded, with the exception of those who lay comparatively near, and endeavour to get them in the following morning under the protection of the Red cross.

50 men of the 34th Poona Horse had been sent up as reserve, and of there 25 occupied the trenches when Captain Robertson-Glasgow's party went out.

The night was wet and blowy.

Casualties.   during day. B.O's Missing 2 &
              Indian Officers --"--   1
              R.& F. ....,--"--   9
              R.& F. ....Wounded.   28

Total to date.   K.   W.   M.
       B.O's. ...   -   -   2
       I.O's. ...   -   2   1
       R.& F. ...   19   126   /9
                      19   128   12

14-11-1914.
In the trenches.
(17th day)

Fine morning and very cold.

Nothing of note occurred. The enemy still appeared busy at his trenches, and during the day our Machine Gun was able to enfilade some men digging E of the LA BASSEE road and killed some 8 or 9 of them.

The enemy used his searchlight a great deal this night, also flares; it seems they are very much on the qui vive after the two attacks on their trenches.

Sniping during the day presistent and accurate as ever.

The new line of entrenchments was shelled vigorously during the day, especially the section on the extreme left., which touches the main road in rear of the position; this road of course forms a good mark for artillery.

Today 2 machine guns of the 4th Cavalry were sent up to occupy the gap between the 1/39th G. and ourselves;

Major. G. H. Taylor.
Capt. A. W. Robertson-Glasgow

14-11-1914.
(continued)

4 platoons of the 2/3rd G.R. from Brigade reserve also arrived, 2 occupying the gap, and 2 being kept in support.
Left flank trenches were subjected to a hot artillery and shrapnel fire during the day.
A party of 50 men from 107th Pioneers came up at dusk and worked on the new alignment of trenches, making head cover etc.
Our guns bombarded enemy's entrenchments from 2.45 p.m. to 3.40 p.m. necessitating the evacuation of my R. flank trenches during that time, but the bombardment was not very severe, and after it had ceased the fire from there trenches was as severe as ever.

Casualties. during day. Indian Ranks wounded 1.
Total to date.   K.   W.   M.
     B.O's.   -   -   2
     I.O's.   2   1
     R.& F.   19   127   9
                   19   129   12

15-11-1914.
In the trenches.
(18th day)

About 5 a.m. our artillery began bombarding the enemy's trenches in front of our R. flank trenches. One of our heavey batteries, evidently mistaking the range, put a number of shells within 15 to 20 of our own trenches, one of them actually falling in the trench, killing 4 and wounding one. News was at once sent to the Brigade to request the artillery to stop dropping shells near our own trenches, and subsequently apologies were received from the C.R.A. for this accident.
A quiet day otherwise till 2.30. p.m. when a short but severe shrapnel fire opened on the buildings round Battalion Headquarters and a hasty move had to be made to the shelter of the support trench, and all sick moved from the hospital shed also. This shrapnel set fire to a haystack, which had been a plentiful source of supply for the trenches, and the farm buildings were soon in a

15-11-1914.
(continued)

blaze,. Some boxes of ammunition stored in the building were moved by Major MacTier to a place of safety. A lot of lose ammunition lying about in the yard kept on going off in the flames, sounding like a miniature action.

The day was blenk and miserable, and a slight fall of snow occurred, with heavy rain.

Casualties. Indian ranks killed 4, Wounded 4.
Total to date.

	K.	W.	M.
B.O's.	-	-	2
G.O's.	-	2	1
R.& F.	23	131	9
	23	133	12

16-11-1914.
In the trenches.
(19th day)

A quiet day, nothing unusual to record, very wet and cold. Usual howitzer shelling of new line of entrenchments.

Searchlights active after dark along our front and front of 19th Brigade.

A small dug-out was made in the support trench behind the R.flank trenches, to accomodate Battalion Headquarters after the fire caused by shrapnel yesterday.

Received news that the 2/2nd G.R. would relieve us on the 17th.

Casualties. Indian Ranks wounded.
Total to date.

	K.	W.	M.
B.O's.	-	-	2
G.O's.	-	2	1
R.& F.	23	132	9
	23	134	12

17-11-1914.
In the trenches.
(20th day)

A quiet day, except for usual shell fire and sniping. Some rain.

British Officers of 2/2nd G.R. came up about 4.30 p.m. to be shewn round the trenches, and given all available information.

Their Battalion was then brought up and the relief was carried out, a slow business as the trenches were very narrow and not made for much traffic, and also very muddy owing to recent rain.

Before the relief actually took place our M.G. opened fire on a group of the enemy whom they saw creeping up the ditch lined with billows about 50 or so from our trench facing E parallel to the LABASSEE road. They shewed up in the light caused by one of the enemy's flares.

The enemy's searchlight was busy this evening during the relief, which made matters worse. Also heavy firing broke out during the relief and this also caused delay.

The 2/2nd G.R. who had lost their M. guns and telephones in their previous fight with the enemy, and had not yet had them replaced, took over our telephones in the trenches for the time being, and our M.guns and detachment complete for one night, as theirs, though issued, were not ready yet.

At 9.30 p.m. the relief was complete, and companies marched off and rendez-voused at RUE DE L'EPINETTE. From here the Battalion marched as a whole to billets at LA TOURET about 4 miles back from the trenches, reaching the place at 10.45 p.m.

The men were comfortably accomodated in brans etc., and the Officers in a large house. The whole deserved their much needed rest, as they had occupied the most important part of the line, the Battalion being specially selected for the important part of the defence. Several complimentary Messages were received from the G.O.C.Brigade; Divisional Commander and Army Corps Commander, which were most gratifying.

Casualties during day. Indian Ranks Killed 1, wounded 2, casualties had been very heavy during the occupation of

17-11-1914.
(continued)

this left section of the defence, totalling 2 B.O's, 3 Indian Officers, and 167 Rank and File.

	K.	W.	M.
B.O's.	-	-	2
I.O's.	-	2	1
R.& F.	24	134	9
	24	136	12

18-11-1914
In Billets
LA TOURET.

A bright warm morning, changed in, to cold during the day. Day spent in general clearring up of rifles and accoutrements after 19 nights and 19 days in the trenches.

During the morning Major General Kerry.C.B.,D.S.O. Commanding Garhwal Brigade visited the Officers in this billet, and also addressed the Indian Officers, and congratulated all on the way the Battalion had worked.

19-11-1914.
In billets. LA-T-
LA TOURET.
and RUE de BOIS.

A cold morning C.O. inspected all rifles at 10 a.m. and went round all the companies.

Received news early this morning that we were to move up to form Brigade reserve to night, and go into billets at RUE de BOIS, vice the 1/9th G.R. who were relieving the 1/39th G. in the trenches, who in turn were to occupy our billets at LA TOURET.

About midday it turned very cold, and began to snow and continued snowing all day and well on into the night.

19-11-1914.
(continued)

At 4.30 p.m. Nos. 1 and 3 D.C's moved off to billets in RUE de BOIS, followed later by Nos. 2 and 4 D.C's. Very comfortable billets for men, Battalion headquarters being situated with Nos. 1 and 3 D.C's.

20-11-1914.
Billets, RUE de BOIS.

A bright fresh morning, cold and tracing snow fairly thick on the ground. C.O. round billets in morning. Nos. I and II D.C's out from 6 p.m. 11 p.m. digging reserve and support trenches near firing line. Casualties Indian Ranks wounded 1 while on fatigue.

21-11-1914.
Billets, RUE de BOIS.

Cold morning, but fresh and bracing. Nothing of importance to record during the day. Nos. III and IV D.C's out from 6 p.m. -11 p.m. as for yesterday. Received orders to move to billets LA COUTURE on 23rd, on relief by 3rd Lahore Division.

22-11-1914.
Billets, RUE de BOIS.

Cold morning. Nothing of importance to record.
Total casualties to date.

	K.	W.	M.
B.O's.	-	-	2
I.O's.	-	2	1
R.& F.	24	136	9
	24	138	12

23-11-1914.
Billets LA Couture.

Cold dull morning, with promise of more snow. Marched from billets RUE de BOIS at 2 p.m. reaching LA COUTURE shortly after 3 p.m. Formed up on open space in village and waited. At about 4.15 p.m. commenced taking over billets from 47th Sikhs Nos. II and III D.C's in big barns, and I and IV and Headquarters in a big house with courtyard. All very comfortable. Remainder of brigade on in reserve of 21st Brigade., reported heavily attacked. Received warm Khaki uniform for men from ordnance today, but too late to issue today.

Other 3 regiments of Brigade despatched to xxxxxxxx reinforce 21st Brigade, where the germans had broken through, about 4 p.m.

It appears verbal orders were sent for 2/39th G. also, but there never reached.

24-11-1914.
Billets LA COUTURE.

A milder morning, and a thaw setting in. D.C's and M.Guns out for a short route march to keep men and animals fit.

Opened up warm clothing, but found it all too small in chest and waist measurements, being only 34" 35" chest, and 32"-33" inch waist, and it would be quite

Hour, Date, Place.	Summary of Events and Information.	Remarks and references to Appendices.

24-11-1914.
(continued)

impossible for men to wear these coats over all their warm clothing. It was therefore all repacked and returned to store.

G.O.C. Brigade went round billets in morning.

25-11-1914.
Billets LA
COUTURE and in
the trenches
FESTUBERT.

Mild morning. Paraded at 12 noon to march to GORRE church, where 350 men of the Battalion had orders to rendezvous to relieve units in the trenches formerly occupied by the 21st (Bareilly) Brigade, arrived GORRE church 1.45. p.m., but found no Staff Officer or orders waiting. Eventually Battalion marched on and halted well in rear of the line at a barn near the village of FESTUBERT. From here C.O. and D.C.C's went on to see the trenches which the Battalion was to take over from the 1/39th G., being the same as those which the 1/39th G., had re-taken from the Germans on the night of 23/24 November. At dusk the Battalion moved up and went into the trenches, A.B.D.G. and H. Coys. being in the firing line, and C. Coy. in support (E. and F. Coys. had remained behind in billets).

The trenches were very bad ones, being very wide and certainly untenable under shrapnel fire. They were constantly crumbling away and needed constant revetting with sandbags. Also the whole line of trenches occupied by the Battalion was one huge grave, a large number of corpses having been buried actually in the trenches and parapet by former occupants of the line. There were also a large number of dead lying close to the trench, both behind and in front, the result of the fighting round this trench on Nov. 23rd, when frontal attacks had been made on it unsuccessfully in an endeavour to re-capture it from

25-11-1914.
(continued)

the Germans, and the night of the 23rd/24th when it was recaptured by the 1/39th G.

It was impossible to do anything to improve the trenches, all that could be done was to patch up bad places with sandbags.

The trenches were full of abandoned German equipment, ammunition, and rifles a large number of the latter being collected and sent to the ordnance depot for disposal.

This particular part of the line was extra ordinarily close to the enemy's trenches, which were no where more than 100 yards distant and in places only about 20 yards. The enemy had dug saps from their lines up to within 4 or 5 yards of ours, and from there saps they threw bombs continually into our trenches. In one part of the line there was actually a trench communicating with the enemy's trench; this was barricaded our end by a barricade made of machine gun shields captured from the enemy.

On the left of the line the Germans and we were occupying the same trench, being divided by about 50 yards of unoccupied trench barricaded and loopholed at each end. From our barricade a short communicating trench ran back to the continuation of our trenches, and here the distance between our trenches and the Germans was only about 20 yards.

As such close ranges sniping was presistent and accurate, and the enemy also made great use of bombs which they threw from their sap heads into out trenches. We retaliated with bombs, thrown into the enemy's sap heads. The enemy also had a machanical bomb thrower worked by a a spring, with a range of about 50 yards, and a trench mortar.

The night of 25th/26th was quiet except for sniping.

A thaw set in to dayp after the recent frost, and the roads were in a very bad condition

26-11-1914.
In the trenches
FESTUBERT.

Quiet morning, except for usual sniping and some bombing. No shelling of these trenches by the enemy taken place, as their own trenches are so close up.
At dusk No.3 D.C. came up from their billets to relieve the 41st Dogras in the trenches. Opposite the line of trench occupied by No.3 D.C. one of the enemy's saps had been driven up to with 4 or 5 yards of the trench. From this sap bombs were continually thrown, and the parapet of our trench was much broken in, necessitating a new trench being dug a few yards in rear. A good supply of bombs was received, and a good many were thrown at the German sap head, but with what result it is impossible to say.
Weather dull, and not very cold.
Casualties. Indian Ranks Killed 2. Wounded 5.

Total to date:-   K.   W.   M
British Officers. -   -   2   2
Indian   -   -   2   1
Rank & File -   26   14   9
                      26   14   12

27-11-1914.
In the trenches
FESTUBERT.

Nothing of note happened during the night, which was followed by a quiet morning. No.III.D.C. section bombed considerably during the day, also the trenches on our extreme left, where 50 men of the Black Watch to be relieved by the 2/8th Gurkhas, and for Lieut.Col. Drake Brockman to take Command of this section of the line. C.O. therefore proceded to Section Headquarter in a house on a road in rear of the position and took over command. During the evening the 2/8th G.R. arrived to relieve the Black Watch, and later on Lieut.Col.Grant, Commanding 2/8th G.R. also arrived and took over Command of the section from Lieut.Col.Drake-Brockman. Some anxietey was shown by the G.O.C.Ferozepore Brigade, under whose orders the Battalion was, regarding the left of the section, part of which was evacuated at lines by closing the men to one flank to avoid the enemy's bombs, but the trenches were never actually evacuated

27-11-1914.
(Continued).

entirely. A strong report was submitted by Lieut.Colonel. Drake Brockman,when in Command of the section about the state of the trenches,especially that portion of the trenches occupied by the Battalion and which had been captured by the Germans and re-captured from them. Some regiment had buries all the corpses Germans and Indian in the fire trench instead of throwing them back/ over the rear of trench for burial by night.

In reply while agreeing with the report the Army Commander sent orders to day to clear the trenches of corpses,and as far as possible remove and bury all corpses in the vicinity.pecuniary rewards and decorations being promised for good work.This was well done by the men and a list submitted of men for favourable notice of G.O.C.and Corps Commander.

The enemy were fairly busy with bombs today against No.III.D.C., several casualties occuring on this account.

Otherwise nothing of note occurred during the day,beyond the usual sniping which caused some casualties.

Casualties. Indian Ranks Killed 1, Wounded 8.

Total. British Officers K. W. M
                              -   2   2
Indian —
Other ranks — 27 149   9
     Total   27 151 12

28-11-1914.
In the trenches
FESTUBERT.

A mild morning.Considerable amount of bombing again,especially against No.III.D.C.and a lot of damage done to the parapet,knocking it down for the length of 3 whole traverses. Bombs also thrown at other parts of the line,but not so much damage done.

Received information that Battalion was to be relieved in the trenches to night by the 2/Leicester Regiment,and the 58th(Vaughans)Rifles.

28-11-1914.
(continued).

Officers from the 2/Leicesters came up in day light to see the trenches, and after dark the relief commenced. This took some time, and it was not till 11.30 p.m. that the relief was complete, and the last D.C.(No.III) left FESTUBERT at midnight, and arrived in billets LA COUTURURE at 1.15 a.m., the other D.C's having marched independently to billets previously.
Some rain fell during the evening.
Casualties. Indian Ranks Killed 4, Wounded 5.
Total during occupation of this part of the line Indian Ranks Killed 7, Wounded 18.

Total to date.

	K.	W.	M.
B.O's.	-	-	2
I.O's.	-	2	1
R.& F.	31	154	9
	31	156	12

29-11-1914.
Billets
LA COUTURE

Weather mild. Muster parade held at midday. Otherwise a quiet day, men resting after their return from trenches.

30-11-1914.
Billets
LA COUTURE.

Weather mild and cloudy. Day spent in cleaning up accoutrements etc. Nothing of note to record.

1-12-1914.
Billets.
LA COUTURE.

Morning wet, but cleared up later. Captain Burton and 100 men went to LOCON, and were there inspected by H.M. The King, together with other Indian Troops.
C.O. went in evening to the trenches near RICHEBOURG originally occupied by the Battalion, to take them over from 59th Rifles.

2-12-1914.
Billets LA COUTRE and in the trenches RICHE BOURG.

Dull morning, cloudy, but weather mild. Paraded 4.30 p.m. to march to trenches, to relieve 59th Rifles F.F. in the same trenches as occupied by Battalion from 29-10-14, to 17.11.14. Arrived in trenches after an hours marching, going slow as the men were carrying a blanket., W.P.Sheet, and a warm sheepskin coat. A.B.C.D.G.H. were in the the firing trenches, E. and F in support. Relief carried out out in an hour. Situation in front of trenches little., if any, different from what it was when Battalion left on 17th November, but inside the support trenches communication had been considerably improved, and a comfortable bomb proof built to accomodate Battalion Headquarters in the orchard near the R.support trench. The loopholes in the trenches had not been well looked after, and required a lot of repairing, as well as the parapet, which had fallen in in many places owing to occupants of the trenches burrowing too much underneath. A quiet night, with considerable sniping. The Battalion had to occupy the trench made in the gap between the 1st Battalion and our line so the line occupied was of considerable length.
The 4th Cavalry M.G. were in the trench also. On our left were the 5

On our left were the 5th Black Watch Territorials, and on our Right the 2/2 Gurkhas.

Casualties Indian Ranks wounded 2
Total to date   K.   W.   M.

```
B.O,s       -     -     2
I.O,s       -     2     1
R&F        31.  156.    9
           ---------------
           31.  158.   12.
```

3. 12. 1914.
In the Trenches.

Mild morning. Everything very quiet in front, except for considerable sniping. No shelling by enemy. Gunner observation officer round trenches in afternoon to see if he could help with guns at all, but not much help possible, as the enemy have no saps up close enough to be dangerous yet

Casualties Indian Ranks wounded...2.
Total to date   K.   W.   M.

```
B.O,s            .-    -     2
Indian Officers. -     2     1
Rank and file..  31   158    9
                 31.  169.  12.
```

(4th December 1914.)
In the trenches.

Fine morning, but cloudy later, and some rain in evening. Usual sniping and one or two shrapnel over support trenches in afternoon, but no damage. Otherwise a quiet day.

Casualties Indian Ranks wounded. . . .6
Total to date . .   K.   W.   M.

```
British Officers..  .  -    -    2
Indian    "  ........  -    2    1
Rank and File ......  31   158   9
                      ---------------
                      31.  165.  12.
```

5th December 1914.
In the trenches.

Wet and Miserable morning, with cold wind. Sniping vigorous and one or two howitzer shells fell some distance away about midday. A few shrapnel also burst in the vicinity of Battalion Head Quarters, but no damage done. Work on improving improving trenches carried on. Trenches very muddy owing to rain, and falling in, needing constant repair.

Casualties Indian Ranks   K.   W.   M.

	K.	W.	M.
British Officers	-	-	2
Indian Officers	-	2	1
Rank and File	31	167	9
	31.	169.	12.

(6th December 1914.)
In the trenches.

Cloudy morning. Sniping as usual, but no shelling, except for three shrapnel which burst in the orchard or near there, near Battalion Head Quarters. Work in repairing trenches continued, planks and beams being collected from houses in the vicinity.

Casualties............Nil.

(7th December 1914.)
In the trenches.

A wet miserable day, rain lasting all day and trenches in an awful state in consequence. Trenches perpetually falling in and needing constant repair. Sniping by day not quite so persistent. A small sap begun from E end of trenches facing south towards a piquet post to be dug to command ditches running due South from here.

Casualties...Indian Ranks...Killed 1 Wounded..2

Total to date

	K.	W.	M.
B.O,s.	-	-	2
I.O,s.	-	2	1
R.& F.	32	169	9
	32.	171.	12.

WAR DIARY or INTELLIGENCE SUMMARY.

Army Form C. 2118.

Hour, Date, Place.

8th December 1914.
In the trenches.

Summary of Events and Information.

Cloudy morning. Trenches in a very bad state after rain and very muddy. Parapets need constant revetting. Sandbags useless for the purpose as they rot so soon. Boards planks, doors etc taken from ruined houses in vicinity & used for revetting. Sniping still persistent, and sand bag loopholes continually being broken down by enemies rifle. Casualties Indian Ranks wounded....1

```
Total to date        K.     W.     M.
        B.O,s         -      -     -
        I.O,s        Nil     2     1
        R & F.        32    170    9
                    ------------------
                     32.    172.   12.
```

(9th December 1914.)
In the trenches.

Cloudy morning with slight drizzel, and trenches terribly muddy. Parapet still in need of constant repair. Sappers and Miners sent a bomb gun to our left flank trenches, and fired several bombs into enemy,s trenches, but actual effect unknown. Enemy appear to be "Jumpy" as they are continually sending up flares at night. A misty day, so not so much rifle fire as usual.
Casualties Indian Ranks Killed 2 Wounded 1.

```
Total to date        K.     W.     M.
        B.O;s         -      -     -
        I.O;s         -      2     1
        R & F         34    171    12
                     34.    173.   12.
```

1 Squdron 9th Hod Son's Horse took over portion of our Right flank trench, with a view to leaming trench work.
Captain Harbord, 44th Infantry, reported his arrival today to be attached to Regiment.

Remarks and references to Appendices.

9th December 1914.
Reinforcements.
158 Rank and file joined this day, under Captain PARKIN 113th Infantry attached for duty.

WAR DIARY or INTELLIGENCE SUMMARY.

(Erase heading not required.)

Army Form C. 2118.

10-12-1914.
In the trenches.

A cloudy morning, but no rain early in the day, but slight drizzle about midday. Bomb gun fired several bombs at enemys trenches, which seemed to have some effect as sniping was certainly considerably less than as former days.

The squadron which arrived yesterday took up the whole of the trench previously occupied by A.Coy., who came into support trenches.

Casualties. Indian Ranks Wounded 4.

Total to date.

	K.	W.	M.
B.O's. ...	-	-	2
I.O's. ...	-	2	1
R.& F. ...	34	175	9
	34	177	12

11-12-1914.
In the trenches.

A raw misty morning. Comparatively little sniping and rifle fire, probably owing to a mist. A few rounds fired from the bomb gun, and our howitzers fired a few rounds in the afternoon. Otherwise a quiet day. Supports out during the day collecting beams, doors, etc., from ruined houses, which were sent up to the trenches at dusk for revetting purposes. Rain began to fall about 5 p.m. and trenches very muddy again, parts under water.

CASUALTIES. Indian Ranks Killed 1. Wounded 3.

Total to date.

	K.	W.	M.
B.O's. ...	-	-	2
I.O's. ...	-	2	1
R.& F. ...	35	178	9
	35	180	12

WAR DIARY or **INTELLIGENCE SUMMARY.**
(Erase heading not required.)

Army Form C. 2118.

12-12-1914.
In the trenches.

Cold and misty morning, remaining misty all day, with some rain. Work of revetting trenches with doors etc., carried on. Some bombing on our right, and enemy fired a few rounds of Howitzer about 4 p.m. which fell in the vicinity of 2/3rd G.R. Headquarters and factory on RUE DE BOIS. A miserable day as regards weather, and sniping not quite so much, probably on account of the inclement weather. Enemy as usual active with flares and search lights at nightfall, bursts of fire breaking out every time a flare went up.

Casualties. Indian Ranks Killed 1., Wounded 3 (one man being killed and 1 wounded while inside a house on the Rue De Bois collecting straw).

Total to date	K.	W.	M.
B.O's. ...	-	-	2
I.O's. ...	-	2	1
R.& F. ...	36	181	9
	36	183	12

13-12-1914.
In the trenches.

Cloudy morning. Work continued on parapet; and trenches in general which still need a tremendous amount of work. Quiet day on the whole, chiefly sniping. Rained again in the evening and trenches still very muddy. Support Coys., worked at widening communication trenches etc.

Casualties. Indian ranks Wounded 7.

Total to date.	K.	W.	M.
B.O's. ...	-	-	2
I.O's. ...	-	2	1
R.& F. ...	37 ⊙	187 ✳	9
	37	189	12

⊙ Includes 1 man (1754 Rfn. Daulat Sing Neg¹) died of wounds on 30-11-14, in Lahore Clearing Hospital LILLERS.
✳ Excludes .ditto.

14-12-1914.
In the trenches.

Fine morning, orders received to carry out a fire attack on enemy's trenches from 10 a.m. to 5 p.m. with a view to assisting advance of a division (which and where unknown) to our North, by holding enemy here and preventing him detaching reinforcements to meet offensive movement above referred to. Fire superiority was gained along practically the whole of our front, the majority of the enemy's loopholes being rendered useless, and his fire slackening appreinably. One of the machine guns put out of action, the barrel casing being perforated by two bm bullets, and the tangent sight elevation screw damaged. Revelting of trenches continued. One of the enemy's bombs blew in a piece of trench occupied by C.Coy., which had just been repaired. Enemy dropped a few howitzer shells about midday near our trenches, but no damage done. Fire maintained throgh earlier part of the night.

Casualties. Indian Ranks wounded 2.

Total to date.	K.	W.	M.
B.O's. ...	-	-	2
I.O's. ...	-	2	1
R.& F. ...	37	189	9
	37	191	12.

15-12-1914.
In the trenches.

Fine morning raining later. Fire attack commenced as yesterday at 10 a.m. and fire superiority gained and enemy's loopholes considerably damaged. During the night a machine gun was received from 41st Dogras to replace the one damaged on 14th a new emplacement was made for the Mahhine Guns., in the time of trenches behind out left flank. Comparatively little fire from the enemy during the day. Work continued in trenches repairing parapet and revelting with boards, doors etc.

Casualties. Indian Ranks Killed 3. Wounded 2.

15-12-1914.
(Continued).

Total to date.
	K.	W.	M.
B.O's. ...	-	-	2
I.O's. ...	-	2	1
R.& F. ...	40	191	9
	40	193	12

16-12-1914.
In the trenches.

Dull morning. At 10 a.m. commenced bursts of fire on enemy's trenches to assist attack of LAHORE Division to the S. Several of enemy's loopholes destroyed. One of our Machine Guns had the foresight shot away, in the dark, early in the morning, but gun still serviceable. Bursts of fire kept up till dusk. News received later in evening that 3rd Division had captured 2 of enemy's sap heads. After dark enemy commenced a continous fire, which they kept up throughout the night, damaging our loopholes considerably. Received orders regarding Major Stewart's appointment as Brigade Major, Garhwal Brigade, vice Major Young died of wounds. Revetting of trenches carried on.
Casualties. Indian Ranks killed 1, wounded 10.

Total to date
	K.	W.	M.
B.O's. ...	-	-	2
I.O's. ...	-	2	1
R.& F. ...	41	201	9
	41	203	12

17-12-1914.
In the trenches.

Cold morning. Enemy suddenly opened heavy fire at 7.30 a.m. on No.I D.C. trenches, destroying the loopholes,

17-12-1914.
(continued)

but otherwise doing no damage. Sniping continous all day, and enemy shelled a house on the Rue de Bois which had been inspected the day before with a view to its being used as an observing station. Sniping very presistent in early part of night, and enemy's searchlight active. Major Stewart left today to take up his appointment as Brigade Major.

Casualties. Indian ranks Wounded 3.
Total to date

	K.	W.	M.
B.O's. ...	-	-	2
I.O's. ...	-	2	1
R.& F. ...	41	204	9
	41	206	12

18-12-1914.
In the trenches.

Cold cloudy morning. G.O.C. Division instructed his intention to visit the trenches this morning, but never came,. C.O's to see G.O.C. Brigade at 12.30 p.m. in Rue de Berceaux. Instructions received for 1/39th G. and 2/39th G. to keep up a heavy fire while 2/ Leicesters, supported by ½ Battalion 2/3rd Q.A.O.G.R. attacked enemy's trenches in their front, at 3.45 p.m. on 19th. This was done, and later news was received (early on 19th morning) that the assault had been successful, a good length of trench being captured, 2 Machine Guns and some prisoners. Otherwise a quiet day, rifle fire being less than usual. No.I D.C. opened a heavy concentrated fire on enemy's loopholes in the trench in their immediate from at 7.30 a.m. and succeeded in closing the magority of them.

Casualties. Indian ranks wounded 8.
Total to date

	K.	W.	M.
B.O's.	-	-	2
I.O's. ...	-	2	1
R.& F. ...	41	214	12
Deduct		1	0
	41	213	12

⊙ No.330 Havr. Siuraj Sing Rawat. Returned as wounded on, but subsequently reported as not wounded, only Mud having been splashed into his eye by a bullet.

WAR DIARY or INTELLIGENCE SUMMARY.

(Erase heading not required.)

Army Form C. 2118.

Hour, Date, Place.	Summary of Events and Information.	Remarks and references to Appendices.
19-12-1914. In the trenches.	A damp cloudy day. Bursts of fire were maintained on enemy's trenches as yesterday, and enemy's fire heavier than usual. A good deal of heavy rifle and gun fire was heard to N. and S., but it was an uneventful day on the whole here. Heavy rain commenced at dusk, and trenches in a very bad state. Rain continued most of the night. <u>Casualties</u>. Indian Ranks wounded 11. Total to date.　　K.　W.　M. 　B.O's.　...　-　-　2 　I.O's.　...　-　2　1 　R.& F.　...　41　222　9 　　　　　　　　41　224　12.	
20.12.1914. In the trenches.	A fine clear morning. German aeroplane appeared over our lines at 9.15 a.m. and almost immediately afterwards the enemy started a very heavy fire attack on our front, presumably to hold us to our trench while attacks were made elsewhere on the line. We replied vigorously. Heavy firing kept up till 10.30 a.m. when it died away. Bursts of rapid fire kept up by us during remainder of the day. Our aeroplanes busy all the morning. Enemy at about midday sent several shrapnel in the orchard when Battalion Headquarter is situated, several bursting quite close, but doing no harm beyond slightly bruising two men in the support trench. Enemy also fired several howitzer shells in vicinity of Battalion aid post, necessitating its evacuation. <u>Casualties</u>. Indian ranks killed 2, Wounded 6. Total to date.　　K　W　M 　B.O's.　...　-　-　2 　I.O's.　...　-　2　1 　R.& F.　...　43　228　9 　　　　　　　　43　230　12.	

WAR DIARY
or
INTELLIGENCE SUMMARY.
(Erase heading not required.)

Army Form C. 2118.

Hour, Date, Place.	Summary of Events and Information.	Remarks and references to Appendices.

21-12-1914.
In the trenches.

Cloudy cold morning. News received that Leicesters had evacuated, by order, trenches captured on 18th also that Seaforths, 2/2nd G.R. and Sirmind Brigade had been driven from their trenches (on our right, near PESTUBERT) and all had been recaptured except those of 2/2nd G.R. Enemy fired very little on our front all day, but heavy artillery fire was heard in PESTUBERT direction about midday. In the evening received orders to keep up fire on enemy in our front on hearing attack of 2nd Brigade (presumably to retake 2/2nd G.R. trenches) commence at dusk. Heavy shelling of enemy at dusk by out artillery, lyddite and shrapnel, several lyddite shells falling on the parapet of the enemy's nearer trench in our front.
The enemy also bombed our R. flank trenches, occupied by No.I D.C., during the day, but did no damage. A good deal of rain fell during the day, and parapet need constant attention. British and French aeroplanes busy during the morning over our lines.
Casualties. Indian Ranks Wounded 3.

Total to date.
	K	W	M.
B.O's.	-	-	2
I.O's.	-	2	1
R.& F.	43	331	9
	43	333	12

22-12-1914.
In the trenches.

Clear morning but cold. Enemy quiet during the morning, only occasional sniping at about midday received news that an aviation had seen 6 Battalions of Germans in readiness at BAS POMMERAU, east of NEUVE CHAPELLE. As this looked like a threatened attack on N. CHAPELLE, preparations were made to meet it, and dispositions arranged in case of a temporary evacuation of the trenches becoming necessary. A quiet day till dusk, when spasmodic bursts of fire broke

Captain Reed transferred to Field Ambulance, SICK.

22-12-1914.
(continued)

out. Occasional heavy firing heard to both North and South during the day.
    Casualties. Indian Ranks Wounded 4.
       Total to date.   K. W. M.
          B.O's. ...   -   - 2
          I.O's. ...   -   2 1
          R.&F. ... 43 236/5 9
                      43 238 7 12.

23-12-1914.
In the trenches.

    Cold morning. A quiet day on the whole. During the morning Major MacTier reported his trench (the extreme left of the line) was being flooded out. The scouts during the night had discovered a small tunnel dug under the LA BASSEE road connecting with a trench running out from the German main trench E. of the road. Down this and through the tunnel and thence down the ditch W. of the road water was flowing and finding its way into our extreme left trench where it joined the LA BASSEE road. That part of the trench occupied by the left section of G.Coy., had to be evacuated as it was flooded and the parapet was subsiding owing to the water. The communication trench leading to the next Bde's trenches on our left being occupied instead, though this trench was also found to be partially flooded and a dam had to be built to prevent further flooding. A sapper officer was sent for, and he gave it as his opinion that undoubtedly the Germans had constructed a well in their trench and were pumping water into the ditch and thence into our trenches. Part of the parapet in their trench was higher than elsewhere and this spot was located as the probable position of the pump. The sapper went along the communicating trench above referred to to go and see if he could find the obstruction which caused the

23-12-1914.
(continued)

water to flow back into our trenches. He did not return, so later on the C.O. sent word over to the regiment on our left (the E.Lancs.) to ask them if they knew anything about him, and they reported that he had been killed in the trench.
Enemy fired several bombs on our right and left flanks after dark, but did no damage. Germans opened several bursts of fire during the night, and kept on sending up flares and using their searchlight as if they apprehended an attack.

Casualties. Indian ranks Wounded 3.

Total to date	K.	W.	M.
B.O's. ...	-	-	2
I.O's. ...	-	2	1
R.& F. ...	43	238	9
	43	240	12.

24-12-1914.
In the trenches.

Fine morning, through cold. Water reported to be still flowing, and difficulty of out let still unsolved. About 12 midday a gunner from a heavy battery came up to observe, from our L.flank trenches the effect of a few rounds of lyddite from a siege battery, on the place in the enemy's trench where the pump was apparently working. A telephone line was run out from the trenches to the gunner observing the back on the RUE de BOIS and thence to the battery so that the observing officer was in direct communication with the battery commander, after waiting 2 hours (2-4 p.m.) for fire to commence the project was given up for today as the battery commander telephoned down to say his guns were required for a more important target.

Fine clear afternoon, and 3 of our aeroplanes were very busy during the after-noon, and were continual fire from enemy's shrapnel and high explosive shells.

24-12-1914.
(Continued)

After dusk working parties were sent out to dig out a broken in culvent on the RUE de BOIS near the spot where the second line trenches hit the road, in the hopes that the water would drain off across the road. This was found to be impossible however, as the ground appeared to slope _upwards_ away from the culvent on both sides of the road. The water stopped rising during the night, and all that could be done was to make a dam in the 2nd line trenches to prevent them being flooded. It was freezing at the time, and the men were working in icy cold water, clearing out the culvent, in bare feet and legs. The water did not rise any more during the night.

The enemy were fairly quiet all day, and sniping alternated with bursts of rapid fire. At 2 a.m. in the mounting a working party of sappers came to improve 2nd line trenches.

Casualties. Indian Ranks Wounded 4.
Total to date.

	K.	W.	M.
B.O's.	-	-	2
I.O's.	-	2	1
R.& F.	43	242	9
	43	244	12.

25-12-1914.
In the trenches.
CHRISTMAS DAY.

A cold misty morning, hard frost. Water reported not rising. About 9 a.m. gunner observing officer came, and 4th Howitzer shortly afterwards started shelling enemy's pump. After 3 or 4 blind shells he reported that he had dropped shells, as far as he could see, within 5 yards each side of the pump, and 1 shell a good deal nearer, and about 10 shells within on 15 yards radius, but it was impossible to estimate the damage.

At 11 a.m. the O C. 5th (British) Brigade and

25-12-1914.
(continued)

the C.O.and Officers Worcesters,came to see the trenches,with a view to relieving us,though no actual orders had been received for relief.

About 3 o'clock the Germans,who had since the morning been shouting and singing in their trenches, made signs to our trenches that they wished to communicate with us,and eventually they began to climb out of their trenches.We did the same,as did also the regiments on our right and left. Both sides fraternised for about an hour,several Germans coming over to our trench and talking and conversing by signs with officers and men, several They gave our men tobacco cigarettes and newspapers,and for about an hour both sides walked about freely outside their trenches and in the open space between the 2 lines.

Opportunity was taken to search for the bodies of the officers and men who were missing after the night attack on the enemy's trenches on the night of the 18th November. Captain Burton found Captain Robertson Glasgow body lying on the parapet of the enemy's trench. The bodies of several men were also found near the trench,but the situation did not admit of a careful search sufficient to indentify them.

About 5.45 p.m.both sides retired again to their trenches,but little or no firing took place for the rest of the day,except an occasional shot. A very quiet night,no firing.Froze hard during the night.Orders received during the evening that such mutual armistices were not to take place in future.

Casualties. NIL.

26-12-1914.
In the trenches.

A fine clear morning,cold and frosty absolutely quiet,no firing by either side till late in the evening,when a maxim gun (enemy's) fired a few rounds.

26-12-1914.
(continued)

A few spasmodic rifle shots in the distance during the day, and distant artillery fire. G.O.C. MXI Division stated to be coming to visit trenches, but he never arrived. German aeroplane over lines during afternoon Captain Robertson Glasgow was buried today.
  Casualties. NIL.

27-12-1914.
In the trenches
and Billets
LACOUTURE.

Cloudy morning. Distant heavy gun fire heard towards south in the morning. Received a message at 12 midnight (26th/27th) that a German deserter had informed 8th (British) Division that the Germans intended an attack on our lines at 12.15.a.m. but nothing occurred. Very little firing during the night of 26th-27th. Received orders during the day that the Worcester Regiment would relieve us in the trenches at 4.30.p.m. They arrived soon after 5, and took over the trenches, the relief being complete at 8 p.m. Double Companies marched independently to Billets at LA COUTURE, the last D.C. reaching this place at 9.30.p.m.

During the day a considerable amount of water rose in the ditch running along the front of C.and D. trenches, and came down the small ditch between these two companies. A dam was constructed in this ditch, but the problem of disposing of this water had not been fully tackled when the relief took place. The water from the German trenches from the E.of the LA BASSEE road continued to flow but the sappers were making arrangements for it to flow out through the E.Lancs. trenches on our left, and also throgh a culvent on the RUE de BOIS which had been blow in by a shell, and had been cleared by our men.

The Regiment had been 25 days and 25 nights in the trenches, and had during the time suffered 100

27-12-1914.
(continued)

casualties (12 killed and 88 wounded) the total casualties
todate (night of 27-12-14) being

	K.	W.	M.
B.O's.	1	-	1
I.O's.	-	2	1
R.& F.	43	242	9
	44	244	11	= 299.

28-12-1914.
Billets
PARADIS.

Left LA COUTURE at 11.30 a.m. reached PARADIS
at 1.15 p.m. a short march, weather wet and squally,
and roads extremely muddy. Met General Anderson, Comdg.
Meerut Division, on the way, who asked the C.O. to congratulate
the regiment on the way they had worked. Fairly comfortable
billets, men rather crowded; wet, raw evening, with
very high wind.

29-12-1914.
Billets
ROBECQ.

Left PARADIS at 11.30 a.m. reached ROBECQ 1.45.
p.m. Route lay through RIEZ de VINAGE to LA BASSEE
canal, thence along canal for about ½ mile to ROBECQ -
Men comfortable in billets. Part of the road was flooded
in the march, necessitating a slight detour. Transport
had to follow another route, as it was not allowed to
use the canal bank, but it arrived v.shortly after the
regiment.

30-12-1914.
Billets

30-12-1914.
Billets
HURIONVILLE.

Left ROBECQ at 11 a.m. reached HURIONVILLE at 2.30 p.m. Route lay throgh LILLERS. Roads good and not so muddy as on previous marches. Very bad billets at HURIONVILLE, which is only a small mining village. In the evening Lieut.Col. Drake Brockman, Captain Burton and Captain Blair left for 7 days leave in England. At HURIONVILLE two G.O's (Sub. Shib Sing Negi and Jemr. Jura Sing Negi) and 24 men joined the Battalion as reinforcements. A damp raw day, with rain in the evening.

31-12-1914.
HURIONVILLE.

Day spent in readjusting billets and finding better places for the men. A good deal of rain during the afternoon and evening. Better billets were found for some companies in the barns etc., evacuated by 1/39th G. the day before, who had moved into the coal mines about 2 miles away.

31/12/14

H.H.Drake Brockman
Lt.Col. 39 G.

WAR DIARY

of 2/39th Garwal Rifles.

From 1st January 1915 To 31st January 1915

WAR DIARY

or

INTELLIGENCE SUMMARY.

(Erase heading not required.)

Hour, Date, Place.	Summary of Events and Information.	Remarks and references to Appendices.
1-1-1915. HURIONVILLE.	Cold cloudy morning with rain and wind. G.O.C. Division inspected all reinforcements at 10-20.a.m., and could only find 4 whom he considered unfit to serve at the front, though these were fit enough for light duty with the train etc. Further adjustment of billets carried out. Rained hard all the afternoon and evening.	
2-1-1915. HURIONVILLE.	Wet morning. Parade ordered for General Wilcocks Commanding Indian Army Corps, at 11 a.m., cancelled on account of the weather. Cleared up about midday but remained cloudy. Day spent in cleaning up accoutrements and rifles etc. A wet afternoon and evening, and very cold.	
3-1-1915. HURIONVILLE.	Another wet morning, but cleared up about eleven o'clock. D.C. parades for practising bomb throwing and passing sandbags up a trench to build a barricade in the trench. Wet in the afternoon. Saw extract from London Gazette in the papers announing the award of a new decoration, the Military Cross, to Sub. Nain Sing Chinwarn, A.Coy., and the 3rd Class Order of Merit to Rifleman Ganesh Sing Sarjwan, D. Company.	
4-1-1915. HURIONVILLE.		

WAR DIARY
or
INTELLIGENCE SUMMARY.

(Erase heading not required.)

Army Form C. 2118.

4-1-1915.
HURIONVILLE.

Wet morning. Brigade paraded at 11 a.m., for inspection by Lieut.General Sir James Willcocks, Commanding Indian Army Corps. He went round each regiment on parade, and addressed each one shortly. He congratulated this Battalion on the good work done, and expressed his pleasure at being able to inspect the regiment and say how pleased he was with the way they had worked. A very brief parade, no march past, and it was all over by 11.30 a.m., Very cold and wet on parade.

Men issued with thick khaki jackets and trousers, and a considerable number with new overcoats.

A cold raw day, with intermittent rain.

5-1-1915.
HURIONVILLE.

Wet morning, with fine intervals. Parades for practising bomb throwing etc. A small line of trench was dug, 20 yards long, to practice throwing bombs from. Wet afternoon, but a clear starlight night.

6-1-1915.
HURIONVILLE.

Fine morning with some sun, but later on rain again. Today 400 men of the Battalion attended baths at LILLERS in the Brewery, and had a good wash, and were issued with clean underclothing. Remainder practised bomb throwing etc. Cloudy afternoon with some rain. Received news today that No.375 Naik Sher Sing Negi died of wounds in Secunderabad Cav. Field Ambulance on 29-11-1914. This makes total casualties now as under:-

6-1-1915.
(continued)

4K. W. M.
45 243 11

7-1-1915.
HURIONVILLE.

A wet and stormy morning. The Garhwal and Sirhind Brigades Paraded on the road side near NURBURE, 2 miles from billets for inspection by the Commander-in-Chief Field Marshal Sir John French. He expressed himself throgh Sir James Willcocks as extremely pleased with the way the Regiment (both Battalions) had worked and the manner they had fought.

At the conclusion of the Inspection General Keary, C,B.,D.S.O., having been promoted to the Command of the Lahore Division, took his farewell of the Battalion and made us all a short speech in a few well chosen words. He was very sorry to leave the Brigade, and would liked to have taken the Brigade along with him; at the conclusion of his speech and after shaking hands with all British and Garhwali Officers, 3 cheers were given for him. The Battalion then marched back to billets. No work could be done owing to heavy rain.

8-1-1915.
HURIONVILLE.

A good deal of rain at intervals during the day. The Battalion paraded at 10.30 a.m., under the C.O., while the sentence of 30 lashes awarded to No.1221 Rifn. Moti Sing Patwal, for sleeping on his post in the trenches, by Summary G.C.M., was carried out. On coclusion of the parade Double Companies were marched off by Double Company Commanders and

8-1-1915
(continued)

practised in Bomb throwing, digging of trenches, putting out parties for digging etc. 16 reinforcements arrived from Marseilles.

9-1-1915.
HURIONVILLE.

Another wet day, heavy showers the whole day with brief intervals.
Parades were under Double Company Commanders who continued practice on the same lines as yesterday.

10-1-1915.
HURIONVILLE.

A bright sunny day with a slight frost in the early morning. Double Companies exercised in capturing hostile trench traverse by traverse by the Bomb throwing method, disposal of captured prisoners in a trench, laying out line of trenches etc. Lieut.Colonel.Blackader, D.S.O. Commanding Garhwal Brigade visited the Battalion Billets and watched the men working.

11-1-1915.
HURIONVILLE.

A bright fine day till about 3.30 p.m., when there was a sharp shower of rain followed by hail. The Battalion marched to a field about 3/4 of a mile from Billets to the North of the FERFAY Road to dig trenches in accordance with a scheme ordered

11-1-1915.
(continued)

by the O.C.Garhwal Brigade, in Brigade Orders.
    Information received of the death from wounds in Meerut Clearing Hospital on 30-11-1914 of No.870 Rifn.Nain Sing Rawat,and No.1711 Rifn.Amar Sing Negi, and the death at Lillers from Pneumonia of No.978 Rifn.Amar Sing Negi,making the total casualties up to date.

This makes total casualties as under.=

	K.	W.	M.
	45	243	11
	+ 2	- 2	-
Grand Total.	47	241	11.

    A party of 26 sick and wounded men from the base rejoined today as reinforcements.

12-1-1915.
HURIONVILLE,

    A dull,cloudy day,but there was no rain.
    The Battalion continued work in the trenches which they commenced to dig yesterday,completing the excavation of a fire trench 200 yards long,and starting to make communication trenches to the rear.

13-1-1915.
HURIONVILLE.

    Another dull day with a little rain about the middle of the day. The Battalion continued work on the same trenches as yesterday,improving them, making head cover and improving the communication trenches.

WAR DIARY or INTELLIGENCE SUMMARY.

(Erase heading not required.)

Army Form C. 2118.

14-1-1915
HURIONVILLE.

Very cloudy and slight rain in the morning but the weather cleared up about noon. The Battalion proceeded to the same rendezvous as yesterday where they were met by a sapper officer who instructed them in extending working parties, sandbag revetments, loopholes, sapping, barricades etc. The work was visited by Lieut. General Sir James Willcocks who seemed very pleased with the work being done.

15-1-1915.
HURIONVILLE.

Cloudy cold morning. Battalion proceeded to same rendezrous as before to practice as for yesterday under guidance of the sapper officer. Some rain during the day.

16-1-1915.
HURIONVILLE.

Very windy morning, but finer than before with a few spells of sunshine. Battalion to same rendezvous where attack on trench with bombs etc was practised. Sapper Officer arrived at 2 p.m., to instruct in throwing a new pattern bomb with a friction fuse, one man was wounded by a splinter during the practice. Some rain in the evening.

17-1-1915
HURIONVILLE.

Brigade Holiday. Battalion out for a short time in the morning to practice bomb attack. Cold day with very cold wind, and some rain in the evening.

18-1-1915.
HURIONVILLE.

Cold day, with wind and less rain than previously in the early morning, though snow and sleet commenced about 11 O'clock. Battalion paraded at 11.30 a.m., to practise a bomb attack under Brigadier General Blackader, D.S.O., Commanding Garhwal Brigade. A wet afternoon.

19-1-1915.
HURIONVILLE

Breezy, cold morning, but no rain. All B.O's., I.O's and N.C.O's went to witness a bomb attack at Brigade Headquarters at 10.45 a.m., Previous to starting all ranks paraded to hear the announcement of awards of the order to Merit and Indian Distinguished Service Medal. The recipients of these rewards were as follows.=

<u>Order of Merit 2nd Class</u> 1541 Rifn. Madan Sing Rawat.
          H. Company.
<u>Indian Distinguished Service Medal.</u>
 Jemadar Lachham Sing Rawat.   A. Coy.
 No. 617 Hav. Bir Sing Danu.   H. "
 No. 939 " Ranjor Sing Pundir.   D. "
 No. 189 " Dewan Sing Padhiyar. A. "
 No. 1480 Nk. Kedar Sing Mahar. A. "
 No. 289 Rif. Kesar Sing Rana.   A. "
 No. 870 " Nain Sing Rawat.   D. "

In the afternoon some B.O's went to see a pattern trench at FERFAY, and discuss certain points regarding trenches generally, the L.G.C. Division being present.

During the morning the L.G.C. Division inspected the three new drafts which had arrived since he last inspected the reinforcements.

At 1.30 p.m., Subedar Galthi Sing Negi and 17 N.C.O's and men arrived as reinforcements. All these men had come from India, with the exception of 1 man who had rejoined from hospital.

WAR DIARY or INTELLIGENCE SUMMARY.

20-1-1915.
HURIONVILLE

Wet cold morning. Paraded 9.40 a.m., to practice bomb attack on trenches. Received orders during the afternoon to march to [CALONNE, en route for the trenches.] All surplus Kit, gifts of warm warm clothing (9 bundles in all) were sent to LILLERS to be stored there. More rain in the evening.

21-1-1915.
CALONNE

Marched at 10.15 a.m., via LILLERS, BUSNES ROBECQ to CALONNE, arriving there at 2.30 p.m., Road good though muddy at the sides. Billets good but scattered. Weather fine, though some rain before starting in the morning, and more rain soon after arriving at CALONNE which continued till late at night.

22-1-1915
VIEILLE CHAPELLE.

Cold frosty morning, and fine weather marched at 11.30 a.m., to VIEILLE CHAPELLE, reaching there at 4.30 p.m., trying march owing to roads being flooded in parts which caused numerous blocks, from which we suffered considerably as regiment was the rear Battalion of the Brigade. Delay who cause by baggage of train taking a separate road and cutting in a head of regiment, which had been held up for nearly an hour by one of the 2/3rd G.R. Carts being upset in some deep water by the side of the road. Good billets, but scattered. Weather fine and clear. Received orders to go at 11 O'clock at night for Brigade to go into trenches on 23rd, 2 Battalions (Leicesters and 1/39th G) in trenches, and 2 Battalions (2/3rd and 2/39th G.) in billets in RICHEBOURG St VAAST. Frosty night.

23-1-1915.
RICHEBORG St VAAST

Fine frosty morning, no rain. Aeroplanes busy all the morning. Marched at 2 p.m., to billet near RICHEBOURG ST VAAST. Billets not very good or clean. Sounds of intermittent gun and rifle fire flainly heard. Cold day, with some rain at night.

24-1-1915
RICHEBOURG ST VAAST

Dull morning and cold. 1st line transport sent back to COUR ST VAAST. The machine guns of the brigade were brigaded under Captain Lodwick 2/3rd G.R., and took up positions in the RUE de BOIS in the top stories of the houses. Remainder of regiment remained in reserve in billets.

25-1-1915.
RICHEBOURG ST VAAST

Cloudy cold morning. Enemy began shelling the village about 7.30 a.m., paying special attention to Brigade Headquarters. Shortly after this a heavy fire attack commenced, lasting till about 9 a.m. Heavy firing broke out at intervals during the day, mostly against 24th (British Brigade) on our left, and on the right in the direction of GIVENCHY. Working parties out at 10 a.m., making redouts in RUE de BERCHAUX, and again after dark improving trenches on RUE de BOIS. Two men were killed by chance shots during the time these working parties were out.
Total casualties to date.

	K.	W.	M.
B.O's.	1	-	1
I.O's.	-	2	1
R.& F.	4B	239	9
	49	241	11

26-1-1915
Trenches
RUE DE BOIS.

Cold cloudy morning. All first line transport was to be sent back to COUR ST VAAST during the day. Paraded at 5 p.m., and marched to 1/39 G. Headquarters, whence Nos.1,2, and 3 D.C.'s proceeded to billets in the ruined houses in the RUE DE BOIS to take over from the 1/39 G, No.4 D.C., being in reserve at Battalion Headquarters.

As the whole country was water logged and all fire trenches and communicating trenches were full of water, it was impossible to either hold the original line of fire trenches or dig new ones, as these filled at once. The system adopted therefore was as follows.= The original line of trenches was held by picquets (1 N.C.O.and 6 men each),2 such picquets beng found from each Double Company. Small defensive breastworks, constructed in the original fire trench, and drained and boarded as much as possible to keep them dry, were constructed for each picquet. The remainder of the troops holding the line lived in ruined houses all along the RUE DE BOIS. Just in front of this line of houses about 40 yards or so, a breastwork was constructed, for firing over kneeling, in case of attack, the picquets having orders to retire on this breastwork under such circumstances. This breast work was worked at by night only as it was of course impossible to do so by day. By day the men worked at putting the houses along the RUE DE BOIS in a state of defence, loopholeing them etc.

In rear of the line several strong redouts were constructed, and a series of breastworks constructed in convenient orchards and gardens to act as a second line on which to fall back in case of necessity. Battalion Headquarters were situated in a farm about 400 yards from RUE DE BOIS.

The reliefs were carried out without incident. Night cold but fine.

The enemy fired a few shrapnel along the RUE DE BOIS shortly after dark, but no damage was done.

27-1-1915
Trenches
RUE DE BOIS.

Cold frosty morning, with a very cold wind. very little firing during the night.
The line held by this Battalion extended from the Cinder track (exclusive) on the left to barricade on RUE DE BOIS, 100 yards E., of CHOCOLATE MENIER corner.

A quiet day with very little firing. Heavy cannonading heard to the South, it being subsequently heard that GUIVENCHY had been heavily attacked by the enemy. As this was the KAISER's birthday it was thought that quite possibly the Germans would celebrate it by an attack. Nothing unusual however occurred, though special vigilance was enjoined on all ranks. Cold & clear night, with frost. Work continued during the day on loopholeing houses in RUE DE BOIS, also on trenches in rear of the line; at night, work on breastwork continued.
Casualty, Indian Ranks, wounded 1.
Total to date.

	K.	W.	M.	Total
B.O's.	1	—	1	
I.O's.	—	2	1	
R.& F.	48	240	9	49. 242 11

Lieut. F.N. Fox and 18 men (12 sick and 6 wounded) rejoined to day, Lieut. Fox having been sent out from India with reinforcements, but had been detained 3 weeks in MARSEILLES.

28-1-1915
Trenches
RUE DE BOIS.

Cold frosty morning, and ice on all streams, also ice on water in trenches, which was broken to prevent it freezing too much. A quiet night with very little firing. Also a quiet day, though our artillery was busy at times, especially the big 6.4's. A german "sausage" observation balloon was seen up during the day in a S.E., direction. Some Officers of the 6th Jats came to Battalion Headquarters during the day to talk over the situation,

28-1-1915
(Continued)

as they are relieving us tomorrow (29th) evening.
No casualties. Work on breast work, houses, and 2nd line
breastwork continued.

29-1-1915
Trenches
RUE DE BOIS

Cold frosty morning, after a very cold
night. Very fine clear day, and ice thicker on all streams.
During the morning four German aeroplanes made a prolonged reconnaissance over our lines, dropping smoke
signals at intervals. Though fired at by our anti-aircraft guns, they suffered no damage, and eventually flew
away on the appearance of some of our machines. For a
long time however they had the field to themselves.
A quiet day, very little firing.
At 5.45 p.m., the 6th Jats arrived to relieve us, their
relieving Coys., marching straight to the trenches.
Reliefs were complete by 8 p.m., and D.C's marched independently to billets at VIEILLE CHAPELLE.
The enemy fired a few shrapnel at about
4 p.m., evidently at a battery close to us which had
probably been located during the aerial reconnaissance
that morning.
Casualty, killed, Indian Ranks 1, (while on
picquet in front line).
The machine gun detachment was also relieved
to day and returned to billets at VIEILLE CHAPELLE.
Total casualties to date.

	K.	W.	M.
B.O's.	1	-	1
I.O's.	-	2	1
R.& F.	49	240	9
Total	50	242	11

WAR DIARY or INTELLIGENCE SUMMARY.

(*Erase heading not required.*)

30-1-1915
Billets
VIEILLE CHAPELLE

Cold frosty morning, followed by slight thaw. Clear, bright day, and our aeroplanes busy during the morning. Companies out during the morning practising close order drill, saluting, turning out guards etc., by order of the G.O.C., Brigade.

31-1-1915
Billets
VIEILLE CHAPELLE.

Cold frosty morning. Working parties out all day at redoubts in RUE DE BOIS, 205 men at 9 O'clock, and 205 men again at 1 p.m.

H.H.Winkelhockman
Lt Col. 785 G.

Serial No 98

121/4719

WAR DIARY

2/39th Garhwal Rifles.

From 1st February 1915 to 28th February 1915

7/3

Original

WAR DIARY
or
INTELLIGENCE SUMMARY.
(Erase heading not required.)

Instructions regarding War Diaries and Intelligence Summaries are contained in F. S. Regs., Part II, and the Staff Manual respectively. Title pages will be prepared in manuscript.

Hour, Date, Place.	Summary of Events and Information.	Remarks and references to Appendices.
1-2-1915 Billets VIEILLE CHAPPELE.	Cold morning, with rain. Companies out for parade during the morning. Heavy cannonading heard during the day. More rain the evening, with a thaw making the roads very heavy.	
W 2-2-1915 Billets VIEILLE CHAPELLE.	Companies out for route march in morning, and officers reconnoitred various defensive works, redoubts etc., in vicinity of LE TOURET, ZELOBES and LA COUTURE. Fine day with no rain. Major Woods. I.M.S. transferred to Field Ambulance to day, sick.	
3-2-1915 Billets VIEILLE CHAPELLE	Cloudy morning. Whole Battalion out as a working party cutting brushwood for the Bareilly Brigade, for revetting purposes etc. Captain Kirwin I.M.S., attached to regiment as Medical Officer vice Major Woods. Fine afternoon and night.	
4-2-1915 Billets RICHEBOURG ST VAAST.	Clear fine morning. 1st line transport moved off at 12 noon to old billets at COUR ST VAAST. Regiment marched at 2 p.m., and arrived RICHEBOURG ST VAAST 3.15 p.m. Billets in main street round church. Battalion was in Brigade Reserve, the 2/Leicesters (½ Bn.) 2/3rd G.R.(½ Bn.) and 1/39th G., being in the trenches, relieving the Dehra Dun Brigade. Big guns busy all day shelling the enemy. A good deal of heavy rifle fire from the south in direction of GIVENCHY was heard, and consider-	

Army Form C. 2118.

4-2-1915
(continued)

able sniping throughout the night. A fine clear night.

5-2-1915
Billets
RICHEBOURG ST VAAST.

Fine morning, though cold. Working parties out during the day improving redoubts and trenches behind RUE DE BOIS position. About 3.45 p.m., enemy commenced shelling houses in RICHEBOURG ST VAAST in vicinity of church. Men billetted there were moved outside in rear of houses; shelling lasted an hour, about 50 shells being fired. A good many houses were struck, and the church was damaged.
Casualties. Wounded, Indian Ranks 4.
Total to date.

	K.	W.	M.
B.O's.	1	-	1
I.O's.	-	2	1
R.& F.	50	244	9
	51	246	11.

6-2-1915
Billets
RICHEBOURG ST VAAST.

Cold cloudy day. Working parties out all day and again at night carrying ~~bundles~~ to RUE DE BOIS, working on redoubts etc. C.O. and Company Commanders up to 1/39th G. Headquarters in afternoon prior to relieving them on 8th.
Casualties. Indian Ranks Killed 1 and Wounded 1.
Total to date.

	K.	W.	M.
B.O's.	1	-	1
I.O's.	-	2	1
R.& F.	51	245	9
	52	247	11.

7-2-1915
Billets
RICHEBOURG
ST VAAST.

Cold cloudy morning. Sir James Willcocks, K.C.B.etc., visited billets in the morning and expressed his pleasure at the appearance of the men, their clean accoutrements etc. A quiet day, no shelling.

8-2-1915
Trenches
RUE DE BOIS.

A cold morning but fine. First line transport back to COUR ST VAAST in the morning. Battalion marched off at 8 p.m., to relieve 1/39th G., in the trenches, D.C's leaving at 10 minutes interval to facilitate relief. Relief completed without incident by 10.30 p.m. Cold night, and very little firing by the enemy. The front occupied was from the orchard redoubt (where Battalion Headquarters were during original occupation of the trenches) exclusive to Factory Chimney road inclusive. The same system of holding the line by means of picquets was adopted, as the trenches themselves were still full of liquid mud and water. 1 N.C.O. and 6 men were placed on Picquet instead of 1 G.O., 1 N.C.O. and 11 men by 1/39th Garhwal Rifles and former regiments.
Lieut. Col. Johnstone of the 8th Battalion West Riding Regiment (Kitchener's Army) joined to night, to be attached to the Battalion for 3 days to see what sort of work Regiments were expected to do.
Nos.2, 3 and 4 Coys., were in the firing line this time, No.1 being in reserve. (See sketch).

9-2-1915
Trenches
RUE DE BOIS.

Cold cloudy morning. C.O. and Col. Johnstone up to RUE de BOIS in the morning to see the work being carried on, loopholing houses, construction of barricades etc., and the general life of a Battalion in the trenches under

9-2-1915
(continued)

present conditions. Enemy fired a few rounds of shrapnel in vicinity of Factory, otherwise a quiet morning. A quiet afternoon and night and not much firing, though heavy firing was heard from the direction of GIVENCHY-LA BASSEE during the evening. Our artillery were busy all day, especially the 6 inch guns.

Casualties. Indian Ranks Killed 1.

Total to date.	K.	W.	M.
B.O's.	1	-	1
I.O's.	-	2	1
R.& F.	52	245	9
	53	247	11

10-2-1915
Trenches
RUE DE BOIS.

Frosty morning, but thawed later. Clear bright sky, but clouded over about midday. Our aeroplanes busy all the morning, and they were fired at a good deal by the enemy but without success. Our own artillery busy all day. Officers of 15th Sikhs came up during the morning, to look round previous to relieving us in the trenches tomorrow. Enemy shelled factory and RUE de BOIS about 4 p.m. Work continued on loopholing houses etc., during the day as usual.

Enemy's rifle fire increased during the evening possibly owing to the fact that the 8th (British) Division on our left were experimenting with some new rockets for flare purposes.

Casualties. Indian Ranks Killed 1, Wounded 2.

Total to date.	K.	W.	M.
B.O's.	1	-	1
I.O's.	-	2	1
R.& F.	53	247	9
	54	249	11

11-2-1915.
Trenches
RUE DE BOIS.

Cold morning. Col. Johnstone left during the morning. Enemy fired a few shells near factory about 9 a.m., and again at 4 p.m., but no damage done. 15th Sikhs arrived at 8.45 p.m., to relieve us; relief completed by 10.45 p.m. D.C's marching independently on relief to old billets at VIEILLE CHAPELLE, the last Coy., reaching there at 12.30 a.m. (12th).

12-2-1915
Billets
VIEILLE CHAPELLE.

Cloudy morning. Day spent in cleaning up accoutrements and inspection of kit and equipment with a view to replacing deficiencies. Reinforcements arrived to day, consisting of 1 British officer (Captain NIXON), 1 Indian officer and 35 Rank and File from the 91st Punjabis, all being Dogras. The remainder (83 in number) had been left sick with mumps at MARSEILLES.

13-2-1915
Billets
VIEILLE CHAPELLE.

Cold morning. Companies paraded for close order drill, rifle exercise etc., during the morning. 9 men rejoined from hospital (8 Sick 1 Wounded) during the day; 12 started from ROUEN but 3 had got left behind at some Station on route, and eventually joined on 14th.

14-2-1915
Billets
VIEILLE CHAPELLE.

Very cold windy morning with rain and sleet, which lasted nearly all day. Nothing of importance to record.

15-2-1915
Billets
VIEILLE CHAPELLE.

Another cold and windy day, with rain and sleet. All companies out for a route march during the morning.

16-2-1915
Billets
VIEILLE CHAPELLE.

Fine bright day with warm sun. Our aeroplanes busy all day, observing for big guns which fired a good deal. G.O.C. brigade round billets during the morning. No.3 Coy., billets vacated during the morning and moved elsewhere, to make room for the 3rd London Regiment., who are due on 17th, and are to be attached to this Brigade, making 5 Battalions in all.

17-2-1915
Billets
VIEILLE CHAPELLE.

A bitterly cold windy day, with continuous rain. Working parties out during the day and night to RUE de BERCEAUX. 3rd London Regiment arrived in billets here.

18-2-1915
Billets
VIEILLE CHAPELLE.

Cloudy day with wind, but milder. 300 men of This Battalion to baths at Brewery during day. British Officers out reconnoitering routes to RUE DE BOIS defences. Working party of 350 men out at 7 p.m. in orchard near old Battalion Head Quarters.

19-2-1915
Billets
VIEILLE CHEPLLE.

Windy morning, cloudy, but no rain. Kit inspection held during morning to see that men were not exceeding the authorised amounts. C.O. went in morning to Head Quarters of Highland Light Infantry in RUE DE L'EPINETTE to see general disposition of defences there, with a view to taking over these trenches from them on 21st instant.

20-2-1915
Billets
VIEILLE CHAPELLE.

Cloudy morning. Coy. Commanders up to RUE DE L'EPINETTE in the morning to see the positions they are to take over from the Highland Light Infantry on 21st. Some rain in the evening.

21-2-1915
Trenches RUE
DE L'EPINETTE.

A cloudy day. 1st line transport and baggage wagons moved to LE TOURET to form a depot there while Battalion was in the trenches. Battalion left VIEILLE CHAPELLE at 5 p.m., together with one Company of the 3rd London Regiment under Captain Moore, which was attached to the Regiment to learn trench work. Head Quarters in RUE DE L'EPINETTE were reached at 6.30 p.m., and the Regiment relieved the 1/Highland Light Infantry in the trenches. The front taken up by the Battalion was bounded by arbitray lines (as shown in attached sketch), in the vicinity of INDIAN VILLAGE to the north, and RUE DE CAILLOUX to the south. INDIAN VILLAGE and the neighbouring picquets and breastworks were held by No.3 Coy., and the Dogra Coy.(32 men only). The 10 "butts" in continuation of and S. of houses A. and B. were held by the Battalion and the 3rd London Regiment alternately, picquets from each Regiment holding every other butt. Houses A. and B. were held by the 3rd London Company, and the Brewery Post by

21-2-1915
(continued)

No.1 Coy. No.2 Coy., was in reserve in billets at DANGER CORNER and No.4 to RUE DE L'EPINETTE.
The relief was completed without incident by 9 p.m. The C.O. and Major MacTier went round the whole position after the relief had been completed. A quiet night, very little rifle fire by the enemy. Work was carried on during the night improving the breastwork and linking up the "butts" by a sand-bag breastwork.

22-2-1915
Trenches
RUE DE L'EPINETTE.

Cold morning with frost, and very misty. G.O.C. Brigade went round trenches in the morning with the C.O. The mist remained all day, and there was very little firing by either side during the day. A thaw set in during the morning and the roads and communications became very muddy in consequence. A quiet night.

23-2-1915
Trenches
RUE DE L'EPINETTE.

Cold foggy morning, but the fog cleared off a little during the day. Very little rifle fire, but enemy shelled the Brewery Post and Indian Village about 3.30 p.m. but did no damage. Brewery again shelled at 11 p.m., but no damage done. Enemy also dropped a few shells during the day along the RUE DE L'EPINETTE but no harm was done. Our big guns did some damage to the enemys breastwork in front of the 3/London Company.
Casualties Indian Ranks Killed one, Wounded one (both in INDIAN VILLAGE, by rifle fire).

Total to date.

	K.	W.	M.
B.O's.	1	-	1
I.O's.	-	2	1
R.& F.	54	248	9
	55	250	11

24-2-1915
Trenches RUE
DE L'EPINETTE.

    Frosty morning, cold and clear, but clouded over about 11 o'clock. Some snow fell about noon, which turned to rain later: a thaw also set in about midday. Enemy shelled Brewery at noon, also RUE DE L'EPINETTE about 3 p.m., but no damage done. Some more snow and sleet during the afternoon. A very cold raw day.

25-2-1915
Trenches, RUE
DE L'EPINETTE.

    Frosty morning with mist, which cleared off later in the day. Snow had fallen about 4 a.m. and some more fell about 9 a.m. but it soon melted. Enemy shelled the Brewery, Danger corner, and RUE DE L'EPINETTE, dropping 18 shells along the latter at noon but doing no damage.
    Very little rifle fire all day.
    The 1/39th Garhwal Rifles relieved the Battalion in the trenches at 7 p.m., relief being complete by 8.45 p.m., without incident. The 3/London Company was also relieved to day.
    The Battalion now came into reserve in billets in Rue DE L'EPINETTE.
    While the Battalion had been in the trenches, considerable progress had been made in the breastworks and so making them accessible at all times from Houses A. and B., though it was only possible to get to these two houses from the Brewery by night, owing to the open nature of the country and lack of covered communications. INDIAN VILLAGE, which was in a filthy state when the Battalion took it over, was cleaned up and made sanitary and habitable, with the aid of all the available sweepers from the Lahore Division.

Hour, Date, Place	Summary of Events and Information	Remarks and references to Appendices

26-2-1915
Trenches, RUE L'EPINETTE.

Cold frosty morning and very misty. A quiet day with little rifle fire. Mist cleared off about 11 a.m. Our aeroplanes were busy all day, three of them constantly circling over the German lines and being heavily fired on without damage. About 3 p.m. the enemy put about 50 shells all along the RUE DE L'EPINETTE but no damage was done. Some shells also fell near the batteries W. of the RUE DE L'EPINETTE, Two of the M.G. Mules were hit; one had to be destroyed. A cold frosty night. 18 men rejoined to day from hospital, 9 sick and 9 wounded.

27-2-1915
RUE DE L'EPINETTE.

Frosty morning, cloudy and very cold with a cold wind. Enemy dropped 6 shells along to road about 11 a.m. but did no damage. Colder towards evening. Captain Burton to Brigade Headquarters to officiate as Brigade Major, vice Major Stewart, on the sick list. A quiet day, though there was a good deal of firing by our guns.

28-2-1915
RUE DE L'EPINETTE.

Cold morning with cold wind. The 1st Battalion Scots Guards arrived about 12.30 p.m. to relieve the Battalion in reserve. While the reliefs were being carried out the enemy started shelling the RUE DE L'EPINETTE, and one shell wounded 4 men in E.Coy., despite the fact that only a platoon at a time was walking down the road in order to lessen the chance of casualties from shell fire.
Companies after relief marched independently to billets near ZELOBES, the last Coy., reaching there at 5 p.m. Billets very crowded.

During the period of occupation of the trenches 2 N.C.O's and 32 men of the M.G. detachment and 1 N.C.O. and 11 men of the Bomb gun detachment had been detached from the regiment, and brigaded with detachments from the remaining regiments of the Brigade; the Brigaded M.G. being under

WAR DIARY or INTELLIGENCE SUMMARY.
(Erase heading not required.)

Army Form C. 2118.

28-2-1915
(continued)

Captain Lodwick 2/3rd Q.A.O.G.R., and the Bomb guns under
Captain Parkin, 113th Infantry, attached 2/39th G.R.
The machine guns were in the front line the whole time,
but the bomb guns were never used.
    Total Casualties to date.

	K.	W.	M.
B.O's.	1	-	1
I.O's.	-	2	1
R.& F.	54	252	9
	55	254	11

WAR DIARY
with appendices.

2nd Battalion 39th Garhwal Rifles.

From 1st March 1915 to 31st March 1915.

121/5114

2ND BN. 39TH GARHWAL RIFLES

1-3-1915
Billets
ZELOBES.

Fine morning but cold. Companies paraded during the morning practising charging and bomb throwing; also physical drill. Short thunderstorm and hail about 3 p.m. Cold night.

2-3-1915
Billets
ZELOBES.

Fine morning; cold and windy. Brigade Armourer Sergeant inspected all rifles in Battalion at 10 a.m. Companies practised charging and bomb throwing. Captain Burton returned from Brigade Head Quarters, Major Stewart having returned from hospital.

3-3-1915
Billets
ZELOBES.

Cold cloudy morning. Companies practised charging and bomb throwing; a good deal of rain fell during the day, and lectures were given in billets to Companies. Lieut. Clarke transferred to hospital today, sick. A wet afternoon and evening.

4-3-1915
Billets
ZELOBES.

Cold cloudy morning, but no rain. Battalion out for a route march under Captain Burton.

5-3-1915
Billets
ZELOBES

Windy morning and dull but no rain. Companies practised bomb throwing and charging in the morning

Hour, Date, Place	Summary of Events and Information	Remarks and references to Appendices

5-3-1915
(continued)

and close order drill in the afternoon.

6-3-1915
Billets
ZELOBES.

A pouring wet morning with strong wind and no parades in consequence. Rain stopped during the afternoon but day remained cloudy. An officer of the Royal Flying Corps alighted close to Head Quarters billets having had engine trouble. After staying about 2 hours and making the necessary repairs he flew off again.

7-3-1915
Billets
ZELOBES.

Cloudy morning, rain commencing about 11 a.m. and continuing on and off all day. The C.O. went forth all B.O's and Company Commanders up to trenches along ESTAIRS-LACASSEE road N., of PORT ARTHUR to reconnoitre ground in vicinity of NEUVE CHAPELLE. A cold raw day.

8-3-1915
ZELOBES
and RICHEBOURG
St VAAST.

Very cold windy day. Preparations made for move, and orders were received to move to RICHEBOURG St VAAST at once at 6.45 p.m. Billets very tight there. A cold night.

9-3-1915
RICHEBOURG
St VAAST.

Cold morning with wind and frost, with some snow during the day. Final preparations made for going into trenches to night, taking over Bombs, ammunition etc.

9-3-1915
(continued)

Orders received to march to position of assembly in 6th Jat trenches along ESTAIRES-LA BASSÉE road at 1.30 a.m. on 10th.

10-3-1915
NEUVE CHAPELLE
and VICINITY.

Left RICHEBOURG St VAAST at 1.30 a.m. and marched to and took up position in 6th Jat trenches. Just before dawn Nos.1 and 2 Coys., left the trenches and filed out in front of main trench and lay in readiness in a small trench just the other side of the road ready for the assault on the German trenches covering NEUVE CHAPELLE. The whole Brigade was to assault in line, the regiments being in the following order from the left

  2/39th G. 2/3rd G.R. Leicesters. 1/39th G.

The front to be assaulted was divided up and assigned to the various regiments of the Brigade as above, the 3/London Regiment being in reserve. The object of the attack was to capture the advanced German trenches, and if possible push on, capture NEUVE CHAPELLE and eventually occupy the original British line E. of the village, known as the Smith-Dorrien line, as being the line taken up by that General's Corps in the fighting round this area in the early days of the war. The 8th (British) Division of the 4th Corps was also to assault on our left, and Brigades of the 1st Corps on our right were also to attack the German trenches in their front. The plan of attack was as follows:-
From 7.35 a.m. to 8.5 a.m. the guns were to concentrate their fire on the front to be assaulted by the Garhwal Brigade; 10 minutes fire being by Field Guns on wire entanglement etc. At 8.5 the attack was to be launched simultaneously along the whole line, though the attack by the 8th Division was timed for half an hour later. At 7.30 a.m., the guns began a terrific bombardment, every kind of gun being used, field siege, and howitzer. The noise was deafening and the fire very accurate. One or two premature bursts caused casualties in the trenches, but these were remarkably few considering the number of guns in action. The German guns also fired a good deal in reply.

10-3-1915
(continued)

Precisely at 8.5 a.m. Nos.1 and 2 Companies rose to the assault, advancing in a very good line across the 100 - 200 yards or so between the trenches, followed by their 2nd Platoons at 50 yards distance, and soon reached the German lines. The barbed wire had been cut a good deal by the fire of the guns, and but little resistance was at first met with. Bombing and bayonet parties worked down the main fire trench and up communication ones and so rounded up prisoners who all surrenderd and touch thus gained with the Berkshire regiment who also were working up the trenches towards us. Several casualties occurred here, but the line pressed on, and reached their objective the line G - H. During this advance 187 prisoners and 3 Machine Guns were captured. Meantime No.3 Company had been sent up to support Nos.1 and 2, and eventually the whole line advanced and passed through NEUVE CHAPELLE and reached the Smith-Dorien line beyond. Touch was gained with the Rifle Brigade on the left, the right Battalion of the 8th Division. A strong line was now established here, the Battalion taking up a position in support of the front line behind the 2/3rd G.R., and facing the BOIS de BIEZ. Sandbags, hurdles, and entrenching tools were found in a house in NEUVE CHAPELLE, evidently a German Sapper depot, and good use was made of all this material to build up a beastwork. A few shells were fired during the day and occasionally a maxim opened on the troops working, but on the whole there was little firing. Jemadar Ghantu Sing Bisht was killed by maxim fire while here.

During the advance, Subedar Shib Sing Negi had been killed, and Subedar Ratan Sing Negi, Jemadar Balbhadar Sing Gusain, and Jemadar Amar Sing Negi had been wounded; 26 rank and file had been killed, and 75 wounded, 31 being reported missing of whom 11 were believed to have been killed. Subedar Khiyali Sing Negi was missing, not traceable at all, so it is presumed he must have been killed by a shell.

The advance had been carried out with great dash and vigour, and the start was well km timed; and this undoubtedly prevented heavier casualties. The men behaved splendidly and were always ready and anxious to advance further.

10-3-1915
(continued)

(For a detailed account of the operations see report, Appendix attached)

About 5 p.m. G.O.C.Brigade sent for the C.O. and he received orders to go and consult with Colonel Swiney, 1/39th G., who had been slightly wounded about consolidating the R.Flank of the line at PORT ARTHUR and to take over both Battalions. Orders were received to be ready to move at a moments notice, and at 12 midnight the Battalion was ordered to proceed to PORT ARTHUR. On the way the Commanding officer was met on his way back from PORT ARTHUR and he ordered the Battalion back to the trenches they had just evacuated. Meanwhile the G.O.C.Brigade had directed Major MacTier, to take over Command of the 1/39th G., vice Colonel Swiney who had been wounded, and Captain Harbord was also transferred to the 1/39th G., as they had suffered heavily today in the attack losing 6 British Officers Killed. The Battalions returned to the breastwork behind the 2/3rd G.R. and got what rest it could.

Casualties during day.
Indian Ranks.
    Officers. Killed. Sub.Shib Sing Negi.
                       Jem.Ghantu Sing Bisht.
             Wounded. Sub.Ratan Sing Negi.
                       Jem.Balbhadar Sing Gusain.
                       Jem.Amar Sing Negi.
             Missing.
             (believed Killed). Sub.Khiyali Sing Negi.
                       6.

Rank & File. Killed. 26
           Wounded. 75
           Wounded
           & Missing. 2
           Missing. 19 (includes 11 believed Killed).
           Total
           Casualties. 122.

Total to date.

	K.	W.	M.
B.O's.	1	-	1
I.O's.	2	5	2
R.& F.	84	322	30
	87	327	33

11-3-1915
Trenches.

At 5 a.m., orders were received placing the Battalion at the disposal of the G.O.C.Dehra Dun Brigade, in connection with operations to be under-taken on the morning of the 11th. The Battalion was ordered to support the Right flank of the Dehra Dun Brigade, which was to attack the BOIS de BIEZ that morning. Accordingly the Battalion marched off once more and reached their appointed position on the R.flank of the Dehra Dun Brigade at about 6.30 a.m. The morning was foggy and cold. The Battalion took up a position in the open ground in front of trenches captured the previous day and now occupied by the 2/Leicester Regiment and the Seaforths. Touch was gained with the 2nd Gurkhas on our left and all was in readiness to support them when they advanced. The prospect was not a pleasing one, as the ground was absolutely open for 800 yards, and it was across this that the Battalion would have to advance. As it was, the Battalion lying out there in the open suffered a good many casualties from rifle fire and snipers, and eventually the C.O.ordered their withdrawal into and behind the trenches, where some dead ground in an orchard afforded a certain amount of cover. Here the Companies entrenched themselves. A report was sent in to the G.O.C.Dehra Dun Brigade explaining the situation and pointing out the extreme difficulty of the task allotted to the Battalion, i.e, to advance under fire from 3 sides across the open ground. Meantime our guns shelled the BOIS de BIEZ heavily the enemy replying occasionally with rifle and machine gun fire. Considerable movement was seen in the German trenches opposite the Battalion, and it was evident that a good number were collecting there. The Bombardment of the BOIS de BIEZ continued practically all day, till about 4 p.m. Rations were brought up for the men by a party of the 2/8th Gurkhas, the first food the men had since leaving RICHEBOURG St VAAST, except what they had in their haversacks with them.

The Germans opened a fairly heavy shell fire all along the line from 4 to 5.30 p.m., but no much damage was done.

At 12 midnight orders were received from G.O.C.Dehra Dun Brigade to march to billets at LA COUTURE. Which was was reached at 3 a.m.

Casualties during this day.

11-3-1915
(continued)

Indian Ranks Killed   4
         Wounded.   27

Total to date.
                K.   W.   M.
       B.O's.   1   0   1
       I.O's.   2   5   2
       R.& F. 88   348   30
               91   355   33.

Ⓞ Captain J.F.Parkin,113th Infantry(attached) had been wounded on 10th instant while doing duty as Brigade Bomb gun Officer through the bursting of one of his own bomb gun while assisting in the attack on NEUVE CHAPELLE.

12-3-1915
LA COUTURE and CROIX
MARMEUSE, and RICHEBOURG
St VAAST.

LA COUTURE was reached by the last Company about 3 a.m., on the way back the Regiment had to march down a road which was being heavily shelled all night by the enemy, and 3 men of the Dogra Company were hit. The road was much congested with traffic, as the Sirhind Brigade were marching up it in one mass into the trenches to relieve the Dehra Dun Brigade. It was afterwards stated that some 300 casualties occurred on this road during the night from shell fire. On the way back the men collected as many of their great coats as they could find, which had been left in the 6th Jat trenches on the morning of the 10th previous to the attack.

The men had hardly settled down in LA COUTURE when orders were received to march early next morning to billets near L'ESTREM. Battalion marched at 7.30 a.m. and reached billets at CROIX MARMEUSE at 10.30 a.m., after a long wait on the road for the billetting officer.

The march was necessarily a slow one as the men were much fatigued after their strenuous efforts of the

12-3-1915
(continued)

the last 3 days. Billets were much scattered here.
At 4.40 p.m. orders were received to march at once to RICHEBOURG St VAAST. The men were cooking at the time, and most of the food had to be thrown away and the Regiment fell in immediately and marched off. The march was very slow, and several men wanted to fall out owing to bad feet. In fact the feet of all the men were in a very bad way and the regiment was in no condition to do any more hard work till it had a day or two's good rest and food. CROIX MARMEUSE was left about 5.45 p.m., and RICHEBOURG reached at 9.15 p.m. and on arrival there billets were allotted but proved difficult to find as there were so many troops in the village and no Staff Officer to shew us till he was seen and fetched out. However sufficient room was eventually found and the men got what rest they could.
All ranks heard with the deepest regret this day that Major MacTier had been killed in action while Commanding the 1/39th G, vice Colonel Swiney, wounded.

13-3-1915
RICHEBOURG
St VAAST and
ZELOBES.

Fine morning. Men's feet still very bad. Heavy gun firing all the morning. During the morning received orders to relieve 1/39th G., in the trenches to night, but these were cancelled and the regiment was ordered back to its former billets at ZELOBES. Left RICHEBOURG St VAAST at 5 p.m., reaching ZELOBES at 7 p.m. 1st line transport hung up on road owing to block in traffic, and did not reach billets till very late; the mess cart was smashed by being run into by some gunner wagons.
Major Woods. I.M.S., rejoined from sick leave, and resumed his duties as M.O., from Captain Kirwan I.M.S. who returned to his Field Ambulance

14-3-1915
ZELOBES.

Cloudy morning. Men rested after their strenuous time. All B.O's went to L'ESTREM in the afternoon to attend the funeral of Major MacTier, Captain Kenny, and Captain Owen (38th Dogras) attached 1/39th G.

15-3-1915
ZELOBES.

Cloudy morning. Nothing of importance to record.

16-3-1915
ZELOBES.

Cloudy morning. Regiment paraded for Lieut. General Sir C.A. Anderson K.C.B., Commanding Meerut Division. He addressed the men, saying that they had made a great name for themselves, which would last for ever, and that the Regiment could not have done better work than it had done. He congratulated all ranks on the way they had worked, and stated that the 1st and 2nd 39th headed the list of regiments which had been submitted to the authorities as having done specially good work.

17-3-1915
ZELOBES.

Fine morning, but clouded over later. Regiment paraded at 11 a.m., for Lieut. General Sir James Willcocks K.C.B., Commanding the Indian Army Corps. He congratulated all ranks on their good work and thanked them all. As he turned away, he said " you are a damned fine regiment " He also made an inspection of the ranks, asking after the mens welfare etc.
Captain J.E. Colenso 2/7th G.R. joined the Regiment today.

18-3-1915.
ZELOBES.

Cold morning and cloudy. Parades under Coy.
Commanders to practise close order drill and charging. G.O.C.
Meerut Division round in evening to see C.O.

19-3-1915
ZELOBES.

A frosty morning. Some snow had fallen during
the night. A very cold day with a cold wind, and intermittent
falls of snow and hail. Coys. paraded for route march and
bomb throwing practice in the morning.

20-3-1915
ZELOBES.

Cloudy day but not so cold. Companies paraded
for close order drill and bomb throwing. Captain Harbord
rejoined Battalion from temporary duty with 1/3eth G.

21-3-1915
ZELOBES.

A beautifully fine morning. Aeroplanes flying
very high passed overhead during morning. A fine warm day.
48 Reinforcements arrived today, including 38 Garhwalis
from Burma Military Police; remainder Sick and Wounded men
rejoined.

Revised list of casualties now stands as
under; since actions of 10th - 11th.

21st March 1915
(continued)

Died of wounds received in action (previously reported wounded).	R.& F.	8
Previously reported wounded now reported killed in action.	"	1
Previously reported missing now reported killed in action.	I.O's. R.& F.	1 (Sub.Khiyali Sing Negi). 1
Now reported wounded, previously not reported.	"	1 (Bomb gun Section).

Total to date.

	K.	W.	M.
B.O's.	2	1	1
I.O's.	3	5	1
R.& F.	98	341	29
	103	347	31

22nd March 1915
ZELOBES.

Fine warm day, but clouded over in the evening. Companies practised close order drill and bombing.

23rd March 1915
ZELOBES.

Cloudy morning. Coys., paraded for close order drill and bomb throwing. Weather generally milder.

24-3-1915
ZELOBES.

Cloudy morning, weather rather muggy. Brigade moved up into Divisional Reserve to Meerut Division, the Bareilly and Dehra Dun Brigades going into the trenches in relief of the 8th (British) Division, the front taken over being from NEUVE CHAPELLE to CHAMPIGNY. The Battalion stayed in present billets, the other 3 Battalions of the Brigade moving up into billets in and around BOUT DE VILLE.

Captains Burton and Nixon left on 7 days leave today.

25-3-1915
ZELOBES.

Cold raw morning with wind and rain G.O.C. Brigade round billets during the morning. Received news of death of one Dogra 91st Punjabis in Hospital at Brighton from wounds received in action. This makes total casualties now

	K.	W.	M.
B.O's. ...	2	-	1
" attached.	-	1	-
I.O's. ...	3	5	1
" attached.	-	-	-
R. & F. ...	91	332	21
" attached.	8	8	8
	104	346	31

26-3-1915
ZELOBES.

Fine morning but cold. Orders received to change billets, but these were afterwards cancelled. Working party of 300 men out from 6 p.m. to 3 a.m., carrying hurdles etc., up to front line for revetting etc.

27-3-1915
ZELOBES.

Cold morning, slight frost; cold N.E. wind with occasional falls of snow all day. Billets changed during day to new farms quite close to former ones, the idea being to concentrate the Brigade move in case of reinforcements being required in front line. New billets scattered but comfortable. Two German aeroplanes over ZELOBES during the morning.

28-3-1915
ZELOBES.

Cold frosty morning, with cold wind. C.O. and all B.O's up to trenches occupied by Bareilly Brigade at 10 p.m. A long walk, and trenches inspected though not much could be ascertained regarding the general situation as it was night, though there was a bright moon. Billets reached at 1.30 a.m. A working party of 300 men was also out to night digging a communication trench up to the front line; this party left billets at 9 p.m., and got back at 5.30 a.m. next morning.

29-3-1915
CALONNE

Cold frosty morning. Garhwal Brigade marched to fresh billets at CALONNE, marching at 12.15 p.m. Battalion paraded at 11.30 a.m. and was rear Battalion of the Brigade: CALONNE reached at 3 p.m. Roads good but dusty, weather very cold. Billets very scattered at CALONNE. Received orders today for the temporary amalgamation of the 1st and 2nd Battalions into one Battalion; to be called "The Garhwal Rifles".

30-3-1915.
CALONNE.

Frosty morning; weather fine and cold. All men of 1/39th G., for transfer to 2nd Battalion on amalgamation paraded for C.O's inspection at 10.a.m. The following numbers were transferred

B.O's. 2. Lieut. A.H.MANKELOW.
Lieut. G.S.ROGERS.
I.O's. 9. (Including 2 with the Tehri
I.S.Sapper and Miners detachment).
O.R.I. 231 of 1/39th G., and 90 men of Tehri I.S.
Sappers and Miners detachment.

2nd Lieut. Rana Jodha Jang Bahadur of the Tehri S.& M., also joined.

This made the strength of the Battalion as under:-

B.O's. 11.
I.O's. 20.
O.R.I. 791.

In addition to the above 5 Indian officers and 134 O.R.I. Dogras, attached 1/39th G., were transferred pending transfer to 41st Dogras on their arrival in the billetting area.

31-3-1915
CALONNE.

Cold morning, with slight frost. Companies paraded for close order drill, bomb throwing etc. Men of 1/39th G., paraded and apportioned off to Companies. Captains Burton and Nixon returned from 7 days leave.

Captain Blair and Lieut. Fox left for 7 days leave.

From

        The Officer Commanding,

            2nd Batt:39th Garhwal Rifles.

To

        The Brigade Major,

            Garhwal Brigade.

No.218/W.A.   Dated 16th March 1915.

        I have the honor to submit the following report on the part played by my Battalion in the attack on NEUVE CHAPELLE on the 10th instant and in subsequent operations.

        The Battalion left billets at RICHEBOURG St VAAST at 1.15 p.m., to proceed to the rendozvous in the entrenchments held by the 6th Jats of Bareilly Brigade. The Battalion arrived and was formed up in the entrenchment ready by 4.30 a.m., the appointed time opposite that portion of the enemy's entrenchment which the Battalion had to attack.

        When reconnoitring the front given me on the previous days, i,e., from the road on centre salient (square S 4 b) exclusive up to N., end of entrenchment in square S 4 a., along the main ESTAIRES-LABASSEE road, I found that owing to the conformation of the ground which sloped down to the ditch. I could get my 2 assaulting lines out without being seen in front of and to the E., of the line of entrenchments and that this would be greatly facilitated if a portion say 6 feet, of the N., end of the hedge of the salient joining the road were cut down or a passage made through it, and in addition a 2 feet deep trench were dug along the E., edge of the ditch which ran alongside of the road.

        Accordingly I arranged with the Officer of the 6th Jats on the spot for this to be done and also officially through the Brigade. By this they were enabled to keep under cover during the bombardment and at the same time have a very much better "take off" and so get off more quickly and make the attack a much greater surprise, which was very essential to the success of the undertaking.

At 5.15.a.m. I directed the first 2 lines to file out in single file into the small trench and lie down close together and wait till the moment came to deliver the assault, which was to be at 8.5.a.m.

This was done very well and quickly and without the enemy getting any idea of its taking place.

In the meantime the other 2 Companies closed up to their right ~~against~~ in the main entrenchment straight behind the front assaulting lines.

As it was very cold I took great coats with me, carried open by the men on the arms, with Waterproof Sheets wrapped on back and these they threw over themselves while lying down in the trench waiting as it was very cold. When the assault took place they were thrown off and left lying in the trench and so the men were very much lighter for the actual assault.

Punctually at 7.30 a.m., the bombardment began, a perfect tornado of shells and was most accurate. The salient of course was vacated as it was impossible for reasons of safety to occupy it during the bombardment.

During the bombardment one German high explosive shell hit the parapet close by where my Adjutant and I were sitting, with my orderly and 1 man of the 6th Jats between us, killing the 2 men and wounding 2 others of my men but leaving us both unhurt, beyond a shaking and covering us with green and a mouthful of green sulphu-vous smoke. 2 men also were killed and 6 wounded by our own shrapnel while lying down in the trench awaiting the moment to advance.

I had given the portion of the front along which ran the hedge of the orchard covering the nearest German trench to one Company and the other portion where the trench ran through the hedge across the open to the other Company (~~vide sketch attached~~).

Punctually at 8.5.a.m., when the artillery lengthened fuse and range my leading line advanced at a steady double across the open towards the objective, followed at 50 yards distance by the 2nd line, which was nearly reached before the enemy was fully aware of the fact and could open as hot a fire as he might have done had he been aware of it from the commencement.

I had directed the right Company whose final objective was the N.E., portion of the long trench marked H.G., not to stop at the first trenches V.W., met with but to press right on to the final objective H.G., as these could be looked after, the Companies, I would push up in support, as I considered it very essential that the objective should be reached as soon as possible and the task given me i.e., to get to this trench H.G., establish myself there and work up from it, gain touch with the British Brigade on my left and double block any communication trenches.

The advance was extremely well carried out by No.1 and 2 Companies under Captains Burton and Blair in line of platoons i.e., on a front of 4 platoons, each leading platoon supported by its second platoon.

The right Company on reaching the trench running along and behind the hedge V V found it empty and pressed on to the next trench where a M.G., was captured with some prisoners. The advance was then continued to the 3rd trench V'.V'., and finally to the objective H.G. It was during the passage across this open space between W.W. and H.G., that many casualties occurred, from fire from direction of H., from a party of the enemy whom the other Company on the left eventually engaged. This trench H.G., having been reached was about to be reversed for firing, but it was 2" deep in water and mud and so a fresh one was commenced on the same alignment. Parties were sent out to the village to scout and link up with the Brigade on our left, and also up the communication trench running out of H.G. In the meantime No.2 Company on the left had advanced at the same time and went straight on clear of the hedge and ditch V.V'., and got into that portion of the main trench W.Y., and began working up this trench bombing and rounding up prisoners towards H., and capturing a M.G., and beyond towards J; also a party was sent up the communication trench ZZ and up H.G., shortly afterwards connection was made with the Berkshires in the main trench.

The enemy in main fire trench finding themselves taken under fire from 2 directions soon began to surrender, but great care had to be exercised as the might have been up to any dirty trick. For instance when surrending, a party in the main fire trench began beckoning to our men to come on. It was found probably that their intention was to get them to come on towards them and as they passed a short piece of trench (not marked on official map) marked Z', they would have come under M.G.fire. Fortunately they were not to be taken in so. This M.G. was captured.

The Companies were now reorganised the objective having been reached. No.3 Company under Captain Wilcox had before been pushed up in support when I thought it was needed, and I kept No.4 Company still in hand for emergencies. Shortly afterwards I pushed up 2 more platoons under Major MacTier to carry on the digging with tools, and very shortly afterwards I pushed up myself with the remaining 2 platoons. On arrival at H.G. I had parties sent out into the village to search the houses for snipers. I saw the Berkshires on our left advancing through the village.

No.1 Company under Captain Burton had by now been pushed on, and swung round S.E., and had commenced digging a support trench on the line approx. S Q., in support of 2/3rd G.R., who had by now occupied the old line of trench T.P. I received a message subsequently to do this, from Brigade Head quarters.

Here at S.Q., I linked up with the Rifle Brigade. I consolidated my support trench S.Q., and was fortunate in finding in a house near S., a lot of ready made burdles sandbags and spades which considerably facilitated my work.

It was now about 9.30 a.m. Work was continued on the support trench S.W., and made by the evening quite strong. I established my telephone station with Brigade Head Quarters in house W2 near R.

About 6 p.m. I was sent for from trench S.Q., to the telephone station as the G.O.C. I was told wished to speak with me. As it was difficult to hear I asked that a message might be sent. This I subsequently received directing me to proceed personally to PORT ARTHUR and consult with Colonel SWINEY who had been wounded and take measures to consolidate our right flank and use both Battalion of the 39th G. I accordingly set forth, but after having gone a short distance fell into a "Black Johnson" hole on the road in the dark and hurt my left knee so that I could not get on just then. I accordingly sent up my 2nd-in-Command Major MacTier to go and see

Colonel Swiney and told him I would follow as soon as I could. This I reported to the Brigade. About 12.a.m. after resting some time I ordered Captain Burton to bring up the Battalion to PORT ARTHUR and I went up on ahead myself to Port Arthur, and after a long time wandering round a maze of trenches in the dark I eventually found the Head Quarters and that Colonel Swiney had gone. I did not meet Major MacTier, but on my return journey to telephone station W2., where I found the Dehrad Dun Brigade had established their Head Quarters, I received a note from Major MacTier saying he had seen G.O.C. Garhwal Brigade who had directed him to take over Command of the 1/39th G.

About 1 a.m., on my return journey I met my Battalion under Captain Burton at the German trench where it crosses the road just in front of PORT ARTHUR and brought it back with me. On arrival at D., where the road leads to house F., and where I understood Garhwal Brigade Head Quarters was to have been established, I halted the Battalion and proceeded to that house. I found only Captain Lodwick there and he informed me that Head Quarters had not arrived. So I returned and took my Battalion back to its trench at S.Q., and sent a message to that effect to Garhwal Brigade Head Quarters. I saw the G.O.C. Dehra Dun Brigade and shortly afterwards received orders for my Battalion to be attached to that Brigade and to guard its right flank during the contemplated attack on the BOIS on BIES on the 11th instant.

Accordingly I took the Battalion over via D., to a position in front of the entrenchments held by the 2/Leicestershire Regiment in front of O., and south of road leading to M, covered by my scouts. Here I formed it up in line 3 Companies in front line and 1 Company in reserve with M.Guns, and lay out in the open in folds of the ground covered by scouts, waiting for the advance to take place.

As however there was a considerable fire coming from the BOIS du BIEZ and many casualties were taking place, I ordered the Battalion to retire to the line held by the 2/Leicestershire Regiment ment and some immediately behind in the orchard where they entrenched themselves. Here we waited all day while a bombardment took place of the Bois du Bies and houses along its N.W. Edge and along road to M.

No advance took place and eventually about 11 p.m. I received orders to go back to LA COUTURE to billets where we arrived 3 a.m. on 12th. I marched next morning at 7 a.m., for vicinity of LESLOBES where billets were apportioned to the Battalion arriving in the forenoon.

During the afternoon at 4.40 p.m. I received urgent orders through Dehra Dun Brigade to march forthwith to RICHEBOURG St VAAST where we arrived 9 p.m., and got into billets. We remained here all the 13th. During the evening I received orders to march at 5 p.m. to billets in the vicinity of ZELOBES where the Battalion is now.

The work of the Battalion throughout the operations had been excellent and the actual attack was carried out splendidly and with great dash. The comparatively few losses are due to the assaulting lines rising without hesitation to the attack precisely at the moment ordered, and to their pressing forward with dash and determination so that they were almost on the leading trenches before the enemy, the majority of whom had undoubtedly withdrawn to trenches in rear during the bombardment, could return back and man their main fire trench. The result was most satisfactory. Comparative few casualties. 3 Officers 187 men and 3 Machine Guns were being captured. Two Machine Huns were actually sent in, one I understand being sent in by the Berkshiere Regiment who came up and linked up with us on our left.

I send in on separate report a list of those whom I consider especially deserving of recognition during the operation.

[signature]

Lieut. Colonel.

Commandant 2nd Batt:39th Garhwal Rifles.

N/S.

7 MEERUT DIV

20 GARWAL BDE

GARHWAL RIFLES
(LATE 1/39 & 2/39 GARHWAL RIFLES)
1914 AUG — 1915 NOV

~~To Egypt~~ ~~1/1916~~
~~NORTHERN CANAL~~

To No 1 CANAL SECTION
EGYPT

121/4046

War Diary
of
1/39th Garhwalis
from 9.8.14
to ~~Oct~~
29/6/14
Volume I
pp 1 to 29

Also from
Intray to 6/4/15
Volume
pp — 6

Meerut Division Aug-Dec 1914

1/39th Garhwal Rifles.

1914 AUG — 1915 MAR

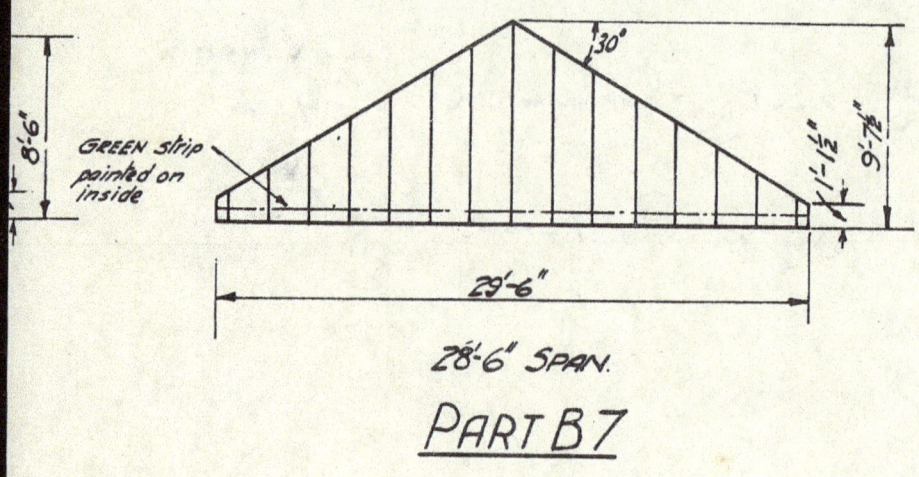

28'-6" SPAN.

PART B7

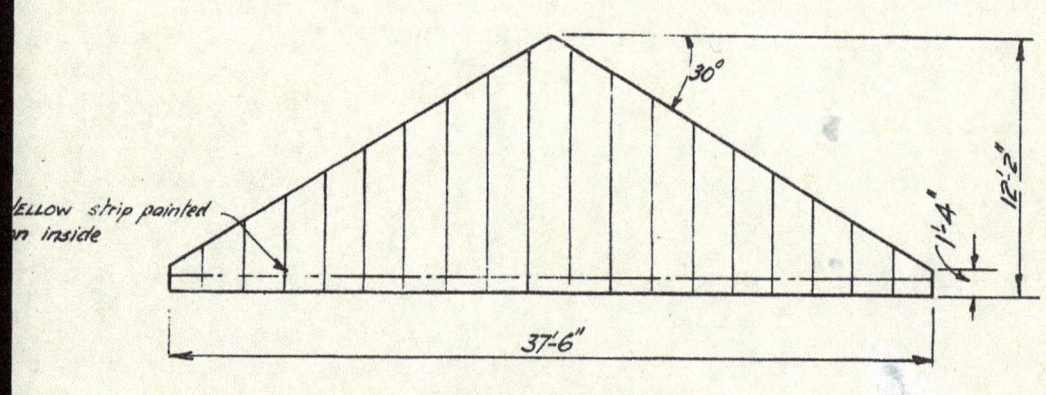

36'-6" SPAN

PART B8

SETS OF EXTERNAL GABLE SHEETING

WHEN FIXED

fixed they conform to the dimensions shown.
be clearly marked by means of a 6" coloured
indicated
× 24 gauge, & to be laid with single side laps.

AMENDED 19-10-38.

SHEETS.   DRAWING No. H. 356/37

WAR DIARY

1st Bn. 39th Garhwal Rifles

(Erase heading not required.)

Hour, Date, Place.	Summary of Events and Information.	Remarks and references to Appendices.
Lansdowne 9-8-1914. 1.30 p.m.	Orders received to mobilise according to allotment tables 1913. The Battalion is to start with 75 men addition_ally to War strength and to leave Depot on scale "A". The above orders were received at 1.30 p.m. Immediately letters of recall to leave and furlough men were stamped and posted catching the 2.30 p.m. post. The following Telegrams were sent (a) to recall all B.O's. on Privilege Leave. (b) To Division requesting recall of B.Os'. on leave out of their India. (c) To Deputy Commissioners of Garhwal and Almora and the Wazir, Tehri State asking them to recall all men on leave and furlough and to order all Reservists to rejoin. (d) To Division requesting recall of any ranks on detached employ. Medical Inspection was completed of all ranks excluding those on furlough and leave.	B.M's. 7391/A. our No. 1524-A. dated 9-8-1914.

Army Form C. 2118.

WAR DIARY

INTELLIGENCE SUMMARY

(*Erase heading not required.*)

Instructions regarding War Diaries and Intelligence Summaries are contained in F. S. Regs., Part II, and the Staff Manual respectively. Title pages will be prepared in manuscript.

Hour, Date, Place.	Summary of Events and Information.	Remarks and references to Appendices.
10-8-1914.	Memo sent to the Assistant Commissioner Lansdowne asking that notices be issued to all villages in his District ordering the recall of all men on leave and furlough and the calling out of Reservists. Measures of interior economy as per Mob. Regs. India taken in hand. Wire sent to Deputy Collector Chamoli asking him to issue orders for the immediate recall of all men on furlough and leave and Reservists. Five Furlough and leave men rejoined. Measures of Interior economy and (Formation of Depôt etc.) continued. Battalion ordered to march to Kotedwara in two marches leaving Lansdowne on the 18th inst.	
11-8-1914.	Report received that equipment not yet available at equipping Station (Roorkee) Jemadar Deb Sing Negi detailed for duty with the S.A.S. Divisional ammunition Column. Telegram sent to D.A.A.G. again requesting recall of Capt. Orton offg. G.S.O. (3) Simla.	

Army Form C. 2118.

WAR DIARY

INTELLIGENCE SUMMARY

(Erase heading not required.)

Instructions regarding War Diaries and Intelligence Summaries are contained in F. S. Regs., Part II, and the Staff Manual respectively. Title pages will be prepared in manuscript.

Hour, Date, Place.	Summary of Events and Information.	Remarks and references to Appendices.
12-8-1914.	Interior Economy arrangements completed as far as is possible till return of Furlo, and Leave men. Fifteen furlough men rejoined.	
13-8-1914.	Orders received from A.G. that Battalion is to move short of strength if necessary. Balance to make up strength to be despatched later. Major Dawes I.M.S. Capt. Lumb Capt. Etherton, and Captain Orton not yet rejoined. Capt. Landie I.M.S. detailed as M.O. to Bn.	
14-8-1914.	Forty furlough men rejoined. Orders received to transfer equipment from Equipping Station (Roorkee) to Kotdwara. Advance Party proceeded to Roorkee today. Telegram received from adjmtstaff 7th Division ordering troops not to leave Lansdowne till orders received from Q.M. General.	

Army Form C. 2118.

WAR DIARY

INTELLIGENCE SUMMARY

(Erase heading not required.)

Instructions regarding War Diaries and Intelligence Summaries are contained in F. S. Regs., Part II, and the Staff Manual respectively. Title pages will be prepared in manuscript.

Hour, Date, Place.	Summary of Events and Information.	Remarks and references to Appendices.
Lansdowne. 15-8-1914.	One hundred and seventy one furlo and leave men still away. Capts. Lumb and Etherton not yet rejoined from leave and Capt. Orton from Army Head Quarters. Extra enlistments commenced today.	
Lansdowne. 16-8-1914.	Telegram sent direct to Capt. Orton ordering him to rejoin immediately. O.C. advance Party reported from equipping station that our consignment does not include socks worsted, Rations men and animals Coats Warm Riflemen or clothing for extra 75 men. Also that there were no indications of a further consignment arriving.	
Lansdowne 17-8-1914.	One hundred furlo and leave men still absent. Report received from O.C. advance Party that equipment from equipping Station and heavy baggage from Lansdowne had both reached Kotedwara.	
Lansdowne. 18-8-1914.	Capt. Orton rejoined from Army Head Quarters. The strength the Battalion could move today is 675 Garhwali Ranks Total of furlough and leave men rejoined to date is 161. The number of Reservists that have come in is 51.	

Army Form C. 2118

WAR DIARY

INTELLIGENCE SUMMARY

(Erase heading not required.)

Instructions regarding War Diaries and Intelligence Summaries are contained in F. S. Regs., Part II, and the Staff Manual respectively. Title pages will be prepared in manuscript.

Hour, Date, Place.	Summary of Events and Information.	Remarks and references to Appendices.
Lansdowne 19-8-1914.	Capt. Landle I.M.S. has not yet reported himself for duty. Orders received from the Adjmtstaff 7th Division by the G.O.C. Brigade that the Battalion is to reach Kotedwara by the evening of the 21st inst. Sixty five furlough and leave men have not yet re-joined. Total of Reservists rejoined to date is eighty.	
Lansdowne. 20-8-1914.	Jemadar Deb Sing Negi and Rifn. (Ward orderly) Sur Sing Pharswan left for Meerut; the former to join the S.A.S. Divisional Ammuni-tion Column and the latter to join no 130.I.F.A. Indian Hospital. Major Mackworth I.M.S. reported himself for duty Capt. Landle I.M.S Having been found Medically unfit. Capt. Burton ordered to rejoin 2/39th Garhwal Rifles. The Battalion marched to Dogadda at 1.15. p.m. Distance 10½ Miles. Strength eight British officers (inluding Medical officer) and 717 Garhwali Ranks. A very hot march. One man fell out.	✱ O.C. Major W.H. Wardell D.C. Comdrs. Major K. Hender--son. D.C. Capt. J. Lane " W.G.S. Kenny " S.B. Orton Adjutant Lieut. Mankelow Q.M. " G.S. Rogers Medical Officer Major, N.W. Mackworth I.M.S.
Dogadda Lansdowne 21-8-1914.	Marched to Kotedwara. No men fell out. camped at Kotdwara near Rail--way Station. Orders received for Battalion to entrain for Karachi on 23rd inst.	

Army Form C. 2118

WAR DIARY

(Erase heading not required.)

Instructions regarding War Diaries and Intelligence Summaries are contained in F. S. Regs., Part II, and the Staff Manual respectively. Title pages will be prepared in manuscript.

Hour, Date, Place.	Summary of Events and Information.	Remarks and references to Appendices.
Kotdwara 22-8-1914.	Advance Party under Capt. Kenny proceeded to Karachi. Orders to entrain on 23rd inst. Cancelled. Battalion to stand fast at Kotdwara till further orders.	
Kotdwara 23-8-1914.	Capt. Etherton rejoined and proceeded to Depot. Total number of Garhwali Ranks ready to entrain here is now 792. Struck Camp near Railway Station and Camped on open ground below Railway. One man returned to Depot suffering from Granular conjunct-vits.	
Kotdwara 24-8-1914.	The balance of men required to make up strength arrived today. Total of Garhwali Ranks is 828. Double Coys. paraded under Double Coy. Commanders.	
Kotdwara 25-8-1914.	Double Coy. parades under Double Coy. Commanders. All ranks receive quinine every alternate day. Very heavy rain fell.	
Kotdwara 26-8-1914.	Double Coy. parades under D.C. Comdrs. Two Reservists returned to the Depot suffering from Conjunctivitis.	

Army Form C. 2118.

WAR DIARY

or

INTELLIGENCE SUMMARY.

(Erase heading not required.)

Instructions regarding War Diaries and Intelligence Summaries are contained in F. S. Regs., Part II, and the Staff Manual respectively. Title pages will be prepared in manuscript.

Hour, Date, Place.	Summary of Events and Information.	Remarks and references to Appendices.
26-8-1914.		
Kotdwara 5. p. m. 27-8-1914.	Special instruction of Reservists in short rifle takes place daily. Double Coy. parades under D.C. Comdrs. Heavy rain during the night.	
28-8-1914.	Parades as yesterday. Telegram came from Control ordering battalion to leave Kotdwara for ~~Gurmukh~~ & Gurwal. Karachi in train No. 27. Block K. Timing 30th on words from Najibabad to Timing C.	useful
Kotdwara 29-8-1914.	Parades as yesterday. One case of Mumps occurred in "B" Coy. The man was sent to the Depot immediately. Captain F. G. E. Lumb rejoined from leave.	

1/39 Garhwal Rifles

30/8/14 – 1/10/14

Army Form C. 2118.

WAR DIARY
or
INTELLIGENCE SUMMARY.
(Erase heading not required.)

Instructions regarding War Diaries and Intelligence Summaries are contained in F. S. Regs., Part II, and the Staff Manual respectively. Title pages will be prepared in manuscript.

Hour, Date, Place.	Summary of Events and Information.	Remarks and references to Appendices.
30-8-1914. 12.30. p.m.	The Battalion left Kotdwara by train for Karachi as follows. First Train Head Quarters, A, B, and portion of C. Coy. M.G. section Officers chargers and all heavy Kit, at 12.30. p.m. Second Train, Portion of C. Coy. D. E. F. G. and H. under the Command of Major Henderson at 2.45. p.m. The first train on reaching Najibabad remained there till the arrival of the Second train when both were formed into one.	
31-8-1914.	On arriving at Lahore, last night we were informed that instead of going by the route which had been issued to us i.e. Via Bhatinda, we were to go Via Lahore. Arrived at Lahore Cantonment (West) at 9.20. a.m. where men Cooked their food for the day. So far it has been rather a hot Journey, but all ranks very fit. Arrived at Rohri at 2.30. p.m. where the men cooked food. Left Rohri at 5.30. p.m.	
1-9-1914.		
2-9-1914. Karachi.	Reached Karachi Rest Camp siding at 12.15. p.m. and detrained.	

Army Form C. 2118.

WAR DIARY
or
INTELLIGENCE SUMMARY.

(Erase heading not required.)

Instructions regarding War Diaries and Intelligence Summaries are contained in F. S. Regs., Part II, and the Staff Manual respectively. Title pages will be prepared in manuscript.

Hour, Date, Place.	Summary of Events and Information.	Remarks and references to Appendices.
3-9-1914. H.T. EKMA.	The R.T.O. there informed us that we were the smartest regiment at detraining and getting clear of the platform that had arrived there so far. Soon after our arrival at the Rest Camp, which is a few hundred yards from the siding, when the men had got settled down and started cooking and order came saying that we were to entrain again and embark that evening. On the C.O. pointing out that this would cause unnecessary in-convenience the Battalion was allowed to remain at the Rest Camp for the night, &&&&&&&&&&&&&& entrain next morning at 6.30. a.m. and proceed to Kiamari Docks to Embark on the H.T. EKMA. On account of some delay in marking the train the Battalion left the Rest Camp siding three minutes after time. It is unnecessary to go into too much detail when marking a train for a journey of a few miles. On arrival at the Docks the Battalion Embarked on the H.T. EKMA. The men are very cramped for Room, while the cooking place and latrines appear to be very inadequate.	

Army Form C. 2118.

WAR DIARY

OF

INTELLIGENCE SUMMARY.

(Erase heading not required.)

Instructions regarding War Diaries and Intelligence Summaries are contained in F. S. Regs., Part II, and the Staff Manual respectively. Title pages will be prepared in manuscript.

Hour, Date, Place.	Summary of Events and Information.	Remarks and references to Appendices.
4-9-1914. H. T. EKMA.	Brigade Head Quarters and Staff, and Head Quarters and two Double Companies of the 2nd 3rd (Q.A.O) Gurkhas will be on board with us. The Battalion was Medically Inspected by the Embarkation Staff Medical officer. He remarked how extremly fit the men looked. There are only twenty five latrines for the use of about 1350 men. This number is very inadequate and may cause illness. Eight sections of an Indian stationary Hospital will also be on board with us.	

Army Form C. 2118.

WAR DIARY
or
INTELLIGENCE SUMMARY.
(Erase heading not required.)

Instructions regarding War Diaries and Intelligence Summaries are contained in F. S. Regs., Part II, and the Staff Manual respectively. Title pages will be prepared in manuscript.

Hour, Date, Place.	Summary of Events and Information.	Remarks and references to Appendices.
5-9-1914. H.T. EKMA.	The rations for the men on board are not of good quality. The Ghi especially being very poor and unfit for issue while a large proportion of the potatoes are bad.	
6-9-1914.	The fever resulting from our ten days halt at Kotdwara, which is an extremely malarious place at this time of year is beginning to come out.	
7-9-1914.	Several more men are down with fever a large proportion, however, of the cases are slight, and the sea Voyage will make the men that have got fever quite fit again. If possible no troops should Camp at Kotdwara during the rainy Season.	
10-9-1914.	The men sleep and cook in the sheds near the ship on the wharf. The animals also were disembarked yesterday. Though in our Embarkation return we pointed out that the men are meat eaters, no meat ration has been provided for them. No Lime-juice has been provided by the authorities. We have, however, provided some Regimentally.	

Army Form C. 2118.

WAR DIARY
of
INTELLIGENCE SUMMARY.
(Erase heading not required.)

Instructions regarding War Diaries and Intelligence Summaries are contained in F. S. Regs., Part II, and the Staff Manual respectively. Title pages will be prepared in manuscript.

Hour, Date, Place.	Summary of Events and Information.	Remarks and references to Appendices.
15-9-1914. 10. a.m.	Troops and followers re-embarked on H.T. EKMA. The M.G. Mules Embarked in the Evening.	
16-9-1914. 6. a.m.	The H.T. Ekma left the wharf to make room for another transport and took up a position in the stream. The ghi referred to before has been changed.	
18-9-1914.	Sub-Assistant Surgeon Sannu Lal Pathak having been found unfit for Field Service has been ordered to report himself to the A.D.M.S. Karachi and is struck off Head Quarters strength of the Battalion. No 2359 R/sh Kundan heyr, transferred to Regtl Hospital of 12/ Bulechis, Kwaka. S.A.S. Ram Krishan Ganpat Shinde reported his arrival and is taken on the strength of the Battalion.	
19-9-14 4. 20-9-1914.		
5.30. p.m.	The H.T. Ekma left Kiamari Docks and took up her station outside the Harbour.	
21-9-1914. 8.30. a.m.	H.M.S. Dartmouth and Harding escorts, and eleven transports left for an unknown destination.	
21-9-1914. to 1-10-1914.	An eventless Voyage so far. The Red Sea was very hot, most of the fever cases are better. There have been a certain number of	

Army Form C. 2118.

WAR DIARY
or
INTELLIGENCE SUMMARY.
(Erase heading not required.)

Hour, Date, Place.	Summary of Events and Information	Remarks and references to Appendices.
	of colic cases caused by the Coarse atta and insufficient cooking accomodation.	
2-9-1914. 5.30. p.m.	Arrived at Suez. One Bugler enteric and Pnemonia case(No.2688 Rai Sing Rawat)and one Rifleman sick attendant (No.2600 Gopal Sing Dokoti) put ashore and transferred to the Hospital Suez. H.T. EKMA remained at Suez for the night.	
3-10-1914. 10.a.m.	The H.T. EKMA left Suez at 10.a.m. Suez Cannal Orders received that, in order to avoid confusion with British Brigades and Divisions,in future we would be known as the 20th Indian Infantry Brigade, Meerut Division.	
4-10-1914. 1.a.m. Port-Said.	Arrived at Port Said Lieut.-Col: Swiney, Major Home,Capt: and Adjutant Mainwaring ^"Lieut Welchman" rejoined today. Remained here for the night.	
5-10-1914. Port-Said.	Col: Swiney took over Command of the Battalion from Major Wardell. Capt: Mainwaring took over the duties of Adjutant from Lieutenant Mankelow, Major Wardell assumed Command of No.II D.C. and Major Home assumed Command of No.III D.C.	

Army Form C. 2118.

14

WAR DIARY
or
INTELLIGENCE SUMMARY.

(Erase heading not required.)

Instructions regarding War Diaries and Intelligence Summaries are contained in F. S. Regs., Part II, and the Staff Manual respectively. Title pages will be prepared in manuscript.

Hour, Date, Place.	Summary of Events and Information	Remarks and references to Appendices.
6-10-1914. PORT-SAID.	Lay off Port Said and Ships took up positions for sailing during the morning. Sailed from Port Said at 5.p.m. under escort of French Warship.	
7-10-1914.	Fine weather.	
8-10-1914.	Early in the morning Sea became rough. Strong wind was blowing by the afternoon and the sea became much rougher towards the evening. Nearly all the men were Sea-Sick.	
9-10-1914.	Sea was much smoother early in the morning:- Some of the men were still sick. Lt: Rogers horse died during the afternoon. The Sea was quite smooth in the evening.	
10-10-1914.	Weather fine and sea quite smooth. Passed MALTA about 9.a.m.	

Army Form C. 2118.

WAR DIARY
or
INTELLIGENCE SUMMARY

(Erase heading not required.)

Instructions regarding War Diaries and Intelligence Summaries are contained in F. S. Regs., Part II, and the Staff Manual respectively. Title pages will be prepared in manuscript.

Hour, Date, Place.	Summary of Events and Information	Remarks and references to Appendices.
11-10-1914.	Sea quite smooth - most of the men quite recovered from sea sickness.	
12-10-1914.	Passed S.E. of SARDINIA - Sea became rough again towards the evening.	
13-10-1914.	Arrived MARSEILLES Ship berthed about 11.30.a.m. No landing berth being available only B.Os. were allowed on shore Orders were received that the Battalion would be re-armed at 7.a.m. the following morning. This order was subsequently cancelled as further orders were received saying that the ship would be berthed and troops disembarked early the next morning.	
14-10-1914.	Ship berthed at about 10.30.a.m. troops immediately commenced to disembark 1/39th G. leading. After piling arms half of each Company was marched off, carrying rifles, to be re-armed at the Ordnance shed (Hangar/h No.7). The whole battalion was rearmed in about half an hour with a similar rifle but which is manufactu- -red to take the Mark VII ammunition.	

Army Form C. 2118.

WAR DIARY

or

INTELLIGENCE SUMMARY.

(Erase heading not required.)

Instructions regarding War Diaries and Intelligence Summaries are contained in F. S. Regs., Part II, and the Staff Manual respectively. Title pages will be prepared in manuscript.

Hour, Date, Place.	Summary of Events and Information	Remarks and references to Appendices.
	Machine Guns and ammunition were also changed soon after rifles had been changed. According to orders 500 men had to be left at the Docks to carry out fatigues from 6.p.m. to 7.a.m. Concequently Nos. II, III & IV D.Cs. remained with their Kits in No. 5 Hangar for the night No. I D.C. marched 2 miles to Camp LA VALENTINE arriving at 7.30.p.m. Before leaving the Docks some difficulty was experienced in loading the transports as the Carts supplied were not capable of carrying the amount of baggage they were supposed to. No. I D.C. had to pitch Camp in the dark Lt:Col: Swiney. Capt: Lumb Capt: Mainwaring and 2nd Lt: Show (interpreter) marched with this D.C.	

Army Form C. 2118.

17

WAR DIARY
or
INTELLIGENCE SUMMARY.
(Erase heading not required.)

Instructions regarding War Diaries and Intelligence Summaries are contained in F. S. Regs., Part II, and the Staff Manual respectively. Title pages will be prepared in manuscript.

Hour, Date, Place.	Summary of Events and Information.	Remarks and references to Appendices.
14-10-14 (contd.)	Machine guns and Ammunition were also changed soon after rifles had been changed. According to orders 500 men had to be left at the Docks to carry out fatigues from 6 p.m. to 7 a.m. Consequently No.s II, III & IV Double Coys remained with their Kits in No 5 Hangar for the night. No I Dt. Marched a mile to Camp LA-VALENTINE arriving at 7.30 p.m. Before leaving the docks some difficulty was experienced in loading the Transports as the carts supplied were not capable of carrying the amount of baggage they were supposed to. No I D.C. tried to pitch camp in the dark. Lt. Col. Swiney, Captain Lumb, Captain Mainwaring & 2nd Lt. Shaw (Instructor) marched with this Double Company.	

Gulab Singh & Sons, Calcutta—No. 22 Army C.—5-8-14—1,07,000.

Army Form C. 2118.

18

WAR DIARY
or
INTELLIGENCE SUMMARY.
(Erase heading not required.)

Instructions regarding War Diaries and Intelligence Summaries are contained in F. S. Regs., Part II, and the Staff Manual respectively. Title pages will be prepared in manuscript.

Hour, Date, Place.	Summary of Events and Information.	Remarks and references to Appendices.
30-10-14 (Contd.)	Machine Guns and Ammunition were also changed from one of the old trench stores. According to orders the men had to be left on the ground carrying fatigues from 6 pm to 7 am throughout. Nos II, III & IV Double Coys remained in the trenches. Relief to No 5 Hanger for the night. Nos 2 & 3C Marched a mile to Pont LA VALENTINE arriving at 7.30pm. Report during the march being difficult were expressed in loading the transport as the two different units were not capable of being supported. The transport of baggage that they were supposed to No 1 D.C. had to find lamps on the dark. At 10. Survey Coy & Pont Coys Marching and 2 & 3 Spare (Butts?) marched with the Double Company.	

Gulab Singh & Sons, Calcutta—No. 22 Army C.—5-8-14—1,07,000.

Army Form C. 2118.

19

WAR DIARY
or
INTELLIGENCE SUMMARY.

(Erase heading not required.)

Instructions regarding War Diaries and Intelligence Summaries are contained in F. S. Regs., Part II, and the Staff Manual respectively. Title pages will be prepared in manuscript.

Hour, Date, Place.	Summary of Events and Information	Remarks and references to Appendices.

14.10.14
(contd.)

Lieut Mountain arrived in Camp at 11.30 p.m. with
Machine Guns and ammunition.
8 Mules were transferred to the 1 F.A at the time.

15.10.14
Camp LA
VALENTINE

Commenced to rain at about 4 a.m. & rained
all day unceasingly
Capt Tea Bennett so far as possible sent as
many tents as were & light to Tuell Lager
The B.H.Qs of the Regt are now out on outline posts
about half way
Camp was fearfully pitched as always - it
was not wonderfully well in spite of the weather
the Camp soon became a swamp

16.10.14
The Weather was again bad & rainfall most of
the day. Message from the Bde Signr —
Picketed by Battalion orders

Extract from Routine Orders
by
Lieut-General C. A. Anderson, C.B.,
Commanding Meerut Div:
At Sea
7-10-14.

x   x   x

11. The procedure for the issue of rations on payment will be as follows:—

Indents will be made on I.A.F.-1026 and will be transferred by Audit Officers after check to Disbursing Officers. Indents at places where accounts are not submitted to Audit will be sent by issuing Officers direct to Disbursing Officers.

Recoveries from Officers in Govt. Service will be effected from their pay. Persons not in Govt. Service will deposit money equal in value to two months rations with Military Accounts Officers at the Base or with the Field Treasure Chest Officers and bring the deposit to this standard at the commencement of each month. Use of I.A.F. F 1026 ipso facto authorises recoveries from pay of Officers in Govt. Service and from deposits of persons not in Govt. Service.

(Authority Q.M.G. in India's No 22/6 W.E.D. 22nd August 1914).

(Sd) A.L. Lindsay Colonel
A.Q.M.G. Meerut Divn

True copy
[signature]
Captain
Acting Adjutant 1/39th G. Rifles

WAR DIARY or INTELLIGENCE SUMMARY

Army Form C. 2118

Hour, Date, Place.	Summary of Events and Information	Remarks and references to Appendices.
16.10.14 (Contd.)	War (Queen of the West" translated & circulated among Companies. F.O.'s kept attached regarding Orders received. 10th. Division 3 pm G.S. began to make attaching F. Coys transferred to the C.T.S.	
17.10.14	Morning: afternoon quick firing & left Air swing Coy on a Very Muddy Extra Dall Labour Firmness. were flooded out during the night No-17. B.O's letter informed that they would possess to leave for F.S. Ration Returned 4 Hundred & expose in the Afternoon about 3 pm	
18.10.14	Battalion Received Orders to entrain at ARENUES (MIRAEILLES) Captain Russo the transport Officer was informed representing all the transport of pre-that no	Divisional Orders nos 11 to 7 10. 14 (with attachm)

Army Form C. 2118.

(2-1)

WAR DIARY

or

INTELLIGENCE SUMMARY.

(Erase heading not required.)

Hour, Date, Place.	Summary of Events and Information	Remarks and references to Appendices.
15.10.44 (contd.)	Wagons were unable to get to Lutakin and in 2 cases unable to attain to Hopin from the ALL. In these lorries were finished. Transport was therefore totally refused from Army and was detailed for the Royal Highlanders who did not take their relief transport. Battalion left camp at about 8 pm. All all ranks & equipt carried by lorries were able to retire exc-loaded in the distance to Meiktuk. Arms and carried nearly over kms during march. ARENG Halt at about 11.35 AM. Several items fallen out. Presumes have had time Hadley burned by a Civilian Driver were from the station. Lieut Wilchner was with it & brought it along to bogoze.	

Army Form C. 2118.

22

WAR DIARY
or
INTELLIGENCE SUMMARY.
(Erase heading not required.)

Instructions regarding War Diaries and Intelligence Summaries are contained in F.S. Regs., Part II, and the Staff Manual respectively. Title pages will be prepared in manuscript.

Hour, Date, Place.	Summary of Events and Information	Remarks and references to Appendices.
19-10-14 (contd.)	Army in a test in first to lead Institute to the train. Otherwise field kit kept to the train. 4 Mess Waggons filled with bread to the train. The train left MARSEILLES at 3.30 April 14th.	
In the Train 19.10.14 to Grande & WILLIAMS	Mens Kits Bandolier Haversack — Arm: A in three at the knee to Ordnance. The following from re-inspection were left on Marseilles Sub-actor Military Make 1 Haversack 1 Linen Haversack 55 Rifles All day Shorts in the the train arrived at CETTE at 11 am. at NARBONNE 2.30 pm etc.	

WAR DIARY
or
INTELLIGENCE SUMMARY

Army Form C. 2118.
23

Hour, Date, Place.	Summary of Events and Information	Remarks and references to Appendices.
19-10-14 (contd.)	Halted over 3 hours. Must treat authorities politest but officer go to the town. Had plenty place to eat and get a good meal. Except for "Bully" I observed men all ready to hand turn in the horses. No horses relieved. Quality had been strict, jack hospitals the opened	
20-10-14	HAYES (MOURDON) no loss where the horses had tea later proceeded to LIMOGES ST SULPICE where we halted for 3 days the men have been again where is good meal. Quads ST SULPICE at 6.15 pm Capt — 9.10 pm.	

Army Form C. 2118.

WAR DIARY
or
INTELLIGENCE SUMMARY.
(Erase heading not required.)

Instructions regarding War Diaries and Intelligence Summaries are contained in F. S. Regs., Part II, and the Staff Manual respectively. Title pages will be prepared in manuscript.

Hour, Date, Place.	Summary of Events and Information	Remarks and references to Appendices.
ORLEANS 23.10.14	Ordered 5 am. Motor lorries were meeting at station to take Baly't Coys which were only 3 to 4 miles away. Weather was bright but no rain fell. A Brigade were allotted to the Battn. bn. An order was issued that no photos were to be taken & that he must never to leave for the front. 3 more reinforcements to Indian Field Ambulance.	
29.10.14	Weather still fine this morning. 3 Riflemen attached as drivers for transport trouops not being sufficient A.S.C. drivers available. These were thoroughly segregated and were accordingly segregated. Battalion hitherto failed was detailed as under. The Quartermaster, Jemr. Apt Sing Rawat & 4 N.C.Os.	

Army Form C. 2118.

25

WAR DIARY

or

INTELLIGENCE SUMMARY.

(*Erase heading not required.*)

Instructions regarding War Diaries and Intelligence Summaries are contained in F. S. Regs., Part II, and the Staff Manual respectively. Title pages will be prepared in manuscript.

Hour, Date, Place.	Summary of Events and Information	Remarks and references to Appendices.
22-10-14 (contd)	21 men mostly suffering from diarrhoea & dysentery were transferred to 1 F.A.	
23. 10-14	Weather still fine. 7 more men transferred to 1 F.A. mostly Dear- -dea cases	
24-10-14	Captain Orton Junior applying to M.O.s to including Capt. of the Battalion left for unknown destination. Capt. Orton travelled by Motor the remainder by rail ——— The White Divisions preceded us & made hard I think about 1 miles. We transfer was made & marched nearly according to schedule. Only 1 inter of the Battalion left the Sours and of them was Major-Manager to	

Army Form C. 2118.

WAR DIARY
or
INTELLIGENCE SUMMARY.

(Erase heading not required.)

Instructions regarding War Diaries and Intelligence Summaries are contained in F. S. Regs., Part II, and the Staff Manual respectively. Title pages will be prepared in manuscript.

Hour, Date, Place.	Summary of Events and Information	Remarks and references to Appendices.
24-11-70 (contd)	to hover to at the desk. Everything the men were very soft whose had to practise this was not to lead the forward. A new man was transferred to the I.F.R. M.O. Could but arrange for the truck heath official only nursing is have lead especially amongst the battalion. Orders West received that health company was in future to be known as a company of the quarts of a battalion of September. The reforms half company was held to the head. On account of the cold & improve has been ordered to always wear warm clothing when outside.	

WAR DIARY
or
INTELLIGENCE SUMMARY.
(Erase heading not required.)

Army Form C. 2118.

27

Hour, Date, Place.	Summary of Events and Information	Remarks and references to Appendices.
ORLEANS 25.10.14	Orders re-entrainment for the front were received	
26.10.14	R. Lothians regarding. Orders received informing the 7.15 pm the BORDER Battn. the 4 Batterys were to be ready at [illegible] 12 B. O. [illegible] change. Three following were the Regtl numbers allocated for the totals Ldrs - F.L. [illegible] Details as Baggage transport - A Row Hosp - 2 Bgge hospitals Wettelung [illegible] - 1 B. O. 1 G.O. 5 M.O.s - 30 M.E. O. above Active Reserve infantry division back to R. [illegible] 4 men following teams through Crossing to a baggage wagon preserving trtgs? [illegible] in lieu of the entraining of [illegible] Cavalry Allocated in the line	

Army Form C. 2118.

28

WAR DIARY
or
INTELLIGENCE SUMMARY.
(Erase heading not required.)

Hour, Date, Place.	Summary of Events and Information	Remarks and references to Appendices.
26.10.14 (contd)	Major Anderson with the Squadron of 54 men of A & B Sqns were left behind. the railway authorities refusing to hire the return waiting a reasonable time.	
27.10.14	The route taken by the train was via MANTES, ROUEN, ABBEVILLE, BOULOGNE, HAZEBROUCK to the South Country town of LILLIERS where the battalion detrained at 7.30 a.m.	Sm.L.H. STUMBER M.A.
28.10.14 CALONNE	The battalion having generals headquarters and remainder of B Sqn to wait for transport however our detail, who had not arrived of yesterday .... the last train pulled in. Arrived behind to march to CALONNE where temporary billets had been allotted by Capt Orr...	

Army Form C. 2118.

WAR DIARY
or
INTELLIGENCE SUMMARY.
(Erase heading not required.)

Instructions regarding War Diaries and Intelligence Summaries are contained in F. S. Regs., Part II, and the Staff Manual respectively. Title pages will be prepared in manuscript.

Hour, Date, Place.	Summary of Events and Information	Remarks and references to Appendices.
28-10-14 (Contd.)	Little other Military interest. The Board of Enquiry into the Road Accident today from the direction of BETHUNE showing the Army Service Corps. Details for a General was [illegible] near LALONNE [illegible] Lewis was ordered to inform the Units [illegible] as a safeguard for the Brigade area. Operation Orders for the transfer to the Lorgies were issued at 10 p.m. + explained to all officers.	Appx I (with [illegible] forwarded with diary Dr 29/10.)

Army Form C. 2118.

WAR DIARY
or
INTELLIGENCE SUMMARY.
(Erase heading not required.)

Instructions regarding War Diaries and Intelligence Summaries are contained in F. S. Regs., Part II, and the Staff Manual respectively. Title pages will be prepared in manuscript.

Hour, Date, Place.	Summary of Events and Information.	Remarks and references to Appendices.
RICHEBOURG VICINITY 7 a.m. LES GLATIGNES 29-10-14	Batt'n. left billets at CALONNE. Batt'n arrived at 10.30 a.m. and halted in two lines - 2 companies in each line facing N.S.E.	Appx I (Ayt 20,000 BETHUNE) " II
2.30 p.m.	C.O. & Adjt were called to the 14th Brigade Head Quarters at C se de Raux, to receive orders as regards taking over trenches from the E. Surrey Regt. Batt'n marched to Rue de L'EPINETTE attack & thence that up a position en At Colonne preparatory to advancing to take over the trenches.	
4.30 p.m.	C.O. & Adjt. & D.C. Cond'rs & M.G.O. preceded escorted by an officer of the 1/E. Surrey Regt to shew the Hd. Qrs. of that Regt. to find out details about taking over the trenches. The portions of the trenches were found to out officers evacuating proceeding to the trenches	

Army Form C. 2118.

WAR DIARY
or
INTELLIGENCE SUMMARY.

(*Erase heading not required.*)

Instructions regarding War Diaries and Intelligence Summaries are contained in F. S. Regs., Part II, and the Staff Manual respectively. Title pages will be prepared in manuscript.

Hour, Date, Place.	Summary of Events and Information.	Remarks and references to Appendices.
RICHEBOURG 29-10-14	After having seen their respective positions on the sketch. The distribution of companies is as shown on our plan sketch of the position	Vide Operation Order No I.
11.40 p.m.	Officers rejoined companies at RUE DE L'ÉPINETTE at 11.40 p.m. and the battalion marched to occupy the trenches at 1.15 a.m.	
30/10/14 1.15 a.m. 5.30 a.m.	All trenches were occupied by 5.30 a.m. — the enemy making 2 feu attacks — the first one a very severe one — while relief was being carried out. There was a heavy downpour of rain during the darkness & the trenches were consequently rendered very uncomfortable and men got chilled.	

WAR DIARY
or
INTELLIGENCE SUMMARY.

(Erase heading not required.)

Army Form C. 2118.

Hour, Date, Place.	Summary of Events and Information	Remarks and references to Appendices.
RICHEBOURG L'AVOUE 30-10-14 9 a.m.	German Heavy Artillery commenced Shelling E & F coys Trenches — also C coys a little later — using high explosive shells — probably 8" Howitzers. These portions of Trenches suffered a great deal of damage, and portions of E, F, & C Coy being cut off from the remainder to their right & left. The German fire was concentrated and actioned by numerous and F company lost 4 killed and 5 wounded from this Shell fire alone. Considering that this was the accurate fire experience of fire if any that they were contemporarily steady. Some N.C.Os & men of E & C coys apparently two or more, as they were cut off from the trenches right and left, retired towards Battr Hd Quarters whence they were immediately sent back to their Trenches. Some of these men approached D company's trenches walking along the CINDER TRACK. This action was immediately rewarded with 3 Salvoes of German Shells, most of which fell beyond G & H companies' Trenches and did very little damage.	These German Howitzer Shells are charged with a very high explosive giving out much flash & smoke. These shells have a very great effect & unless they burst either very close to the parapet or in the trench do very little damage. It is remarkable that the German Infantry did not open fire on the men retiring from or returning to Trenches on the open ground. See Sketch I. 1/39 G Trenches Weather - fair - very little rain
Noon.	Shelling ceased about noon.	
31-10-14	Casualties this day were pretty heavy — mainly due to Sniping from that part of the enemy's trenches in front of E and C companies. Total 4 killed, 24 wounded. Early part of the night fairly quiet. Trenches in wet condition — a good deal of sniping during the morning.	
5.30 p.m. 6 p.m.	A short fire attack by the enemy. Sappers & Miners arrived and commenced work on C.M.C. Trench in GAP between C & D companies	

On His Majesty's Service.

39th Gurkha Rifles

31/10/14 — 23/11/14

Army Form C. 2118.

WAR DIARY
or
INTELLIGENCE SUMMARY.
(Erase heading not required.)

Instructions regarding War Diaries and Intelligence Summaries are contained in F. S. Regs., Part II, and the Staff Manual respectively. Title pages will be prepared in manuscript.

Hour, Date, Place.	Summary of Events and Information	Remarks and references to Appendices.
RICHEBOURG L'AVOUÉ 31-10-14.	Fairly quiet night on the whole – Snipers were active. Sappers carried the C.M.C. trench from left of D Coy to within a few yards of the rear of the right flank of C Coy. Rations received during the night consisted of Dhal & biscuits only.	Sketch I. 1/39 G Trenches Casualties: 14 wounded
1-11-14	A fine morning. Enemy's howitzers nearly struck the machine gun pit in rear of the LEFT PICKET with two H.E. Shells – no damage was done however. No. 7 Battery R.F.A. ranged with great accuracy on the enemy's trench in front of C Coy stopping the sniping which had caused so many casualties in that Company.	No. 7 Battery R.F.A. was some 1000 yards in rear of Battn H.Q. and was of the greatest assistance to us in keeping down the enemy's rifle fire during the whole period we were in trenches at RICHEBOURG L'AVOUÉ i.e. from 29-10-14 to 19-11-14. Casualties: 5 wounded
8 p.m.	The men received a good "atta" ration as well as Beans. Reported by Major Henderson on our right that he believed the Yeomanry were sapping towards the junction of our right flank with 2/3rd Gurkhas left. 400 waterproof Sheets brought up by the Quarter-Master – they added greatly to the comfort of men in trenches. Rained heavily during the night.	
2-11-14	All companies employed in improving trenches and making comfortable places in which to sleep for men to rest in. There was practically no shelling during the day.	Casualties: 1 killed 4 wounded

Army Form C. 2118.

WAR DIARY
or
INTELLIGENCE SUMMARY.
(Erase heading not required.)

Instructions regarding War Diaries and Intelligence Summaries are contained in F. S. Regs., Part II, and the Staff Manual respectively. Title pages will be prepared in manuscript.

Hour, Date, Place.	Summary of Events and Information	Remarks and references to Appendices.
RICHEBOURG L'AVOUE 3-11-14 10 p.m.	Weather fine. Nothing of any importance occurred during the day except some shelling by German howitzers which had no effect. Enemy opened a very heavy fire attack directed mostly against 1 G.H. Company. The attack it was preceded by the advanced post opening and covering fire on German trenches. G & H companies replied vigorously and No 7 battery opened fire on which the Germans came firing. B Company under Capt. Lewis moved up into the C.P.C. trench between C & D companies & consisted of into a fire trench sapping & driving entrenchment in front of B company. No entrenchments in front of B company. Practically no artillery fire during the day.	A Company under Dhan Sing Negi joined the Brigade Reserve, so the battalion was left with no supporting company. Casualties 2 killed, 1 Wounded.
4-11-14 4 p.m. 7 p.m.	Commenced to rain. A party of Scouts sent out by Capt. Lewis were charged by a large party of the enemy who succeeded in rushing the 99s on B company's left. Capt. Lewis withdrew a section from B company who Jemadar Ajab Sing Rawat, who charged the Germans who immediately fled. This party of Germans was about 80 strong and could easily have rolled up Capt. Lewis's flank had they pressed the attack but the prompt action on the part of Capt. Lewis & Jemadar Ajab Sing put an end to any further offensive action, and showed that the Germans were not keen to meet the bayonet.	Casualties 4 Wounded

Army Form C. 2118.

WAR DIARY
or
INTELLIGENCE SUMMARY.
(Erase heading not required.)

Instructions regarding War Diaries and Intelligence Summaries are contained in F. S. Regs., Part II, and the Staff Manual respectively. Title pages will be prepared in manuscript.

Hour, Date, Place.	Summary of Events and Information	Remarks and references to Appendices.
RICHEBOURG L'AVOUÉ 5.11.14 6 a.m.	Fine weather again. Fulbh Dhan Sing then west off "A" company arrived. Still no artillery fire in our direction.	Sketch I
5 p.m.	Quiet day — no artillery fire in our direction. "A" company relieved "C" company. Previously one section of "A" company had been sent to pulay. B company's left so there was now a continuous line of fire trench between the CINDER TRACK and the LEFT PICKET ditch. C company retired to the Support trench — so the	Sketch II
7/11 a.m.	distribution of companies from 7 p.m. on this night was as follows (see Sketch II) ① + ② — G + H (Kerr & Paxton) companies ③ — D company ④ + ⑤ + ⑥ — A + B companies & one section 'H' company ⑦ — E + F companies Machine guns as shown — H on sketch.	Major P.M. Horne admitted to Hospital & sent home on sick list.
6-11-14	Nothing of any importance occurred during the day.	Casualties 2 wounded
7-11-14	Night 7.6th-7th November a quiet one. All companies employed throughout the day in improving their trenches and D company entered the Stella trenches already commenced.	Casualties Nil.
6.30 p.m.	Enemy's Scouts advancing against E & F companies were driven back by fire, a few sniping shots No firing by enemy beyond a few sniping shots before midnight.	Casualties 1 Killed 1 Wounded

WAR DIARY
or
INTELLIGENCE SUMMARY.

(Erase heading not required.)

Army Form C. 2118.

Instructions regarding War Diaries and Intelligence Summaries are contained in F. S. Regs., Part II, and the Staff Manual respectively. Title pages will be prepared in manuscript.

Hour, Date, Place.	Summary of Events and Information	Remarks and references to Appendices.
RICHEBOURG L'AVOUE 8-11-14	Major Wardell carried out a careful reconnaissance with field glasses from the roof of the ruined cottage and located German Trenches at (C) & (D).	Sketch II.
11 a.m.	D Company were employed in strengthening the CINDER TRACK PICKET, which was important as at covered the only means of approach to our position, i.e. the CINDER TRACK ditch. 2nd Rifle Battery shelled German Trenches (C) & (D) but their shots were nearly all of too long a range. A quiet morning and afternoon.	
11.30 p.m.	Capt. Lane reported Germans digging a new trench on his left front facing and threatening the gap between our position and the 2/39.G. Capt. Lane requested that "A" Coy. might relieve his company in the LEFT PICKET (F.A) to enable him to extend men along the GAP TRENCH (FA) as an advance would threaten his rear.	Sketch II.
9-11-14 3 a.m.	Capt. Lane asked to arrange with Capt. Lewis as regards relief of picket. This relief having been carried out Capt. Lane extended 12 men along the gap and informed the missing ditch making loopholes.	Sketch II.
9 a.m.	A report on the present by the new German Trench (C) was sent to the Brigade. The G.O.C. accordingly ordered that this trench was to be assaulted and destroyed. Arrangements were accordingly made with O.C. 2/39.G.	Appx. IV F.S (B.M. 194) " V
7.30 p.m.	For a count of how attack was arranged a carried out see Staff Lewis account. Congratulatory letters from Indian Army Corps Commander and Divisional Commander are attached to Appendices	" VI Casualties 2nd Lieut Tate wounded, other ranks 2 wounded, 1 missing

Army Form C. 2118.

WAR DIARY
or
INTELLIGENCE SUMMARY.

(Erase heading not required.)

Instructions regarding War Diaries and Intelligence Summaries are contained in F. S. Regs., Part II, and the Staff Manual respectively. Title pages will be prepared in manuscript.

Hour, Date, Place.	Summary of Events and Information	Remarks and references to Appendices.
RICHEBOURG L'AVOUE		
10-11-14	The trench captured was found to be shallow. Larger than expected. So Major Taylor ordered a retirement on trench filling it in.	Casualties. Jemdr. Kushal Sing Takuli & 5 N.C.Os & men killed - 7 men wounded. 3 missing.
8 a.m.	Capt. Lane reported the Germans from the entrenching then new trench (G) towards his right. Enemy worked with the greatest rapidity. It was thought they were making this trench with a view to carrying out a sudden attack on the gap and the trenches right and left of it. A company from the Bde. Reserve (2/3 of Gurkhas) was sent up to remain in the vicinity of the gap during the night-which proved to be a quiet one.	Sketch II
4.30 p.m.		
11-11-14 5 a.m.	German trench (G) reported to be 120 yards long in front of the 1st Battalion. Brigade was informed that Sappers were necessary to make obstacles in front of gap (T.1) which was quite unprotected.	Casualties 1 killed & 4 wounded Sketch II
11.20 a.m.	One of our own howitzer shells fell in 4 company's trench and luckily did no damage.	
4/5 p.m.	Capt. Alexander 2/3rd Gurkhas with 2 platoons of his Battn. arrived at Battn. H.Q. & was guided to the (T.1) when he remained in support all night. Enemy made two attacks during the night which was a very stormy one, a great deal of rain falling between nothing.	Casualties Nil.
12-11-14 NEUVEVE CHAPELLE		
5.30 a.m.	A fine morning at dawn. The trenches were however in a bad state, in many places the parapet had given way damaging loopholes.	

Army Form C. 2118.

WAR DIARY
or
INTELLIGENCE SUMMARY.
(Erase heading not required.)

Instructions regarding War Diaries and Intelligence Summaries are contained in F. S. Regs., Part II, and the Staff Manual respectively. Title pages will be prepared in manuscript.

Hour, Date, Place.	Summary of Events and Information	Remarks and references to Appendices.
RICHEBOURG L'AVOUÉ		
12-11-14 10 a.m.	German field batteries searched up and down the main road of R'Bourg L'Avoué	Appx VII F.S.
Noon 1.30 p.m.	Reports and sketches of field glass reconnaissance received from Major Henderson –	Appx VIII F.S. Sketch I.
3.30 p.m.	E company having vacated a portion of their trench near the G.A.D trench (T.A) our heavy artillery shelled the German trench (G) with no marked success.	Casualties 3 wounded.
4.30 p.m.	(T.A) re-occupied by our men.	
" "	2 Platoons 2/3rd G.R. Sent up to re-inforce (T.A).	
13-11-14 9 a.m.	C.O. summoned to Bde. H.Q. to a conference concerning attack to be carried out against German trench (G)	Appx IX F.S.
3.30 p.m.	Our howitzers again shelled trench (G) with no apparent effect.	
	Rockets were received from the Brigade – there was only to be fired in case of sudden artillery support being required.	
9/5 p.m.	The 2/3rd Gurkhas commenced their attack on the German trench (G) – Our companies were ordered to man loopholes & remain ready to attack to repel any counter attack on the part of the enemy.	
	The 2/3rd Gurkha attack was not wholly successful and as all our companies were at their loopholes we could not assist except by keeping down the enemy's fire.	Casualties 1 Killed.
	The enemy did not fire on our centre or right to any great extent during the night.	

Army Form C. 2118.

WAR DIARY
or
INTELLIGENCE SUMMARY.

(Erase heading not required.)

Instructions regarding War Diaries and Intelligence Summaries are contained in F. S. Regs., Part II, and the Staff Manual respectively. Title pages will be prepared in manuscript.

Hour, Date, Place.	Summary of Events and Information	Remarks and references to Appendices.
RICHEBOURG L'AVOUÉ 14-11-14	The Germans re-occupied the trench G apparently soon after midnight. Orders were received in the evening that the 1/39.G. were to take over the trench (7.A) i.e. up to the right of the 2/39.G. and the 2/3rd Gurkhas were ordered to hand over the two trenches O & 2. The close proximity of the Germans in their trench G necessitated the loopholes in O & 7.A being manned all night in case of a sudden attack and E & F companies consequently had very little rest.	
15-11-14 2 a.m.	Enemy in front of E company attempted an advance which was stopped by our fire just in front of G the German parapet.	
5.30 a.m.	2/3rd Company vacated (7.A) and E company took on the whole of the GAP trench which also held the 2 machine guns of the 4th Cavalry. 2/3rd occupied trenches O & 2. G company returned to the support trench while H company with Major Henderson retired to Bn. H.Q. Then we had F & H platoons Wilkinson in reserve, and therefore as the situation in front of German trench G, but a screen drawn on the companies, knowing in their flank, the C.O. decided that these companies should be relieved every 24 hours.	

WAR DIARY
or
INTELLIGENCE SUMMARY
(Erase heading not required.)

Army Form C. 2118.

Instructions regarding War Diaries and Intelligence Summaries are contained in F.S. Regs., Part II, and the Staff Manual respectively. Title pages will be prepared in manuscript.

Hour, Date, Place.	Summary of Events and Information	Remarks and references to Appendices.
RICHEBOURG L'AVOUE 15-11-14 3 p.m.	Orders were received that we were to retake over Trench ② from 2/3rd Gurkhas. Owing to a misunderstanding and delay caused by the C.O. requesting the Staff Captain to ask G.O.C. if the 2/3rd might remain in ② the trench in question was not taken over during the night. G company were employed most of the day in improving the Support Trench ⑧ and lengthening it towards ②.	Sketch I.
16.11.14 10.30 a.m.	Heavy rain fell during the early hours before dawn. Orders again received to take over the trench ② which was accordingly done. A full report after personal inspection by Major Henderson was made by him on the state of our trenches and communicators. He advised abandoning the left C&C trench ① as far as ② and using the cinder track as a trench for the whole of our trenches as communication with our left could be maintained via Support trench ⑧ and its prolongation to ②. The C.O. gave orders that the various latrines suggested by Major Henderson for all companies should be carried out. H. Coy. made a dug-out from the cinder track to behind a house near the barricade enabling our German frontier.	Sketch II. Casualties 4 Wounded Sketch II
17-11-14. 6 a.m.	Heavy rain during the night & early morning. Report received from companies stated that the night had been a quiet one not practically no firing on either side. German trench ⓖ had been extended as far as in front of our LEFT PICKET.	"See Major Henderson's report Appx I." Casualties 1 killed 2 wounded

WAR DIARY
or
INTELLIGENCE SUMMARY.

Army Form C. 2118.

(Erase heading not required.)

Hour, Date, Place.	Summary of Events and Information	Remarks and references to Appendices.
RICHEBOURG L'AVOUE 17-11-14 2.30 p.m.	To see Major Henderson, Report on the progress of work on the left of our line. Afternoon and evening quite uneventful for a few snipers Scots.	Appx XI F.S.
18-11-14	Reports stated that enemy had done nothing beyond a little sniping during the early part of the night. C.P.C. trenches had been much improved flooring of the trenches with leaves was commenced on the left. All trenches would a lot of cleaning some of them being ankle deep in mud	
1.30 p.m.	Message received from K/Col. that the 119th Gurkhas would relieve us in the trenches on the evening 19th 20th.	
4 p.m.	C.O. & officers 119th Gurkhas arrived at our H.Q. & were escorted by the Adjutant to the trenches & shown them all. Enemy fired a few shots during the night but nothing further of note occurred.	Appx XII F.S. XIII "
19-11-14	Orders were issued & circulated in trenches giving directions for the relief of companies and machine guns and for the march to billets well Bde. Headn. Ordr No. 5 (S)	
5.30 p.m.	Snow commenced to fall soon after first relay & by the evening there was about a couple of inches on the ground. 1st Parties 38/119th Gurkhas arrived and the reliefs were carried out according to the machine guns did not accompany their There was a good deal of delay in carrying out the reliefs, and the enemy to further duty, supporting trust to meet. The LEFT PICKET but were driven back by the Henderson's repeat his M.Gun. past the left of the LEFT PICKET.	Appx XII F.S

Army Form C. 2118.

WAR DIARY
INTELLIGENCE SUMMARY.

(Erase heading not required.)

Hour, Date, Place.	Summary of Events and Information	Remarks and references to Appendices.
RICHEBOURG L'AVOUE LE TOURET 20-11-14	Snow continued to fall at intervals. All details had reached their billets by 10.a.m after a very slow march - the men feet were in a very bad state, nearly all of them suffering severely from chilblains. The roads were in a very slippery condition due to the snow and frost. The Battalion was now part of the Brigade Reserve. A fine day all day. All ranks had an opportunity of getting their kit cleaned and giving their feet a good rest. Nothing of importance occurred during the day or night.	Casualties 1 wounded
21-11-14	Rain morning and evening hard. 2 German Biplanes descended on account of engine trouble quite near our billets. I questioned 2 German officers who were made prisoner by 2/Lt. Shaw & M. Largues (our interpreters). The known was deputated to G.H.Q and the battalion placed a guard on the machine.	Casualties Nil.
4 p.m.	A court of enquiry was held to investigate the causes from which rations were received short in the trenches on several occasions.	
22-11-14	Capt. Orton, 2/Lt Shaw, Jemadar Ajit Sing and billeting N.C.os proceeded to LA COUTURE & VIEILLE CHAPELLE to arrange billets for the battalion for the next day. This party returned to LE TOURET the same evening.	Appx XIV F.S.
23-11-14	A.T. Cart had to make 2 journeys to LA COUTURE to return tools etc. The Battalion was ordered to march at 3/p.m. to Billets at LA COUTURE-VIEILLE CHAPELLE.	

Army Form C. 2118.

WAR DIARY
or
INTELLIGENCE SUMMARY.

(Erase heading not required.)

Instructions regarding War Diaries and Intelligence Summaries are contained in F. S. Regs., Part II, and the Staff Manual respectively. Title pages will be prepared in manuscript.

Hour, Date, Place.	Summary of Events and Information	Remarks and references to Appendices.
LA COUTURE 23-11-14 3:10 p.m.	Battalion left billets when entering LA COUTURE village at 3.40 p.m. a message was received this Brigade from MEERUT Division to the effect that the Battalion was to march at once to GORRE & sending a mounted officer on ahead, to report to General MACBEAN. For narrative of events and the action which followed consequent on the above message see full reports sent in by the C.O.	Appx IV F.S. and accompanying sketch

Appx XVg

From
The Officer Commanding
1/39th Garhwal Rifles

To The Brigade Major
Garhwal Brigade

Reference attached sketch.

On the 23rd November at 3.40 p.m. when entering the village of LA COUTURE I received a message ordering me to proceed at once to GORRE and report to General MACBEAN sending on an officer for orders.

At about 5.30 p.m. I reached GORRE where we were ordered to halt till the 2nd/Leicesters closed-up on our rear, and then move on to FESTUBERT and report to GENERAL EGERTON.

We moved on at about 6 p.m. and reached General E's H.Q. at about 7.30. We moved slowly owing to the men carrying 200 rounds and an extra blanket, I had ordered for the short march from LE TOURET to LA COUTURE.

General E. explained to me that a portion of his trenches had been lost in the forenoon and partially retaken at dusk and that he wished my battalion to re-capture the remainder.

Accompanied by Col. Grant, commanding his Centre Section he took me to the point "A" and explained that he wanted me to replace the 107th Pioneers in the supporting trench C and then keeping my left on a road which Colonel Grant would indicate, attack frontally the French M.D. over a distance

estimated at 600x, taking a front
of about 300x and moving forward with
the 107th Pioneers prolonging my right.
This order with my strength meant a thin line
and practically no depth.

I ordered my battalion up to the point A
and meanwhile made a personal reconnaissance
as far as possible from B & C. I found the
ground over which we were to advance
was flat & coverless & snow covered and movement
across it fully visible for 300x in the starlight.
Just then Lieut. Orchard, attached 2/8th Gurkhas
came in from ahead where some portions
of his battalion had remained hung up in a
ditch halfway towards the enemy since
their dusk counter attack.

I must mention that at first General E
told me he had reason to believe the
Germans had left the captured trench, as the
right portion had been re-occupied
after being found empty. Lieut Orchard
however gave a very different account. He
said the Germans were still there in force
with several Machine Guns and that a
frontal attack would be risky and
strongly urged oblique attacks on the right
& left of the lost trench from view of the inner
flanks of the battalion on its flanks.

I then asked General E to reconsider his
orders and he ordered us to stand fast while
he did so. Shortly after Col. Grant returned with
orders for us to carry out the attack as originally
directed immediately.

I then moved 3 Coys into trench C and
1 Coy as support into a ditch B.

A delay then occurred as the Coy in B.
had to go back to FESTUBERT to the
1st line Carts which had only just come up,
to fetch entrenching tools. On their return I
ordered them to go to the left of C and follow
the attack up the right of the road there

which we then believed to be the road on which we were to keep our left & which was said to lead up to the enemy's right. A reconnaissance however then showed that this road ended abruptly at D. As we were evidently not in the right place, I thought it imperative to go back to FESTUBERT and request further and better information and if possible a guide as we were on unknown ground in the dark and possibilities of attacking the rear of our own line either right or left of our objective by starting in a wrong direction, was a grave danger.

Colonel Grant returned with me as guide. On my convincing him that the road ending at D was not the right one, we went off in search and shortly after struck the latter at E.

I then decided to move the Battalion less one company up the right hand ditch of the road as far as possible, then deploy to the right and attack. I ordered the fourth Coy, each man carrying two tools and stretcher bearers to move up by the communication trench to the point of and stand ready there to move in as soon as our objective was attained. This Company under Major Henderson struck the communication trench at about F and moved to G, where it found the Reserve Company & Bn. H.Q. of the 129L Baluchis under Col. Southey. On hearing what was planned Colonel Southey expressed the opinion that so weak a frontal attack under the circumstances had no chance of success. Colonel Grant then

then arrived, and after discussion Major Henderson asked him if he would authorize the advance being stopped while a reference was made to the General suggesting

(a) that the 1/39th should be authorized to attack from M instead of frontally; or as an alternative,

(b) that if a frontal attack was required Colonel Southey wished the General to know that he considered it from his local knowledge impossible by a force smaller than two battalions with a third in Reserve.

Colonel Grant authorized Major Henderson to send me his authority to stand fast while he himself went back to Genl. EGERTON. I received the orders to halt when the head of the battalion was about the point K and the rest in single file down the ditch on the right edge of the road. This was about 1·30 a.m.

About 2·30 a.m. Lt. Grant returned and asked Major Henderson to give me the General's order that it was imperative the 1/39th should attack without further delay, but that I might do it as I best thought fit. With this important latitude, which I had previously received, I then decided to attack from M and not frontally. The supporting Coy then moved to the point H ready to move up the line of the road which, since the losing of the touch in the morning the 57th Rifles & 129th Baluchis had lined as a refused flank.

The rest of the Bn. moved via H, G and L to M.

Major Wardell's Company by Lt. Robson

The Sappers and Miners led the advance from M where the right of the 57th rested up the communication trench into the lost trench. These two Officers with a few men worked their way forward helped by bombers at first and later with the bayonet, followed by the rest of the company under Captain Orton. They thus took about 2 traverses and captured 30 or 40 prisoners. Meanwhile Captain Lumb with his company had moved forward about 20 yards to Major Wardell's right in a ditch with about a section and a half, the remainder having got jammed in the communication trench by Major Wardell's prisoners and escort. Captain Lumb about 50ˣ forward found the ditch getting shallow and a cross fire bearing on him. He therefore wheeled to his left and jumped into the trench arriving in the midst of Major Wardell's leading men. With this section and a half he then moved forward along the trench ahead of Major Wardell's company and rushed it traverse by traverse, taking more prisoners. His further progress then began to leave a gap between himself and Major Wardell's company which depleted by escorts to prisoners had come to a stand still manning such length of the captured trench as it was able to. Lieut. Welshman then brought the rest of Capt. Lumb's company past Major Wardell's and the prisoners and found Captain Lumb whose whole company then completed the capture of the trench till they met the left of the 107th Pioneers just after day light.

When Lieut. Welchman and the bulk of Captain Leumb's company were jammed about the point M, Lieut Welchman received a verbal report from the right that Captain Leumb had been wounded and his men driven out of the trench to the rear. Meeting at this moment Major Henderson who had come up for the rear to enquire about the situation and see if his company was required, he gave him the information, which was borne out by a heavy fire fight in the open ground in rear of the re-captured trench. Major Henderson at once returned to his company and requested the O.C. 129th Baluchis to send this information to the General as he considered it important if the attack had failed that support should be provided in rear. I have since been told by an officer of the 2/Leicesters that part of the 2/Leicesters who retook the trench on the left of the 107th Pioneers by frontal attack, were obliged to retire, and it was evidently their retirement which lent colour to the report received by Lt. Welchman and forwarded through Major Henderson. Shortly after this report was sent, Captain Orton passed though wounded and was able to authoritatively contradict it, and this contradiction was then passed to the General by the O.C. 129th Baluchis.

Major Wardell's company now moved on and took post on Capt. Leumb's left in the re-captured trench.

On his way to the rear wounded Captain Orton had previously passed me near the point M. Telling me re-inforcements were needed I then sent forward

Captain Lane's Company. In taking up the left of the re-captured trench this company came under enfilade fire at the point O where the straight line of the main trench runs on to the left a head of the curved position in rear forming a D-shape. The curve of the "D" of the trench to the right of O was in our possession, but the left of the straight part of the "D" was still held by the enemy who came down a sap. Captain Lane then closed this position by a barricade under a heavy enfilade fire.

The following captures were made in the trench:—

2 Machine Guns, 1 Trench Mortar, over 100 Rifles & bayonets, 105 prisoners (including 4 "Unter Offiziers") and much equipment & many tools. There were 32 dead Germans in the trench, and five or six of the prisoners were wounded. There were also many dead Germans outside the trench on both sides.

Our losses were as follows:—

1 Indian Officer ⎫
19 Rank & file ⎭ Killed.

1 British Officer. Missing. (Believed wounded & admitted to Hospital)
1 N.C.O.   "

1 British Officer ⎫
2 Indian Officers ⎬ Wounded.
17 Rank & file ⎭

P.T.O.

I wish to bring the names of the following
for specially favourable notice —
    Major W. H. Wardell
    Captain F. G. S. Lunch
    —   J. T. H. Lane

Also the following Indian ranks —
 No 1810 Havildar ALAMSING NEGI.
This N.C.O. was at the head of his Coy
and the.

107th Pioneers

57th Rifles

A FESTUBERT

Sketch to accompany Appx XV

39th Garhwal Rifles
9th Dec — 29th Dec 14

On His Majesty's Service.

Air Ministry

Account of Travelling etc., Expenses.

2 Cavendish Sq.

Army Form C. 2118.

WAR DIARY

of

INTELLIGENCE SUMMARY.

(Erase heading not required.)

Instructions regarding War Diaries and Intelligence Summaries are contained in F. S. Regs., Part II, and the Staff Manual respectively. Title Pages will be prepared in manuscript.

Hour, Date, Place.	Summary of Events and Information.	Remarks and references to Appendices.
NIGHT REPORT 9-12-14 LIBOURG	Major Kershaw made a tour of the horse and mule lines in the Evening and all is O.K. Personal attention necessary owing to employees for grass suggest. Forecers not enough also there should not be of grass horses and one horses 1/2 of picket's and rugs. Can out move much to improve shelter but the weight and make some arrangement. Employing S.W.E.R.A. with Service II at not to burn at any rate chauffeurs etc have taken place also were no available trucks 10-1-14. There are no rugs to shelter during the day. Suffices horses but certainly a great in one head added to right feet in milling. Free trench cut down a big break day to rest up horses. Et Caralley & G. was posted in the gap Caralle.	

Army Form C. 2118.

WAR DIARY
or
INTELLIGENCE SUMMARY.
(Erase heading not required.)

Instructions regarding War Diaries and Intelligence Summaries are contained in F. S. Regs., Part II, and the Staff Manual respectively. Title pages will be prepared in manuscript.

Hour, Date, Place.	Summary of Events and Information.	Remarks and references to Appendices
NIEMERQUE LABOURÉ S/F N 9-12-14	9th Bengal Lancers. The Squadron of the 30th Lancers arrived in the morning and relieved the whole of D Sqn. but no section of C Sqn. found. (3) This squadron was fresh from the base and had been sent to work for French work. The whole of D Sqn and one section of C were relieved at 10.30. Remainder owing to reliefs by cavalry.	
10-12-14	Nothing of note to report. Enemy visible but some snipers reported from left to right. Casualties. Killed nil. Wounded Two. Missing Nil. A squadron of 30th Lancers reinforced trenches. Casualties. The squadron which had lost two men was thoroughly [illegible] cavalry having nearly seven hours service to [illegible] as the trenches are always full [illegible] at [illegible] right [illegible] took all night	

WAR DIARY
or
INTELLIGENCE SUMMARY.
(Erase heading not required.)

Hour, Date, Place.	Summary of Events and Information.	Remarks and references to Appendices.
RICHEBOURG L'AVOUE 10.12.14.	to settle down and rest badly in reference of French work before they were near relieved. Note Company Commander came in and Lieutenan & Corpl HEARICH Cpl TATUM still had been placed. Casualties Killed nil. Wounded nil. missing nil.	
11-12-14	Heavy gun fire nearly my little infantry teams shewn to us. After the hour the left and next he got that enemy were putting out Chevaux de Frises along the front of their trenches. Later having been warned to take over trenches that had been taken that night by 2nd Inf. Bde & Dept arthur Colonel Murray thereof was ordered to take up the gap trench on the left of the cavalry there & 67 men 1 pm HQ. Crel and 16 to this. Work was carried on demean of work. Track CrC Trench.	

Army Form C. 2118.

WAR DIARY
or
INTELLIGENCE SUMMARY.
(Erase heading not required.)

Instructions regarding War Diaries and Intelligence Summaries are contained in F. S. Regs., Part II, and the Staff Manual respectively. Title pages will be prepared in manuscript.

Hour, Date, Place.	Summary of Events and Information	Remarks and references to Appendices.
Richebourg to L'Avoué 12-12-14	Not by what light count slaughtered the [illegible] in UPPER TOWN. All companies were [illegible] [illegible] night-day slaving trenches. One howitzer rifle damage by own. Mr Hat [illegible] [illegible] to fairly heavy fire after dark from long distance rifle shooting. A man in extra party B Company was shot dead. Casualties. Killed one. Wounded not missing nil.	
13-12-14	[illegible] an entire [illegible] number of bullets came from houses of CHAPELLE [illegible] and [illegible] from house. CHAPELLE [illegible] [illegible] [illegible] [illegible] during the afternoon as H.Q. [illegible] [illegible] [illegible] [illegible] [illegible] [illegible] mortally wounded.	

Army Form C. 2118.

WAR DIARY
or
INTELLIGENCE SUMMARY.

(Erase heading not required.)

Instructions regarding War Diaries and Intelligence Summaries are contained in F. S. Regs., Part II, and the Staff Manual respectively. Title pages will be prepared in manuscript.

Hour, Date, Place.	Summary of Events and Information	Remarks and references to Appendices.
RICHEBOURG L'AVOUÉ / 14-12-14.		
10 a.m.	According to orders received piers opened & light arty. all day with a view to harass enemy & trenches in front of mounted attack delivered by French & Lahore division. Fire near Rue Lorraine Givenchy. Results first from enemy's trenches very slight. Orders were issued for an attacking party from the battalion to be cut. 2nd Gurkhas Bhawan at all costs. Suggested that be composed of 25 men in attacking line with Several Bombs in support.	
5.30 p.m.	2nd Lt. Kalan Bay & coy. sent out searching party & looked into trench. The party returned without loss, but no information. Officially enemy trenches held as strongly as ours. Wounded 3, missing nil. Casualties killed nil. Wounded 3, missing nil. Jemadar Darcent S. Q. NGO & party of 25 men started for attack to obtain	
15-12-14 / 1 a.m.		

Army Form C. 2118.

WAR DIARY
or
INTELLIGENCE SUMMARY.
(Erase heading not required.)

Instructions regarding War Diaries and Intelligence Summaries are contained in F. S. Regs., Part II, and the Staff Manual respectively. Title pages will be prepared in manuscript.

Hour, Date, Place.	Summary of Events and Information	Remarks and references to Appendices.
RUE DU BOIS LAVOUE 15-12-14	German prisoner. Account of attack & failure thereof as intimated to Bde. Major A. Butler arrived from General Henry Horne's Staff Section having been to South Staff's Sec E. Rugeley Division. Hours 1 & 2 non: but stating that to keep up the parity had done well. Further orders were regard to keep up bursts of fire during the day. Casualties killed nil. Wounds Two. missing nil.	Appx I Went
16-12-14	Times spend & kept up all day on probably enemy supply way lights thrown by but seemed heavy during the night - sent up till after dark, enabling, & putting of heavy when in front of their trenches by the aid of a flare until fire was opened on the same way set in this. One German Coffe [illegible] seen to fall.	

Gulab Singh & Sons, Calcutta.—No. 22 Army C.—6-8-14—1,07,000.

Army Form C. 2118.

WAR DIARY
or
INTELLIGENCE SUMMARY.
(Erase heading not required.)

Instructions regarding War Diaries and Intelligence Summaries are contained in F. S. Regs., Part II, and the Staff Manual respectively. Title pages will be prepared in manuscript.

Hour, Date, Place.	Summary of Events and Information	Remarks and references to Appendices.
RICHEBOURG L'AVOUE 16-12-14	4 wounded to Indian Field Ambulance first - Inchcape took over duties of Adjutant Capt Patrick took over duties of B.G. Officer. Casualties Killed nil. Wounded Six. Missing nil	
17-12-14.	Improvements of 2 sepoys to trenches progressed with today. Enemy fired very little during the day but kept up a considerable fire throughout the night - O.C. No 3 Coy suggests sniping out from Capt Pregent's Casualties Killed nil. Wounded Seven missing nil. Total of Casualties to date since 9-13 the Richebourg Doubled 23 missing Rehung - Killed One 9 O 23 9 wounded.	

WAR DIARY
or
INTELLIGENCE SUMMARY.

(Erase heading not required.)

Army Form C. 2118.

Instructions regarding War Diaries and Intelligence Summaries are contained in F. S. Regs., Part II, and the Staff Manual respectively. Title pages will be prepared in manuscript.

Hour, Date, Place.	Summary of Events and Information	Remarks and references to Appendices.
RICHEBOURG L'AVOUE 18-12-1914	Nothing of interest to report during the day. At 3.20 a.m. enemy opened a heavy fire on our centre, which replied. Enemy attack at 3.45 a.m. its trenches made constant on enemy trenches on our right at 4 a.m. in accordance with orders received from the Brigade we opened a heavy fire all along our front in continuation of the Brigade. The attack succeeded and 300 yards of the enemy's trench was captured. Capt. Cane & Lt. Kleat were wounded. Three Mustafis Capt. Pollard killed a German sniper.	
19-12-1914	Situation unchanged today except that Capt. [?] and another several Mustafis Ghurung? and other Peers were slightly [illegible] killed on Seward from heavy fire.	

WAR DIARY
or
INTELLIGENCE SUMMARY.
(Erase heading not required.)

Army Form C. 2118.

Instructions regarding War Diaries and Intelligence Summaries are contained in F. S. Regs., Part II, and the Staff Manual respectively. Title pages will be prepared in manuscript.

Hour, Date, Place.	Summary of Events and Information.	Remarks and references to Appendices.
RICHEBOURG L'AVOUE 20-12-1914	Situation unchanged. Dehra Dun Brigade lost some ground on right some of which was retaken. We engaged the enemy with a few rifles - Shrapnel was set up. Some of our shrapnel was falling short but was moved out over enemy trenches. Held ground until some hundreds of Germans seen filtering back into position. Situation remained the same. Fired about 872 rounds indirectly one a 5-1 when 6/2 Field Brigade occupied enemy with fire, fuse 10 ft. at which would covering were resumed. Our German Infantry dropped some 17 E Shell in our trenches, buried two men about a dozen out - about the way trophies fell. Casualties safe under 150 We have had several men wounded from rifle and shrapnel fire, details being fastened below.	
21-12-1914		

Army Form C. 2118.

WAR DIARY
INTELLIGENCE SUMMARY.
(Erase heading not required.)

Instructions regarding War Diaries and Intelligence Summaries are contained in F. S. Regs., Part II, and the Staff Manual respectively. Title pages will be prepared in manuscript.

Hour, Date, Place.	Summary of Events and Information	Remarks and references to Appendices.
RICHEBOURG L'AVOUE		
21-12-'14.	Enemy's parapet's obtained. Casualties killed nil. Wounded five missing nil.	
22-12-1914.	No change in the situation. Communication trench & was prepared for defence in case of trouble on our left, and a course of action formulated. Casualties killed nil. Wounded three. missing nil.	
23-12-1914.	No change in situation. Casualties killed nil. Wounded one. Wounded three missing nil.	
24-12-14.	No change in situation. Casualties killed one. Wounded two missing nil.	
25-12-14.	[illegible]	A/Ajd: H

Army Form C. 2118.

WAR DIARY
or
INTELLIGENCE SUMMARY.
(Erase heading not required.)

Instructions regarding War Diaries and Intelligence Summaries are contained in F. S. Regs., Part II, and the Staff Manual respectively. Title pages will be prepared in manuscript.

Hour, Date, Place.	Summary of Events and Information	Remarks and references to Appendices.
25-12-14. RICHEBOURG L'AVOUÉ	An unofficial armistice took place between No 2 Coy & the regiments on our left & the Germans. Casualties killed one, wounded nil. Missing nil.	
26-12-1914.	No change in situation. Casualties nil.	
27-12-1914.	No change in situation. Battalion was relieved by the Oxfordshire & Bucks L.I. after dusk & marched to billets at LA COUTURE. Germans to our front hardly fired at all while relief was taking place.	
25-12-1914 to 14 PARADIS.	Marched to PARADIS. The relieving company now in reserve to the firing line.	
25-12-14.	Marched to ROBECQ	

Adjt 1/39G   Appx: I

After personal reconnaissance by daylight with Jemdr Saulatu from the PIQUET (see attached Sketch), and on the report of Scouts that there was a more or less detached piquet of the enemy similar to ours in the same ditch, I ordered him to rush it. It was also reported to contain a maxim, which was laid to fire down the ditch. To avoid this and approach & attack from a flank, I ordered the Jemadar to move as shown by red arrow line, i.e. to B & thence turn sharp to the left to the piquet, which was believed to be a few yards our side of A. I ordered them to crawl on their stomachs as far as possible, and then to charge silently, & to come back as soon as they had one prisoner.

In order to get a compact handy formation I ordered the party of 25 to move in the following formation

```
                • Jemadar.
        • • • • • • •        6 men
              2 yards         6 men
        • • • • • •
              2 yards
        • • • • • •           6 men
              2 yards
        • • • • • • •         7 men
                              ───
                               25
```

At B they were to turn to their left thus presenting a front of 4 short columns of 6 men in single file for the charge.

I saw them off at 1 am & went to the telephone as ordered by the C.O. Captain Lumb was at PORT ARTHUR with Ward Orderly and 4 Street - Church

Up to 3 a.m. we had no sound except desultory odd shots apparently not more ticeminous than go on all along the line all night. But just before 3 a.m. 4 flares were sent up from near A, which showed the enemy suspected or had discovered something.

At 3 a.m. I sent to Capt. Lumb and directed him to enquire if our picquet had seen or heard nothing. In reply I got a message to come at once.

I found 2 men of Jemdr. Daulatti's party with him, who said the Jemadar a Havildar & several men had got separated & touch had been lost & the remainder under Havr Parkins were lying in the open & wanted orders what to do. They reported one man wounded.

As it was evident the enemy were now on the alert & the party was now much weakened, I ordered them to withdraw. From questioning many men separately I have arrived at the following narrative.

The advance was conducted as ordered as far as B. But there the party wheeled instead of turned to its left, thus affording a shallower, broader, & less broken target.

In this manner they moved still undetected till they struck the end of the entanglement round which they moved to within 4 or 5 yards of the enemy's loopholes. Still undetected, the Jemadar (someothers) then looked into the trench & found it to be a large continuous trench fully manned.

Jemdr. Daulatti then said "This is not a picquet, but the enemy's main trench" and detailed two men of the front six to move down the ditch towards our

piquet & fires the enemy's supposed advanced
piquet.

This evidently involved some delay and
a good deal of whispering which resulted
in detection; for as soon as the two men
had moved off fire was opened, and the
sole survivor of the remaining front
four men Rfn JITU states the two on his
right were killed at once, leaving him
and Havr Bhawanu; with Jemadar Daulatu
just behind them.

Jemr Daulatu then passed back the
order to retire, which the three squads behind
him complied with. Meanwhile Havr Bhawanu
had said to Jitu " Tell the Jemadar
we ought to charge" Jitu looking round
saw he & Bhawanu were alone & said
so, whereupon they also decided to retire,
They evidently had not heard the Jemadar's
order.

Bhawanu then raised himself
on his elbow & was at once killed.
Jit kept flat on his belly and managed
to crawl back; as he did so he says
some one behind him was shot & fell,
and he thinks it was the Jemadar.
Jitu then worked along the ditch to our
piquet & got back quite alone last of
all.

Mean while Havr Parding and the
remainder collected some way off and
sent in for orders, & were joined
as they came in by the two men originally
sent off to look for the enemy's piquet
who finding after a time that they
were alone, made their way back
they saw no piquet, and I have little

doubt none exists.

The failure is therefore due to the non existence or missing of this piquet and to the impossibility of a party of this strength rushing a portion of a strong & fully manned hostile trench.

I submit that it is impossible to make prisoners except by attack on a large scale, or else by rushing detached posts or lying up for scouts. There are no detached posts in our front and the surprise of scouts is a thing which must await opportunity and cannot be done any time to order.

The following are the casualties

Jemdr. Danlola Nesz
No 1609 Havr. Bhawani Bhandari ⎫ Missing
— 2623 Rifn. Umrao Gusain   ⎬ Believed
— 2308 Rect. Fateh S. Bhandari   ⎭ Killed.

No 1816 Rect Dewan S. Nesz, Wounded.

(Sd) K Hutchinson Major
1/39 G R

True Copy.
[signature]
Captain
for Acting Adjutant 1/39 G. Rifles

Appx II

To
The Adjutant 1/39th G.

In compliance with your telephone message, I have the honour to submit the following report as regards the men of my section of defence leaving their trenches and approaching & fraternising with the Germans this afternoon.

At about 2.30 p.m., as far as I am aware, a Rifleman came and told me that many of the enemy were standing up on their parapet unarmed & shouting to us. I went to the "Gap" & there saw about 40 or 50 of the enemy as described. One or two called to us in English to come out & speak to them. Then one German came about 10 yards out of his trench & put a box of cigars on the ground. Lt. Welchman who was then with me, & he gave orders for all sentries to remain on the lookout at their posts. A British Cavalry Soldier attached to 4th Cavy. Machine Guns, who was about 10 yards on my left, came out of the Gap trench & went towards the enemy. I then noticed that others on my left from the 2/39th Garhwalis were out of their trenches & moving towards the enemy's trenches. On the impulse of the moment I also went out & Lt. Welchman, Capt. Pearse 4th Cavy. & some of the men came out too. About 12 or 15 Germans approached us & came up & shook hands with us & wished us the compliments of the Season. One or two spoke English & I ordered them not to come nearer our line than half way. I then asked permission to bury the dead that were lying there; this was accorded & our men buried on the spot 1 Jemdr. & 4 Riflemen of the 2/3?? & Jemdr. Karbal Thapa?? & Riflemen Thapru F Coy. 1/39th G. their identity discs were searched for but not found. One dead man was lying right at the foot of the German parapet & 3 men of F Coy. were permitted to go right up to the German trenches there

One or two others of our men were given
bread & cigarettes right close to the German
trench.

Afterwards 2 German Subalterns came out
and spoke to us. The men were all of
the 16½ Saxon Regt. I asked them this
(as I can talk a little German) They
told me they were Saxons & not Prussians.
I did not notice any other regiment
amongst the men. Shortly after this
I was told that Major Henderson
was calling for me & I went back
to him & he ordered me to bring all
the men back into the trenches.
Unfortunately I then noticed that a party
of 4 or 5 Germans had come up to about
10 yards from our trench. I had previously
given orders for no one to approach
us closer than half way. But these men
could not have seen into our trenches
as our barbed wire would have prevented
them. They could not have located our Mac-
-hine Guns as these are dismantled
& hidden during the day.

Captain Burton 2/39½ Gs told me that he found
the body of Captain Robertson – Glasgow
2/39½ Gs.

I wish to make it clear that a German
first came up to half way between the
two trenches, & a British Cavalry Soldier,
attached to 4½ Cav. Machine Guns, then
went up to him & shook hands. Whereupon
more Germans came out & then more of our
men.

I attach herewith a report on the German
trenches, seen by our men & corroborated
by 2 British Cavalry Soldiers, who also
went up to the German parapet
& helped to bury a dead Gurkha

Lt: Welchman noticed a printed postal address on a box of cigarettes, which a German soldier had been handing round — on it was printed the man's name, Army Corps (7th), Division (14th) & Regt: (16th)

Both the British Cavalry Soldiers who helped to bury the dead Gurkha on the German parapet, state that at that time the Germans had completely evacuated their trenches, & were all outside & unarmed.

Lt: Welchman & I estimate the number of the enemy we saw opposite the Gap & slightly to the left opposite the 2/39th G. as about 100

(Sd) W. G. S. Kenny Capt.
1/39th G.

25th December 1914.

True Copy

J. _____
Capt.
for Acting Adjutant 1/39th Garhwal Rifles.

App II

Report on German Trenches Opposite
1/39th Left Section of Defence.

The German trenches in Depth, width & general form resemble our own. The travers curved close together, about 6 yards apart, but were not built right up to ground level. The parapet is very thick at least 6'. Loopholes very strong & well made. Some with strong wooden sides tops & bottoms, the side walls of such loopholes being in some instances 3" thick. Other loopholes were made of galvanized iron, sides, tops, & bottoms.

There are 2 Machine Guns in epaulments opposite the centre of the Gap, 6' separating the two epaulments. There is another Machine Gun opposite a point 20 yds from the Right corner of the Gap.

The men's shelters are like ours & cut out underneath the parapet. It appeared that there were considerably more men than loopholes. The trenches were clean & dry. There were no wire entanglements anywhere. There is a Chevaux-de-frise opposite the Left centre of the Gap, but it is a good deal damaged. There were several ladders run on the rear wall of the trench, but none on the front wall. But the ladders were movable & not fixed.

(Sd) W. C. S. Kenny Capt
1/39th G.

25-12-14

True Copy
J. Ceruns
Captain

for Acting Adjutant 1/39th Garhwal Rifles

appx II.

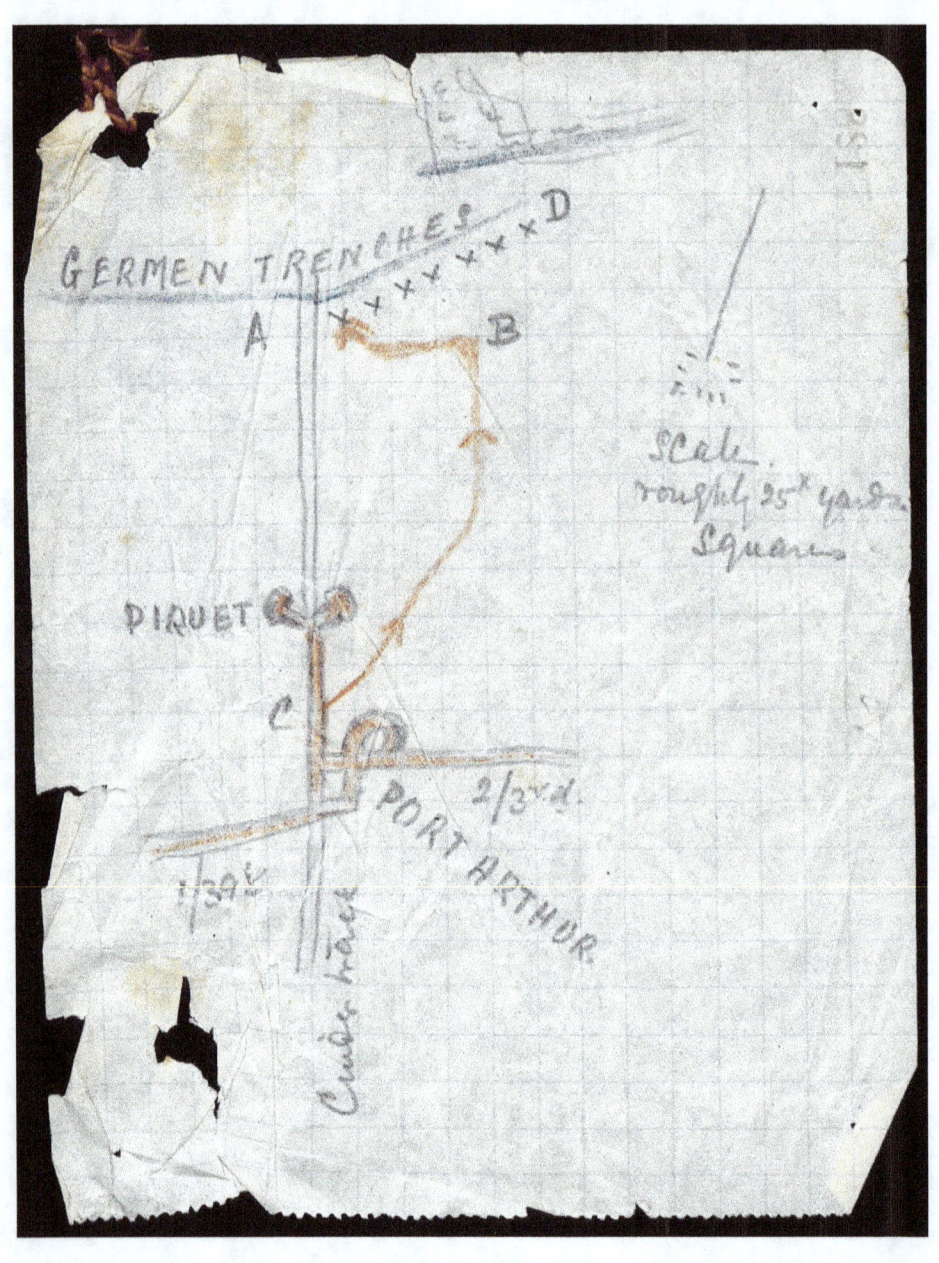

39th Garhwal Rifles

30th/12/14 – 31/1/15

On His Majesty's Service.

~~Major Beavour~~
~~Egerton Beck Esq~~
~~War Cabinet~~

Historical Section, (Military Branch)
2. Cavendish Square
W.1.

BY HAND.

While F coy: were digging on redoubt yesterday 30th Jany - a fire broke out in the farm occupied by the Headquarters of the Seaforths, about 300ʸ away. The coy: doubled across & with the help of a few of the 3rd S.& M. coys assisted in suppressing the fire. They 1st got out about 9 sacks of bombs & placed them a safe distance from the building. A line was then formed & the straw & dried haricot plants passed out from the adjoining loft, part being thrown out through a hole which was made in the tiles of the roof. 1 N.C.O. & 3 men stood ready to put out sparks which might catch a haystack close by.

When there was no further danger from falling tiles & timber from the gutted roof the line passed along waters & extinguished the burning debris.

JL. 31.1.16.

WAR DIARY
or
INTELLIGENCE SUMMARY.
(Erase heading not required.)

Army Form C. 2118.

Hour, Date, Place.	Summary of Events and Information	Remarks and references to Appendices.
30-12-1914.	Marched to permanent billets at FOSSE NO 3 DE TERTAY.	
FOSSE No 3 DE TERTAY. 31-12-14 to 3-1-15.	Nothing of interest to note.	
4-1-15.	The Brigade was inspected by the Corps Commander who was very complimentary as to the good work the Battalion had done during the time it had been in action. Havildar DARWAN SING NEGI V.C. was called out by the Corps Commander in formed him that he was to be sent to the Base for recruiting purposes.	
5-1-15. 6-1-15.	Nothing to note. The draft of 7 2nd reinforcement was in spected by the A.D.M.S. Doctor. 19 men are to be returned to India as unfit; nearly 80 nesifs, while 25 are too old & only fit for work on the L. of C. 2 yr years in too long for a Reservist to serve for Reserve.	

Army Form C. 2118.

1/39 Garhwal Rifles.

WAR DIARY
or
INTELLIGENCE SUMMARY.
(Erase heading not required.)

Instructions regarding War Diaries and Intelligence Summaries are contained in F. S. Regs., Part II, and the Staff Manual respectively. Title pages will be prepared in manuscript.

Hour, Date, Place.	Summary of Events and Information	Remarks and references to Appendices.
7-1-1915. FOSSE No 3 DE FERTAY.	The Brigade was inspected by the C in C. Major K. Henderson has been appointed Brigade Major, Garhwal Brigade, and left the Battn to take up his new appointment.	
8-1-15 to 13-1-15	Instruction in Trench digging, making head cover, etc. etc. Also in bomb throwing.	
14-1-15.	R.E. Officer came to superintend work on F[ire] trenches lines: (i) Extending working parties. (ii) Construction of Machine Gun emplacements. (iii) Revetting. (iv) Sapping out from fire Trenches, & construction & Observation Posts. G.O.C. Indian Army Corps came to inspect the	

Army Form C. 2118

WAR DIARY
or
INTELLIGENCE SUMMARY.
(Erase heading not required.)

Instructions regarding War Diaries and Intelligence Summaries are contained in F. S. Regs., Part II, and the Staff Manual respectively. Title pages will be prepared in manuscript.

Hour, Date, Place.	Summary of Events and Information	Remarks and references to Appendices.
FOSSE N°3 DE FERFAY		
15-1-15 16-1-15	Trenches & work already done, & expressed himself as being exceedingly pleased with what he saw. Practical construction of Trenches etc. under supervision of R.E. Officer as on 14th inst.	
17-1-15	Sunday. 2 hours work on construction of communication trenches. Remainder of day given up to rest.	
18-1-15	Practiced attack on Trenches opposite our own, which has been dug by 2/39 G. Brigadier was present.	

Army Form C. 2118.

WAR DIARY
or
INTELLIGENCE SUMMARY.
(Erase heading not required.)

Hour, Date, Place.	Summary of Events and Information	Remarks and references to Appendices.
FOSSE No 3 DE FERFAY.		
19-1-15	All B.Os, G.Os, N.C.Os & Bomb-Throwers witnessed bombardment by bomb-mortars, bomb attacks on trenches &c carried out by 2nd Leicester Regt, 1st Seaforth Highlanders & 2/3rd G.R. on Leicester Regt entrenching ground.	
20-1-15	Practice under Company arrangements. Orders were received for the march next day to CAUCHY.	
21-1-15	The Battalion left billets at 9.45 a.m. & marched via LILLERS and BUSNES to CAUCHY arriving in billets at 2.30 p.m.	
CAUCHY 2.30 p.m.	Weather cloudy and light rain falling for the last two hours of the march which was one of about 11 miles — only 8 men in the Battalion fell out on the march	

Army Form C. 2118.

WAR DIARY
or
INTELLIGENCE SUMMARY

(Erase heading not required.)

Instructions regarding War Diaries and Intelligence Summaries are contained in F. S. Regs., Part II, and the Staff Manual respectively. Title pages will be prepared in manuscript.

Hour, Date, Place.	Summary of Events and Information	Remarks and references to Appendices.
CALONNE 22-1-15 11.20 a.m.	Fine morning and frosty. The Battalion marched for VIEILLE CHAPELLE via LESTREM and ZELOBES.	
VIEILLE CHAPELLE 3.30 p.m.	Battalion arrived at billets - which were the same as occupied on 23-11-14 and en route to billets at the end of December. A large number of aircraft (allies) were seen during the march. The battalion marched for the first time with great coats in slings - blankets being done up in bundles and carried on baggage wagons.	
RUE DE BERCEAU 23-1-15 5.30 pm	Battalion marched from VIEILLE CHAPELLE at 4.30 p.m. and took over trenches from 5.9th Rifles the same evening. The trenches being unable the advanced line is now held by 6 piquets each of 1 N.C.O. & 6 men; the remainder of the battalion being held in readiness in the houses in the RUE DU BOIS immediately in rear. Two platoons are kept in support with Battalion Head Quarters in the RUE DE BERCEAU. The line of this sector is thoroughly wet - sodden - boggy & all the trenches & ditches are full of water. This being	

Army Form C. 2118.

WAR DIARY
or
INTELLIGENCE SUMMARY.
(Erase heading not required.)

Instructions regarding War Diaries and Intelligence Summaries are contained in F.S. Regs., Part II. and the Staff Manual respectively. Title pages will be prepared in manuscript.

Hour, Date, Place	Summary of Events and Information	Remarks and references to Appendices
RUE DE BERCEAU 23-1-15	During the day Breastworks are being constructed in places where we are exposed. JGH	
RUE DE BOIS. 24-1-15	Nothing of note occurred. No rain but very cold. No casualties. JGH	
25-1-15	At 8 a.m. enemy's guns opened fire on RT. Sherwoods on our present line and also on RICHEBOURG ST VAAST. Shortly afterwards heavy rifle fire was opened on the left by the 8th Div. This continued for an hour. Two casualties both slight. The day was again cloudy and but no rain fell. JGH	
RICHEBOURG ST VAAST 26-1-15	The day passed off quietly. Two men slightly wounded. During the evening the Battalion was relieved by 2/3.9 Gurkhas Rifles. The relief was accomplished without any accidents. The Battalion then marched to billets in RICHEBOURG ST VAAST where it will remain in support until further orders. JGH	

(73989) W4141—463. 400,000. 9/14. H.&J.Ltd. Forms/C. 2118/10.

Army Form C. 2118.

WAR DIARY
or
INTELLIGENCE SUMMARY.

(Erase heading not required.)

Instructions regarding War Diaries and Intelligence Summaries are contained in F.S. Regs., Part II. and the Staff Manual respectively. Title pages will be prepared in manuscript.

Hour, Date, Place	Summary of Events and Information	Remarks and references to Appendices
RICHEBOURG ST VAAST 27-1-15	The Battalion in Brigade Reserve all in billets & employed during the day on 3 redoubts in second line of defence in R'BOURG ST. VAAST. After dark working parties were sent out to the front line	
28-1-15	As for 27-1-15	One man wounded
29-1-15 2/0 p.m.	The battalion was relieved by the 2/2nd Gurkha Rifles at 2/0 p.m. and marched to our old billets at VIEILLE CHAPELLE which we had occupied several times before	
VIEILLE CHAPELLE 30-1-15	During the day from 9 a.m. until dark the battalion supplied working parties in relief at RICHEBOURG ST VAAST. During the time when Z company under Capt. Lane was employed there a fire broke out - a description of this and how it was extinguished is given as an appendix	Appx.

Appx.

Army Form C. 2118.

WAR DIARY
or
INTELLIGENCE SUMMARY.
(Erase heading not required.)

Instructions regarding War Diaries and Intelligence Summaries are contained in F. S. Regs., Part II. and the Staff Manual respectively. Title pages will be prepared in manuscript.

Hour, Date, Place	Summary of Events and Information	Remarks and references to Appendices
NEILLE CHAPELLE 31 – 1 – 15	Battalion in billets & detailed as Outlying Battn. for the Brigade until 3 p.m. Companies paraded under company commanders – for rifle exercises, drill etc.	

WAR DIARY

With appendices.

OF

1/39th Garhwal Rifles.

From 1st February 1915 TO 29th March 1915.

WAR DIARY
or
INTELLIGENCE SUMMARY.
(Erase heading not required.)

Army Form C. 2118.

Hour, Date, Place	Summary of Events and Information	Remarks and references to Appendices
VIEILLE CHAPELLE		
1 – 2 – 15	In billets – parties worked on company entrenchments	
2 – 2 – 15	"	
3 – 2 – 15	9 a.m. — not available men were sent to ZELOBES under Lt Mackley to cut revetments which were taken by the carts to Regimental coy to LE TOURET	
2 p.m.	MM CoL L.V. + Company commanders proceeded to RICHEBOURG L'AVOUÉ to H.Q. of 9th Gurkhas to arrange for the taking over of trenches the following day. Batts came in late billeting duty.	
4 – 2 – 15		
6.10 p.m.	Batts. marched at 5.15 p.m. arrived at 9th Gurkhas Head Quarters	
10 p.m.	Relief of companies were completed. Enemy kept up a sniping fire between 6 p.m. and 9 p.m. wounding one man in B company. German Field battery shelled near Batt. German Head Quarters at 7.30 p.m. doing	

WAR DIARY
or
INTELLIGENCE SUMMARY.
(Erase heading not required.)

Army Form C. 2118.

Hour, Date, Place	Summary of Events and Information	Remarks and references to Appendices
RICHEBOURG L'AVOUÉ 5-2-15	No damage. Report sent to Brigade H.Q. reporting guns right.	
7 a.m.	1 N.C.O. & 3 men for company sent to witness execution of 3 men proved guilty of cowardice. German Field Battery fired a few shrapnel over Battn. H.Q. — no damage.	
9 a.m.	Distribution of Companies:- No II. D.C. under Capts Clarke ?? & Patrick on the Right. No I. D.C. under Capts Trent & Gibson in Centre " IV " Capt Kenny & Lt Welchman on left F Company under Capts Lane & Murray at Battn. H.Q. Our original line line held by Irish guards two of which were filled with water Officers & men in these for guards relieved every 12 hours & sent back in to Batln H.Q. to dry their clothes. After remaining at H.Q. for a few hours and having thoroughly dried their clothes details of ? sergeants returned to their companies.	See Sketch.

WAR DIARY
or
INTELLIGENCE SUMMARY.
(Erase heading not required.)

Army Form C. 2118.

Hour, Date, Place	Summary of Events and Information	Remarks and references to Appendices
RICHEBOURG L'AVOUÉ 5.2-15	One man wounded in No 3 Picquet - bringing him in delayed return of this picquet for some hours.	
6.2.15	A good deal of sniping between dusk and 10 p.m.	
10 a.m.	From dawn until 9.30 p.m. very quiet - no firing at all.	
10.30 a.m.	Enemy commenced shelling R. du Bois. Several shrapnel fired at or near R. du Bois - no casualties. I.D.C.'s horses.	
1.30 p.m.	Received message from Bde informing us that heavy bombardment of Enemy's position was about to take place near CINCHY.	
3 p.m.	2/39th officers arrived at our H.Q. to find out dispositions of our line with a view to taking over on 8-2-15.	
7-2-15	All companies in front line employed during the day in improving defences in R. du Bois. During the night materials were sent out to advanced picquets for their improvement - towards were used for showing up picquets - needed constant repair.	

WAR DIARY
or
INTELLIGENCE SUMMARY.

Army Form C. 2118.

(Erase heading not required.)

Hour, Date, Place	Summary of Events and Information	Remarks and references to Appendices
RICHEBOURG L'AVOUE 7-2-15	During the forenoon all companies strengthened buildings & loopholed walls in the RUE DU BOIS, and improved the abatis & cleared them. All available men were employed on the treatworks in rear of the factory. Loopholing and clearing RUE DU BOIS was continued during the afternoon.	
5.30 p.m. to 9 p.m.	Snipers & German trenches very active. Remainder of the night fairly quiet.	
8-2-15	The morning was very quiet and work as on the previous day was continued throughout on defence line	
11.30 a.m.	Company Commanders 2/39 Gurkha Rifles who were relieving us the same evening arrived to examine the local conditions. Germans opened shrapnel fire with one field gun at house in RUE DU BOIS – no casualties occurred from this fire. Arrangements were made with 2/39 G.R. for the relief to take place at or	

WAR DIARY
or
INTELLIGENCE SUMMARY.
(Erase heading not required.)

Army Form C. 2118.

Hour, Date, Place	Summary of Events and Information	Remarks and references to Appendices
RICHEBOURG L'AVOUE 8.2.15	After 9 p.m. no hostile shelling and rifle fire was sustained from 5.30 p.m. to about 8.30 p.m. A fine day and evening.	
8.30 p.m.	Company and Bugler guides of 1/39 G. Rifles 2/39 G. Company at cross roads of S.B.C. at 8.30 p.m. — Companies marching up to Rue Du Bois at 10 minutes intervals.	
11 p.m.	Reliefs were complete, all Rajputs having marshalled at centre of Cutter Subeatan by the Jemadar Adjutant and marched to RICHEBOURG ST. VAAST under the orders of the Adjutant.	
RICHEBOURG ST. VAAST. 9.2.15	Battalion had to supply working parties day and night. Both collecting wood in P.B. ST VAAST and working after dark at or near the Rue du Bois. Enemy shelled with shrapnel on the even street of P.B. ST VAAST — but beyond killing the Church steeple did no damage.	
10.2.15 10 a.m.	Battalion again employed all companies in working parties. Court Martial held on for trial of No: Rifm GANGA BISHT — sleeping on his post in the trenches.	

Army Form C. 2118.

WAR DIARY
or
INTELLIGENCE SUMMARY.
(Erase heading not required.)

Hour, Date, Place.	Summary of Events and Information	Remarks and references to Appendices.
RICHEBOURG ST.VAAST 10.2.15 11.2.15 2p.m.	Working parties were again employed from this battalion. Garhwal Rif. relieved by the Tochundon Rifles. The battalion on relief by the 39th Sikhs in billets, marched to LA COUTURE and occupied the same billets as before.	
LACOUTURE {NEUVE CHAPELLE 12.2.15.	Capt. W. OWEN — Subadar CHABSAH SINGH, Jemadar LACHMAN & SAWAN and 168 N.C.Os & men of the 38th Dogras arrived and were formed into "C" & "D" companies, i.e. No II Double Company. The Garhwali "C" & "D" companies being broken up & substituted throughout the battalion in A, B, E, F, G & H companies. The arrival of this draft brought the battalion strength to over 600 men. Parades under company arrangements.	
13.2.15 14.2.15 3p.m.	Battalion came on "Flying duty" for the Brigade for 24 hours."	

Army Form C. 2118.

WAR DIARY
or
INTELLIGENCE SUMMARY.
(Erase heading not required.)

Instructions regarding War Diaries and Intelligence Summaries are contained in F. S. Regs., Part II, and the Staff Manual respectively. Title pages will be prepared in manuscript.

Hour, Date, Place.	Summary of Events and Information	Remarks and references to Appendices.
15. 2. 15.	Parade in the Orchard arrangements.	
16. 2. 15.		
17. 2. 15.	1 Battalion came in Billets ready for the Brigade	
18. 2. 15.	to take over.	
19. 2. 15.	Orders received to take over from Sirmoor & field Cav. Rifles	
	16 [?] to [?]	
	(No 2758) 1st Bn Gurkha Rifles [Hd Qrs]).	
	Parade under Company arrangements.	
20. 2. 15.	Battalion marched at 1.30 p.m.	
21. 2. 15.	Orders at [?] on the [?] to be brought [?]	
RUE DE L'EPINETTE	which were carried out + Relieved in trenches	
TO	by 2/39th Garhwal Rifles & Sirmoor Rifles	
25. 2. 15.	Battalion [?] over [?] TUCKER.	
	1st Battalion relieved by 2/3rd Gurkha Rifles	
	The Battalion came in from [?] (24-2-15) & [?] in Billets Rue Kuno	
	during this time the Battn took over [?] in the trenches opposite	
	BREWERY — INDIAN VILLAGE + DANJER CORNER.	

25. 2. 15.

Army Form C. 2118.

WAR DIARY
or
INTELLIGENCE SUMMARY.
(Erase heading not required.)

Hour, Date, Place.	Summary of Events and Information	Remarks and references to Appendices.
15.2.15	Parades under Company arrangements.	
16.2.15	"	
17.2.15	"	
18.2.15	Battalion came on inlying Duty for the Brigade for 24 hours.	
3 p.m.	Stood in front parade held at 12.30 p.m. today to promulgate notices of Summary (General Field Court Martial) (No 2758 Rifleman Ganga Bahdl 139 G.)	
19.2.15	Parades under Company arrangements.	
20.2.15	Battalion Punch'd at 1 p.m. Arrived at 4/5 p.m. at H.Q. Connaught Rangers Relief was carried out & Battalion in reserve to 2/39 G., right section, Garhwal Bde relieved Sinhind Brigade.	
21.2.15	1st line reserved at TOURET. The Battalion are forming part of Brigade Genl Reserve.	
RUE DE L'EPINETTE	During this period (21st to 25th) the enemy shelled both the Rue de L'EPINETTE & Rue du BOIS causing little damage.	
25.2.15	Battalion relieved 2/39 G. in the trenches at BREWERY — INDIAN VILLAGE — DANGER CORNER	

Army Form C. 2118.

WAR DIARY
or
INTELLIGENCE SUMMARY.
(Erase heading not required.)

Instructions regarding War Diaries and Intelligence Summaries are contained in F. S. Regs., Part II, and the Staff Manual respectively. Title pages will be prepared in manuscript.

Hour, Date, Place.	Summary of Events and Information	Remarks and references to Appendices.
25-2-15.	No 4 Company exercising in trench drill. Battalion reserve.	
26-2-15.	Lieut R L Lemon schooling 91 Singh branch late Capt 98 N.C.O.s men of the 30th Rajputs arrived + went straight to the trenches from Battalion.	
28-2-15.	Brigade relieved by the 1st Infantry Brigade. Battalion relieved at night by the Cameron Highlanders marched to billets 10 km area arriving at 11 pm.	
1-3-15.	Parades under Company arrangements.	
2-3-15 (3pm)	Battalion came on "playing Duty" for the Brigade 24 hrs.	
3-3-15.	Parades under Company arrangements.	
4-3-15.	" " " "	
5-3-15.	" " " "	
6-3-15.	" " " "	
7-3-15. 3pm	Battalion came on "playing Duty" for the Brigade 24 hrs. Parades under Company arrangements.	
8-3-15. 7pm	Battalion marched to billets at NEUVE CHAPELLE in rear No IX X I + III M.G. Section of firing line.	

Army Form C. 2118.

WAR DIARY
or
INTELLIGENCE SUMMARY.
(Erase heading not required.)

Instructions regarding War Diaries and Intelligence Summaries are contained in F. S. Regs., Part II, and the Staff Manual respectively. Title pages will be prepared in manuscript.

Hour, Date, Place.	Summary of Events and Information	Remarks and references to Appendices.
25-2-15.	No 11 Infantry remaining in forward trenches Battalion reserve.	
	Lieut F.S. Lappin	
28-2-15.	1.95 N.C.Os returned to 59th [Regt?] having reported [sick?] [...] to hospital in the [...]	
Locon.	Relieved [...] 1st [...] Infantry Brigade by 1st Cameron Highlanders.	
1 — 3 — 15.	Battalion arrived at road [...] [Citata?] 20 [...] arose arriving at 11 p.m.	
2 — 3 — 15.	Battalion came on [...] Aug. Ir. 1 [...] [...] Parade [...] a day [...]	
3 — 3 — 15.	"	
4 — 3 — 15.	"	
5 — 3 — 15.	"	
6 — 3 — 15.	"	
7 — 3 — 15.	[...] portion [...] on [...] to [...] at [...] [...] [...]	
8 — 3 — 15.	[...] [...] [...] at [...] M.G. [...] of the [...]	

Army Form C. 2118.

WAR DIARY
or
INTELLIGENCE SUMMARY.
(Erase heading not required.)

Hour, Date, Place	Summary of Events and Information	Remarks and references to Appendices
VIEILLE CHAPELLE 9.3.15.	Battn. in billets here all day. Various orders & messages were received during the day in relation to the attack to be carried out in the vicinity of NEUVE CHAPELLE the next day. The notification received from Bde according to orders received at 11.0 p.m. for the resistance of events which followed up to the end of the battle of NEUVE CHAPELLE see notes, sketch map et all attached as Apple. VIII	Apple. VIII

Army Form C. 2118.

WAR DIARY
or
INTELLIGENCE SUMMARY.
(Erase heading not required.)

Instructions regarding War Diaries and Intelligence Summaries are contained in F.S. Regs., Part II. and the Staff Manual respectively. Title pages will be prepared in manuscript.

Hour, Date, Place	Summary of Events and Information	Remarks and references to Appendices
L'EPINETTE (LESTREM AREA) Sunday 14-2-15 5 p.m.	Battalion arrived in billets from NEUVE CHAPELLE at 5 p.m. & went into rest immediately. The C.O. r. Officers, together with party of men came from the 2/13 G.R. to be present at the burial of Major McIvor, Capt. Wg of KENNY, & Capt. Wynne OWEN (39th N.Ghas) attend? The procession started from the cross roads ("Epinette") marching thence through LESTREM to the Cemetary, where the bodies were laid to rest. Capt-Revd. the Chaplain of Meerut Division officiated. Officers present:— Colonel Dick-Cunyngham Capt Bailey " Lyall " Wilson " Cosgrave " Hartinard " Lyon " Fox Major Manisty Lieut Rogers " Shaw 1bg H.Q. 2/2. 1 bg H.Q.	(2/10 Gunthnos.) (125thF.G.J. Stanley) (Revd Penjetoi) (30th K.G.O. Baluchis) (53rd Sikhs) attached 1bg N 9.

Army Form C. 2118.

WAR DIARY
or
INTELLIGENCE SUMMARY.
(Erase heading not required.)

Hour, Date, Place	Summary of Events and Information	Remarks and references to Appendices
L'EPINETTE (LESTREM AREA) Sunday 14-2-15 5 p.m.	Battalion arrived at L'EPINETTE from NEUVE CHAPELLE at 5 p.m. + went into billets immediately. The C.O., Officers together with half of men went from the 21st of Feb to be buried at M. Lunel. Major Moore took in Lt J. KENNY & CAPT WYNNE OWEN (1st Bn appointment). The interview started from the cross road L'Epinette meeting where through LESTREM to the Convent where the cross roads in + laid to rest. Capt. Nixon the Captain of Mount Division arrived. Officers present — (Genl. Davis — Brigadier Col. Col. " Farnan Major " Hall Capt. Milmore " Bonnyman " Montgomery Major Ford Lieut Capt. " Montieory Lieut Rogers " Shaw M.I. Jones Capt. Jack " Mary Lieut. Collie) (2/Lt. Purdon) (Capt. Purdon) (Capt. Purdon) (Lieut R.G.L. Bamford) (2nd Welsh) attached 1st Gr. F. attached 1st Gr. F.

WAR DIARY
or
INTELLIGENCE SUMMARY.

(Erase heading not required.)

Army Form C. 2118.

Hour, Date, Place	Summary of Events and Information	Remarks and references to Appendices
L'EPINETTE. 15.3.15	The following Special Order of the day by Br. Gen'l C.G. Blackader D.S.O. Commdg. Garhwal Brigade was read. The following has been received from the G.O.C. Sir J. Willcocks K.C.B. K.C.S.I. K.C.M.O. D.S.O. Commdg. Indian Army Corps & to be communicated to all ranks of Garhwal Brigade.	"Please convey to all ranks of your (Garhwal) Brigade my hearty thanks & congratulations on their splendid work at NEUVE CHAPELLE. You indeed brigade is hard to have outdone itself in the demands of my command. Notwithstanding their great efforts they are prepared for still further in the immediate future Jr.
16.3.15. 9.0 a.m.	The G.O.C. Meerut Division (Lt. Genl. Anderson K.C.B.) made an informal inspection of the Battalion, congratulating them on their splendid work at NEUVE-CHAPELLE.	It were more than enterprising to dwell upon the fifteen's victory by Garhwal Lifts splendid example by have shown of gallantry, dash, endurance & discipline in the operations of the last few days. The behaviour of first every member of the Brigade is not only proud of the decision they have achieved, but also of history added fresh lustre to the finest traditions of their Units.
17.3.15. 10 a.m.	Strong & possible parade at 10 a.m. The Army Corps Commander inspected the Battalion & congratulated them on their fine work at NEUVE-CHAPELLE.	
18-3-15.	Parades under Company arrangements.	

WAR DIARY or INTELLIGENCE SUMMARY

Army Form C. 2118.

Hour, Date, Place	Summary of Events and Information	Remarks and references to Appendices
L'EPINETTE 15.3.15.	Telegram of congratulation received from Major Gen'l G.C. Anderson D.S.O. Comm'g Indian Cavalry Brigade [?] [?] [?] [?] from Maj Genl Sir Henry [?] KCB K.C.S.I KCVO DSO Comm'g Indian Army Corps to be communicated to all ranks of 1 Garhwal Brigade.	(1) Please convey to the rest of your gallant Brigade my hearty [?] congratulations on the splendid work of NEUVE CHAPELLE. Your Indian Brigade I found to have not the equals in the [?] it [?] [?] my command. Notwithstanding what [?] they are prepared for still greater [?] in the immediate future."
16. 2.15.	The G.O.C. Meerut Division (Major Gen'l Anderson K.C.B.) visited [?] and instructor to the Battalion congratulating them on their gallant work at NEUVE-CHAPELLE	I am now anxious to state to Brig. Anderson's Brigade [?] splendid example before shown of gallantry [?] and discipline in the operations [?] last few days. The [?] that every member of the Brigade is not only proud of the success [?] have achieved, but also of having added fresh honors to the past traditions of their units.
17.3.15. Strong parties [?] at 10 AM the Army Corps Commander inspected the Battalion + congratulated them on their fine work at NEUVE-CHAPELLE.		
10 A.M.	Parades under Company arrangements.	

15-3-15.

Army Form C. 2118.

WAR DIARY
or
INTELLIGENCE SUMMARY.
(Erase heading not required.)

Instructions regarding War Diaries and Intelligence Summaries are contained in F.S. Regs., Part II. and the Staff Manual respectively. Title pages will be prepared in manuscript.

Hour, Date, Place	Summary of Events and Information	Remarks and references to Appendices
19—3—15.	Lieut. C.M. LONGBOTHAM 73rd Punjabis reported his arrival for attachment to the Battalion. Parades. Route Marching Bomb-Throwing & Physical Drill.	
20—3—15.	Captain C.A. James assumed command of the Battalion from 9 a.m. of 20-3-15 vice Major G. ROOKE 2/10th G.R. transferred to 2nd G.R. Parades. As for 19-3-15.	
21—3—15.	Lieut. BURNE. (INDIAN ARMY RESERVE of Officers) reported his arrival for duty 2/Lieut. RAMA JODA JUNG (NATIVE INDIAN LAND FORCES) rejoined his annual training with this Regt, bringing with him 2 IOs in charge and a draft from Indian of State 1 N.M. as reinforcements. 4 96 Rank & File from Indian of State. Parades. Route Marching & Physical Drill.	
22—3—15.	The Batt had orders for its to New Bridle lines = The Tetris District of B.M. Area No 3 DC under Colonel Murray consists of 2 lt Rajputs & Jungs No 1 & 4 DCs consist of Jabalpur & No 1 BC consisting of Dogras of the 38th D & 39th D attached to the Battalion.	
23—3—15.	Parades under B.C. Commander.	

WAR DIARY
or
INTELLIGENCE SUMMARY.
(Erase heading not required.)

Army Form C. 2118.

Instructions regarding War Diaries and Intelligence Summaries are contained in F.S. Regs., Part II. and the Staff Manual respectively. Title pages will be prepared in manuscript.

Hour, Date, Place	Summary of Events and Information	Remarks and references to Appendices
24-3-1915. EPINETTE	Battalion marched from Epinette to VIEILLE CHAPELLE, arriving at later billets about 4 P.M. Garhwal Brigade was attached to Divisional Reserve to BAREILLY + DEHRA DUN BRIGADES who were in the trenches. 2 Batts of the Brigade were detailed daily as "flying Battalions".	
25-3-1915 VIEILLE CHAPELLE	Battn under the Commander. Batt Marching, Bayonet Fencing, Physical Drill, Bomb Throwing etc. —	
26-3-1915. VIEILLE CHAPELLE	do — do — do	
27-3-1915 VIEILLE CHAPELLE	In alarm + camping + working parties into estaminets to 2 AM.	
28-3-1915. VIEILLE CHAPELLE	+ training locally under Lt Byron for 1 PM. BAREILLY + being employed on fortification + field works through the night. Sections — CO. Adjt + Dees proceeded via 10th Gurkha Rifles Redoubt to trenches which the BOGRAS through LITTLE Redoubt and trenches of BAREILLY BRIGADE	
29-3-1915. VIEILLE CHAPELLE and CALONNE.	Battn marched to CALONNE 12.15 PM via LA TOSSE, LESTREM + PARADIS + arrived at new billets 3.30 PM. Transport & Ammunition to 1st + 2nd line at 1st offs with the title "Mounted Inspection by Indian Army Corps Commander + Intimidation Received to Battalion to prepare to return to England. Rifle orders. S 38, B + 30° Plywood & transfered as working. Possible to 41st Brigade	

"Message dated 9.3.15"   App.xe XVII

- 2/Leinsters
- 3 Londons
- 2/3rd Gurkhas
- 1/39 cy.
- 2/39 cy.
- No 3 Coy S&M.

B.M. 654.

All units will make up numbers of sandbags in possession to be 2 per man of fighting strength, the number required being drawn today from R.E. depot No 3 Coy S&M. aaa Units will also draw & place in advanced amm depots the following Nos of Sandbags prepared in bundles for carrying gun. 2/Leinsters 400 aaa 2/3rd 400 aa 1/39 G. 1000 aaa 2/39 G. 800 The following stores will also be each unit except Londons aaa 12 loophole Shields aaa 16 boxes of Pipe grenades for distribution to companies & 16 boxes for placing in reserve at advanced Amm. depots aaa Leinsters will also draw 50 billhooks The balance of grenades available for the brigade will be taken over by & returned with the Amm. Reserve aaa

Addressed to all units of Garhwal Bde & repeated to 3rd Coy S&M.

From   Garhwal Bde
      9 a.m.

(Sd) J.K. Stewart Major.

Secret

Copy No 4.

Operation Order No 25
by
Brig. Genl. C.G. Blackader D.S.O.
Comdg. Garhwal Bde.

Reference 1/40,000 BETHUNE Sheet
1/5000 Sketch Map No 589.

Garhwal Bde. H.Q.
9 March 1915.

Information. 1 (a) No further information has been received regarding enemy.

(b) The Indian Corps & 4th Corps are to co-operate in an attack on NEUVE CHAPELLE on the 10th March. The 8th Division is to attack from the 4th Corps front & the Meerut Division from that of the Indian Corps.

The Artillery of the two Corps will bombard the area to be attacked for 35 minutes before the Assault. This bombardment will commence at 7.30 a.m. & cease at 8.5 a.m. Artillery fire continuing with increased fuse & range.

Intention. 2. The GARHWAL Bde. (simultaneously with 8th Div. attack) will assault the enemy's trenches east of the ESTAIRES — LA BASSÉE road at 8.5 a.m. as follows — assembling beforehand as detailed in Table. A.

3. Distribution of Attacking troops.

P.T.O.

3. Distribution of Attacking troops.

Units	Objective	Limits of Zone of Attack	Lines to be occupied & immediately consolidated	Special Points to be made good and occupied
1/39 G.	C.	Left. Line drawn from N.E. exit of RUE DU BOIS from PORT ARTHUR X road D.N. where it crosses R. des LAYES.	S.E. Corner of PORT ARTHUR through C to road D-N at crossing of R. des LAYES.	Junction of enemy trenches at B.
2/Leicesters	Group of Houses round X roads at D.	Right. As per left of 1/39 G. Left Natural ditch running ↙ towards enemy's lines from ESTAIRES - LA BASSEE road 300ˢ from PORT ARTHUR X roads	Road D-N at crossing of R. des LAYES to C and then to road (inclusive) 100ˢ N.E. of cross roads at D.	
2/3rd G.R.	Group of Houses at road junction at F.	Right As for left of Leicesters. Left Road S.4.b.3.2 to NEUVE CHAPELLE (inclusive).	From road (inclusive) 100ˢ N.E. of X roads at D. through G to road (inclusive)	200ˢ from G in enemy trench which runs parallel to road to NEUVE CHAPELLE.
2/39 G.	Line G.H.	Right as for left of 2/3rd G.R. but road exclusive.	From left of 2/3rd G.R. (road exclusive) to H.	To join hands with 8th Divn.

On the objective (column 2 above) being attained all trenches leading towards the enemy will be double blocked (beyond bombing distance) and then cleared beyond the barricades made.

<u>Brigade Reserve</u>
4. 1/3 London Regt. in the most westerly breastwork parallel to and 200 yards from Est ESTAIRES - LA BASSEE road - to move forward to the breastwork 100ˢ East, when it is cleared after the bombardment.

<u>Machine Guns</u>
5. Each assaulting battalion will have 2 machine guns. The remaining machine guns will be disposed under the orders of the Bde. M.G.O. to support & guard the left flank of the attack.

<u>Right flank Protection</u>
6. Bomb guns will be disposed to support and guard in co-operation with

rifle & machine gun fire of the ....
Bde, the right flank of the attack.

Ammunition etc. to be Carried
7. Each man will carry 150 rounds of S.A. Ammunition, 2 sandbags, emergency ration, and unexpended portion of the days rations, each assaulting coy will carry 192 bombs.

Reserves of Ammunition and bombs
8. Magazines of S.A.A. and bombs have been formed with 100 boxes S.A.A. & 192 bombs in each of the following points - Southern portion of PORT ARTHUR, Northern portion of PORT ARTHUR, Southern Portion of Advanced post at S.4.b.3.2. and Northern Portion of advanced post at S.4.b.3.2.
Twenty boxes S.A.A. are also stored for Bde. M.Gs. at S.4. a 8.7.
The Bde Amm. Reserve will be at Bde H.Q. (with some additional bombs. Company Ammunition mules with Amm. will be at Bde Amm. reserve. Battalion Ammunition carts will be with the First line transport, animal, ready to load in.

9. In order to indicate to artillery & to units supporting the attack by fire the locality reached by attacking troops, coloured flags (pink for flank battalions, & light & dark blue for centre battalions) will be placed by leading bodies of troops on the side of enemy trenches or buildings captured.

Communication
10. Telephone & visual signalling will be maintained between Bde H.Q. & H.Qs. of units

First Line Transport
11. First line transport (less Amm. mules & medical equipment) at LA COUTURE

Dressing Station
12. At existing aid Posts in Rue des BERCEAUX (S.8.6 & S.3.c)

Reports. 13. Reports to farm at 83 a 52, where Bde. H.Qs have been established.

Issued this signal return at 6.30 p.m.

(Sd) J.M.K Stewart
Major
D.M. Garhwal Bde.

Copy No 4 to 1/39.G.

TABLE A.

(with Operation Order No 25 of 9.3.15.

Unit	Place of Assembly	Route	Time of passing Starting point Road junction at S.2.C.22.
2 Leicesters	Trenches from PORT ARTHUR road junction to 300ᵡ N.N.W. along LA BASSÉE road, & southern half of front breastwork parallel to and 100ᵡ west of ESTAIRES - LA BASSÉE road.	Edward Rd. Rue du Bois, Roome's trench.	Night 9ᵗʰ/10ᵗʰ 11.30 p.m.
2/3rd G.R.	Trenches on line of ESTAIRES - LA BASSÉE Rd. from left of Leicesters to road junction S.4. & 3.2. and Northern half of front breastwork parallel to & 100 yards W. of ESTAIRES - LA BASSÉE road	S.3.C.42 Rue des BERCEAUX to S.4 a 04 thence across country	12.30 a.m.
1/39.G.	Part of PORT ARTHUR S. of Rue du Bois & in Roome's trench	As for 2 Leicesters	1 a.m.
2/39.G.	In trenches on line of ESTAIRES - LA BASSÉE road N.N.W. of road junction S.4. & 3.2.	As for 2/3rd G.R. to S4 a 04 thence continue along Rue des BERCEAUX to destination	1.30 a.m.
1/3 London Regt.	Second breastwork parallel to and 200ᵡ from the ESTAIRES - LA BASSÉE road leaving 60ᵡ at Southern end clear for Pioneers	EDWARD Rd. and thence across country.	1.15 a.m.
Bde. M.Gs.	Trenches at S.4. a 8.9.	As per 2/39.G.	Verbally created to Bde. M.G.O.

Secret

Addition to Operation Order
No 25
by
Brig. General C.G. Blackader D.S.O.
Comdg. Garhwal Bde.

Information

1. The General Object of the attack is to enable the 4th & Indian Corps to establish themselves on a more forward line to the East, the eventual objective being the high ground from AUBERS to LIGNY LE GRAND.

The Dividing line between the 4th & Indian Corps is point where Dividing line between squares M & S cuts NEUVE CHAPELLE — Cross roads in S6a 6.9. — Cross roads at LA CLIQUETERIE Fe.

The 1st Corps is assaulting the enemy's line N.E. of GIVENCHY.

The subsequent objective to the line C.O.G.H. which the Bde is to assault will be

(a) The first available line in the East side of the PORT ARTHUR — NEUVE CHAPELLE road

(b) The Eastern edge of the Bois de BIEZ and

(c) Line thro' LE HUE & LIGNY LE GRAND to LA CLIQUETERIE Fe (inclusive)

During these several advances all Commanders must bear in mind the necessity for being prepared to specially protect the right flank of the movement.

The 8th Division's assault on the village of NEUVE CHAPELLE will commence at 8.35 a.m.

The Dehra Dun Bde will be in close support of the Garhwal Bde.

The Bareilly Bde will continue to hold the present line of trenches.

Parties of Sappers & Miners & Pioneers have been ordered to put localities in a state of defence.

Assembly 2. All battalions will be in position by 4.30 a.m.

Prisoners 3. Any prisoners taken will be sent back in parties under escorts to be specially detailed (and not by individuals on their own initiative) to the front line of the Bareilly Bde to whom the prisoners will be handed over, escorts returning to their units immediately.

(Sd) J.M.S. Stewart Maj
BM.
Garhwal Bde.

Battle of NEUVE CHAPELLE — Appx XVII

Share of ~~Forces~~ 39.B. in the Operations

According to Operation Orders No 25 issued by the O.O.C. Garhwal Bde. the battalion was in position by 4.20 a.m. on 10th March 1915.

Distribution — The following distribution of companies in the attack were made by me

Front line attacking Companies
  No 2 Company under Capts Clarke (Comdg) & Owen.
  No 4 Company "   "   Kenny & ") & Lt. Welchman

Supporting Companies
  No III Company under Capt. Murray (Comdg) & Lt. Lemon.
  No I Company "   "   Sparrow.

No 2 Company keeping its left on the line marked in pencil on the accompanying sketch, so as to keep touch with the 2/Leicesters right flank, was to attack the German trenches straight to its front.

No 4 Company keeping its left on No.2. Coy.'s right was to attack & capture "C"

No III Company 2 Platoons under Capt. Murray were to follow immediately in rear of Capt. Clarke's i.e. No 2 Company. The remaining two platoons staying at Bn. H.Q. in the front breastwork of PORT ARTHUR under ~~and~~ Lt. Lemon to be used as a battalion reserve in case of emergency & to take up tools etc. after a successful assault.

No I Company was ~~unseen~~ to support Capt. Kenny's i.e. No 4. Company, and follow immediately on their heels.

Machine Guns — 2 Machine Guns under Lt. Mankelow were detailed to remain under C.O's orders in PORT ARTHUR to be sent up, after the assault as occasions required.

Assault. At 8.5 a.m. i.e. at the time given for the bombardment on the German front line trenches to end the 2 leading companies commenced the assault

Assault.
(Contd)

No. 2 Company under Capts Clarke & Owen immediately bore too much to the right & thus caused Capt. Kennys No 4 Company to also bear too much to the right, the consequence being that a large portion of the German front line trench i.e. from the Rue du Bois to nearly 200 South of this road was not attacked, the Germans still holding it in force.

I should mention here that during the artillery bombardment the German trench had hardly been touched by our shells all along the front to be attacked by the battalion, while the barbed wire was practically intact. The two leading companies managed after some fighting & clearing obstacles in face of a very heavy fire to capture a portion of the trench some 200 yards in extent immediately to the right of "C".

Seeing that the battalion attack had swerved too much to the right & not knowing to what extent of the trench was still held by Germans I ordered Capt. Murray to support with his 2 platoons immediately in rear of No 2 Coy which had suffered heavy loss. Capt. Sparrow with 2 platoons only had followed immediately behind No 4. Company leaving 2 platoons in the right salient.

I do not know why he did this unless it was that he thought that as the "jumping off" place in the trench could not hold more than 2 platoons — he had better get ahead with the two platoons ready & in

3.

a good position for advancing.

Assault (contd)
Anyhow he had apparently given orders to 2 platoons under Jemadar Bije Kandari to remain in support.

Seeing that the large portion of the trench still in the hands of the Germans could not be assaulted by the few men I had left, especially as it would have to be carried out across 100 yards of open ground, swept by rifle fire from the uncaptured portion of the German trench and enfiladed by machine guns in the enemy's trenches from the vicinity of the ESTAIRES - LA BASSÉE road, I sent the Adjutant to the salient of PORT ARTHUR on the right to give orders that no men were to attempt to advance until I received reinforcements sufficient to assault the German trench.

I was not able to find out for some time as to what had happened to all the British Officers of the attacking companies, but after some delay I ascertained that they had all been killed and that the survivors of the attacking companies were holding the captured trench under the command of Garhwali Officers.

I was unable to get at these men or to give them any assistance - they were however in a fairly good position and they held their ground all day in spite of a few German attempts to dislodge them by means of bombs etc.

I telephoned to Bde. Hdrs. at about 8.45 a.m. and explained the situation asking for reinforcements at once. I asked for 2 companies.

(2)

Assault
(Contd)

About 10 a.m. I received a lacerated wound on the inside of my left thigh – field dressed it & managed to carry on.

Soon after this I received 2 companies of the 3rd London Regt. (T.F.) as reinforcements and was informed that the Seaforth Highlanders & 2nd Gurkhas (Dehra Dun Bde) were going to assault the uncaptured portion of the trench from the direction of "D", that is from the inner flank. I was given to understand also that as soon as I saw this attack developing I was to send forward my 2 companies of the 3rd Londons together with the remainder of my own men.

There had been a good deal of shell fire directed on to PORT ARTHUR & in consequence there had been several casualties. Capt Taylor I.M.S. the M.O. of the Battalion came up to PORT ARTHUR where he did excellent & unceasing work in attending to the wounded all that day & most of the night, altho' under shell fire most of the time.

The attack of my two leading companies together with the supporting platoons under Capts Sparrow and Murray was I consider carried out with the greatest dash & bravery the Officers & men being fired at from two sides as well as their front – Also as I have mentioned before the chevaux-de-frise entanglements were almost intact along the whole front of the German trench from ① to ③ (see sketch.) ① to ② shews roughly the portion of the trench which should have been captured by us in the first place, ② to ③ shews the portion captured in the first assault.

(5)

The attack of the Seaforth Highlanders did not develop until about 5 p.m. at which time a bombing party commenced advancing down the trench from ⓒ i.e. the right flank of the German trench captured by the 2 Leinsters towards ⓒ the left flank of the portion held by my battalion.

As soon as I saw the leading platoons of the Seaforth Highlanders advance from the group of buildings near "D" I ordered the advance of the 2 companies of the 3rd Londons — also the remainder of my own men. All these carried out the assault with the greatest dash altho' losing heavily all the time. On the attack nearing the German trenches the remainder of the enemy some 3 officers & 80 men surrendered & were taken prisoners & sent to the rear.

I sent Capt. Mainwaring (the Adjutant) & Lt Mankelow (machine gun offr) forward to the captured trench where the companies were collected & work was continued in reversing the trench etc.

I was unable to go any further on account of the wound in my leg.

Major MacIver of the 2/39th was sent to relieve me in command of the battalion at about 10 p.m. after he had arrived to confer with the Brigadier in the Salient of PORT ARTHUR

I left at about midnight 10th/11th March in a stretcher accompanied by the medical officer.

The remainder of the account of the battalions share in the battle up to the afternoon of

12th March is supplied by Captain Mainwaring the Adjutant of the battalion

The remainder of the night 10th & 11th was spent in cleaning up the captured trench & in reversing the parapet - also in blocking the C.T.C. trench at ③.

The night was a quiet one there being no shelling or firing at our position of the trench.

The whole of the 11th March passed off quietly except for a little shelling up to nearly midnight when a fairly heavy shell fire was directed on PORT ARTHUR & in the vicinity of our trenches i.e. ② to ③. This shelling was kept up until nearly dawn.

At dawn a heavy fire broke out on our left and almost immediately a movement in our front was evident. It was a hazy morning and difficult to see any distance. A Very pistol was fired & revealed German attacking columns charging our position in 3 lines. A rapid fire with rifles & machine guns was opened immediately & the enemy's attack never reached our position. The firing was soon controlled and stopped when it was ascertained that the attack on our front had failed but the enemy had succeeded in getting round our right flank and even a short way in our right rear where they were mostly accounted for by the Machine guns of the Black Watch.

During the night 11th/12th working parties had been employed in digging a trench (which was still not more than 3 feet deep) from ③ to the main road immediately to the right of this point.

Up this shallow trench the enemy managed to creep as the working parties through an error on being given the order to stand to arms before dawn had evacuated this short piece of trench. The right flank of our line at ③ was thus exposed altho defended by a picket at that point. The enemy commenced a bombardment with trench mortars on this flank to try & drive it in but the men with great gallantry in spite of severe losses managed to drive all attacks back. The machine gun placed at this point i.e. on our flank was splendidly served and was the chief means of stopping all attempts on the part of the enemy to rush the position. I would here add that the work of the machine guns in spite of very severe losses were admirably handled by Lt. Hankelow & his men who served the guns splendidly man after man being shot while necessarily exposing himself to work the guns. The O.C. the Seaforth Highlanders on our left sent his bombing party to help in driving back the enemy who had advanced down a communication from the direction of "B". It was soon discovered that the enemy were hiding behind the cover of a bend in the trenches South of "B" & were not in the trenches themselves. So Lt. Kenny commanding the bombing party ordered his men to retire as it was impossible for them to dislodge the enemy. This bomb party did excellent work however in relieving the pressure on our right flank. Major Martin was I regret to say then killed during the early part of the German Counter-attack. The Command of the battalion being taken by Capt. Harbord who had joined from the 2/3Q.G. the previous day.

The enemy did not attempt any further attacks on our line but shelled the vicinity incessantly all day & the trench we were holding at about 4p.m. causing some casualties.

The Garhewales ranks behaved throughout this trying period with the utmost gallantry never giving a yard of ground in spite of very heavy casualties & in constant danger of being surrounded & rushed on the right flank.

Lt. Mankelow & his machine guns contributed mostly in repelling the German attack in the morning and the gun on the extreme right of our line was splendidly served & was the means of driving back all attempts of the enemy to push back our right

12th March. Captain Mainwaring was wounded in the afternoon & was removed to the Aid post. I therefore attach Capt. Harbord's (who joined the Battn from 2/39.G. on 11th March) account which gives full details of the operations on 12th & until the battalion was relieved. The following casualties occurred during the operations 10th - 12th March.

Officers	Killed	Wounded	Missing
	Major Blackten	Bt. Col Swiney	Nil
	Capt. Sparrow	Capt. Mainwaring	
	" Clarke	Lt. Haukelow	
	" Kenny	" Lemon	
	" Owen	Capt. Taylor I.M.S.	
	" Murray	Subdr. Bije Kandari	
	Lt. Welchman	Jemdr. Guman Sing Negi	
	Subdr. Deb Sing Mahar		
	" Chabbi Sing		
	Jemdr. Prem Sing Negi		
	" Jit " Negi		
	" Deb Sing Negi		
	" Tawahin Burwan		

Rank and File: 98 killed, 190 wounded, 22 missing

E.V.H. Swiney
Bt Col
Comdg 1/39 G.

Report of Operations from 10th March to 8 a.m. 11th March 1915.

About twenty minutes before our artillery bombardment commenced and when we were ready in our positions for the attack the enemy commenced to shell PORT ARTHUR somewhat heavily and inflicted several casualties on us.

In advancing to the attack the Company under the command of Capt CLARKE bore away too much to the right thereby loosing touch with the Leicestershire Regt: and causing a gap of about 300x to 350x yards to occur between the latter and our selves which was still held by the Germans. During the attack we were enfiladed by Machine Gun fire coming from our right which together with the fact that the chevaux de frise was still almost intact accounted for rather a large number of Casualties. Captains CLARKE, MURRAY SPARROW and OWEN and Lieut WELCHMAN were killed before the German trench was reached. Captain KENNY though twice wounded reached the trench but was killed shortly afterwards. Col: SWINEY and Lieut LEMON were both wounded early in the day in PORT ARTHUR but the former continued to direct operations and did not leave till after midnight. Late in the afternoon two companies of the 3rd London working in conjunction with the 1st Seaforths, who attacked from the left flank, assaulted and gained the 300 yards of trench which the Germans were still holding between our selves and the Leicestershire Regt.

About Midnight Major MACTIER 2/39th G arrived to take over the command of the battalion in the meantime I had completed the reversing of the parapet which was then thickened. Pickets were posted and communicating trenches blocked, a listening patrol was also put out. We were shelled by the enemy during the night but the shelling was neither heavy nor effective. Captain HARBORD 2/39th G arrived to join the battalion about 8 a.m. on the 11th which made the total of British Officers with the battalion four.

Captain Taylor I.M.S. Medical Officer of the Battn. was dressing the wounded under a heavy shellfire and very frequently went into very exposed places to do so. Several lives were saved by his prompt attention on the spot.

A.D. Wanchelow?

Report of operations from 8 am 11th March to 8 pm 12th March.

Duplicate

I was sent over to the 1/39 G.R. from the 2/39 G.R. on the morning of the 11th - during that day except for shell fire all was quiet. The night of the 11th the collecting of dead and burial of same was carried out as far as possible by a working party, the remainder of the Regt. being employed in digging a trench back from our right to the LA BASSÉE road to connect up with the "Crescent". The tools having been left behind at the "jumping off" point and not being recovered work was carried on with the entrenching tools and hence was very slow. However by the morning a certain amount of cover had been obtained - a party had been sent back to the "jumping off" point to recover the entrenching tools but they were not to be found. Just before dawn on the 12th about 5.30 am while work was still being proceeded with the German counter attack commenced in three lines on our front and on our right - that to our front was easily repulsed with machine gun and rifle fire the enemy suffering heavy loss - as regards the right the enemy managed to work up a communication trench which was in continuation of our own trench but which had been double blocked though to block it effectively was difficult on account of the tortuous nature of the trench - here the enemy covered by a trench mortar got to within 40 yards of our main trench where they were held up by our machine gun and later by our trench gun - this latter though it was in position early in the attack was unable to be fired owing to there being no fuzes or powder with the gun - these arriving later. Major MACTIER 2/39 G.R. who was commanding, was killed at the commencement of the attack and the command devolved on me. We were suffering somewhat severe losses at this time from the enemy's trench mortar and his fire from communication trench on our right and to our right rear - these losses were heavier than they might have

have been owing to the fact that we were very much overcrowded in our trench. There hardly being room to move. At about 8am the officer commanding 1st Seaforths sent up a bombing party (all our bombers having become casualties) to clear the communication trench - they got up about 20 yards and then returned as they found the enemy were no longer in the communication trench but outside it behind the parapet. We then turned our machine guns on to the enemy and cleared our right flank. A local counter-attack was arranged in conjunction with the 1st Seaforths but it did not materialize. In the afternoon we were very severely shelled by the enemy's artillery and suffered heavy loss especially on our right and in the trench refused back to join up with the "Crescent" - we with drew from the right till the shelling was over as we were being enfiladed - the trench was again occupied later in the afternoon - the enemy did not follow this bombardment with an attack. We were relieved with the exception of the machine guns in the evening of the 12th by the 1st Seaforths and went into dugouts taking the place of the relieving company. The men were very done up from the prolonged strain having been on the go without rest from the evening of the 9/10th to the evening of the 12/13th.

In conclusion I would draw attention to the splendid work of the machine gun section under Lieut MANKELOW, to the magnificent way in which the men stood their ground under the enemy's shell fire and also to the splendid conduct shown by the men all through the operation.

Ros Harford, Capt
alt O.C. 1/39 G R

Meerut Division
Garhwal Brigade

Garhwal Rifles
April – Nov. 1915

121/5504

WAR DIARY
OF
Garhwal Rifles.

From 1st April 1915 To 30th April 1915

WAR DIARY or INTELLIGENCE SUMMARY.

(Erase heading not required.)

Army Form C. 2118.

Hour, Date, Place	Summary of Events and Information	Remarks and references to Appendices

1-4-1915
CALONNE.

Cold morning, slight frost. Companies paraded as usual. Captain Blair and Lieut. Fox departed on 7 days leave.

2-4-1915
CALONNE.

Good Friday. Weather milder, and no frost. The Lord Bishop of London held a service for troops in the Brigade Area during the afternoon. At 4 p.m., reinforcements arrived, consisting of Captain GATHERER 2/10th G.R. and Captain ETHERTON 1/39th G., with 1 Indian officer and 62 Burma Military Police. Some Dogra reinforcements also arrived, originally intended for the regiment, but these were marched straight to the 41st Dogras. During the morning all the Dogras who had previously attached to the two battalions were transferred to the 41st Dogras (5 Indian officers and 159 other ranks).
Captain Wilcox left on 7 days leave today.

The Lord Bishop of London visited CALONNE Today, held a service in the afternoon.

3.4.1915
CALONNE.

Cloudy morning; weather mild. Companies paraded as usual. A wet afternoon and evening.

4.4.1915
CALONNE.

a Ester Sunday. A wet raw day. The G.O.C. Meerut Division inspected all reinforcements (who had joined the Battalion since January) during the afternoon. These consisted of the Tehri Sappers and Miners and the two detachments of Burma Police who had recently joined. He also saw, and recommended their return to India, 22 men whose length of service or chronic ailments rendered them unfit for the campaign.

5.4.1915
CALONNE.

Wet morning and rain continued all day. Orders came to day appointing Captain James to the Battalion, and for the remaining Officers of the 1st Battalion to proceed to various regiments. As the Battalion was very strong, the Army Corps Commander sanctioned 14 British officers being posted.

6-4-1915.
CALONNE.

Fine day but cloudy and a high N.W.Wind. Companies paraded as usual. Loading baggage Wagons practised. Route March. Lieut.Col. Drake Brockman, Captain Lyell and Captain Berryman proceeded on 7 days leave to England.

7-4-1915.
CALONNE.

Dull, cloudy day high wind, rain in afternoon. Companies paraded as usual. Route March and Bomb throwing. Maps of new line of trenches received.

8-4-1915.
CALONNE.

A cloudy day, very high wind. Companies paraded as usual. The Bomb throwers practised with live bombs. Sir Douglas Haig, Commanding 1st Army, saw all C.O's. of the Brigade and congratulated the Garhwal Rifles on their splendid achievements.

9-4-1915
CALONNE.

A wild rainy windy day. Captains. Blair, Wilcox and Lieut. Fox returned from leave. 2nd Lieut. Shaw Interpreter 1/39th G.R., joined the Battalion on from leave. Sir John French, the Commander-in-Chief, was to have inspected the Brigade, but the parade was cancelled at the last moment owing to a violent snow storm. Lieut Saunders, I.A.R., was posted to the Battalion.

10-4-1915
VIELLE CHAPELLE.

Fine sunny day. Roads very greasy and muddy from recent heavy rains. The Battalion marched at 10 a.m., to billets at VIELLE CHAPELLE and was second Regiment in Brigade.

2nd Lieut. Watney (Interpreter) rejoined from leave.

11-4-1915
VIELLE CHAPELLE.

Fine bright day and much warmer. The Regiment was detailed as Inlying Battalion.

2nd Lieut. Watney, Interpreter, was transferred to 40th Pathans in a similar capacity.

12-4-1915
VIELLE CHAPELLE.

Fine day; weather mild. Parades as usual. Lieut. Colonel Drake Brockman, Captain Lyell and Captain Berryman returned from leave.

13-4-1915.
XXX LA COUTURE.

Fine day; weather mild. Regiment marched to fresh billets in LA COUTURE at 2 p.m. Commanding officer and 2 G.O's (Subr. Bishan Sing Mawat and Jemr. Sangram Sing Negi) went to Brigade Headquarters at 2.45 p.m. to meet Lord Curzon.

14-4-1915.
LA COUTURE.

Wet morning and intermittent rain all day:
parades as usual. During the afternoon several War Correspondents came round, saw and sketched some of the men and were subsequently conducted round some trenches near the RUE DU BOIS by Captain Burton. A wet evening.

15-4-1915.
LA COUTURE.

A warm fine day. Parades as usual, our aeroplanes active towards evening.

16-4-1915
LA COUTURE.

A fine warm day. Parades as usual. Captain D.A.Blair joined Meerut Division Headquarters today as attached in D.A.A.G's branch.

17-4-1915
LA COUTURE.

Fine warm day. Parades as usual, and 300 men of the Battalion had baths in Divisional Baths at VIEILLE CHAPELLE.

18-4-1915
LA COUTURE.

Fine sunny day. Parades as usual. The Brigade Signalling Officer inspected Signallers during the afternoon: results good.
Captain J.E.Colenso, 2/7th G.R., was transferred today to 2/2nd G.R.
3 Working Parties, 400 men in all, sent out at 8.30 p.m., for digging and carrying purposes to RUE DU BOIS trenches. Returned 3 a.m.

WAR DIARY or INTELLIGENCE SUMMARY.

Army Form C. 2118.

19-4-1915
LA COUTURE.

Fine sunny day. Parades as usual.
At 6.45 p.m. No.4 Company under Captain Gatherer and Lieut. Saunders marched to occupy work A.1., together with one Company of the 2/Leicesters, in reserve to the 3/Londons who held the RUE DU BOIS trenches from the LA BASSEE road to the ORCHARD redoubt.

20-4-1915
LA COUTURE.

Cloudy morning, colder than usual, but bright and sunny later. Parades as usual. Two working parties one of 260 men and one of 200 men, out at 8 p.m., carrying revetting materials up to RUE DU BOIS trenches. Returned 2.30.a.m. While out with one of these parties Jemadar GUMAN SING NEGI (1st Battalion) was killed by a chance shot.
Total Casualties to date.

	2/39th G.			1/39th G.		
	K.	W.	M.	K.	W.	M.
B.Os. ...	2	1	1	...		
" attached.	3	5	1	...	1	
I.O's. ...	91	332	21	...		
O.R.I. ... }att	8	8	8	...		
Total.	104	346	31	1	—	—

21-4-1915
LA COUTURE.

Cloudy morning, but cleared up later. Parades as usual. Cold evening.

22-4-1915
LA COUTURE.

Cloudy morning and weather rather colder generally. Parades as usual.

WAR DIARY or INTELLIGENCE SUMMARY.
(Erase heading not required.)

Army Form C. 2118.

23-4-1915
LA COUTURE - CALONNE.

Cloudy morning with cold wind. The Brigade marched at 12.30 p.m., to former billets at CALONNE reaching there at 4 p.m.

Captain Harbord and Lieut. Rogers departed on leave today but about an hour after they had left orders came cancelling all leave and recalling Officers already started. But they, having left by rail, were not recalled.

No.4 Company in redoubt A.1., were under orders for relief at 8.30 p.m. to night, but were subsequently told to stand fast.

Orders were received for Major C.A.James, to be transferred to day to 129th Baluchis. He left at 7 p.m. to join them.

Received orders at 9.30 p.m. to return to LA COUTURE the following morning. No.4 Company was not relieved from Work A.1.

24-4-1915
CALONNE,
LA COUTURE.

Cloudy morning with wind. The Brigade left at 10 a.m., for the return march to LA COUTURE, the regiment being the last in order of march. LA COUTURE was reached at 1.30 p.m. and the same billets were occupied as had been evacuated on 23rd instant. Weather cold towards evening, with strong wind.

25-4-1915.
LA COUTURE.

Some rain fell during the night, and it was a cloudy morning with a slight drizzle. The C.O. and Adjutant went at 7 a.m. to see the trenches occupied by the 4th Seaforths in front of NEUVE CHAPELLE with a view to relieving them eventually. A fine afternoon and evening. Three working parties (436 men all told) were out in the evening at 7 O'clock, carrying revetting materials and digging in the vicinity of the RUE DU BOIS, returning at 3 a.m. During the time these parties were out working, two men were

25-4-1915
LA COUTURE.

were wounded by chance shots.(one of 1st Bn.and one of 2nd Bn.).

	2/39th.			1/39th		
	K.	W.	M.	K.	W.	M.
B.O's.	2	-	1	-	-	-
"attached.	-	1	-	-	-	-
I.O's.	3	5	1	1	-	-
" attached.	-	-	-	-	-	-
O.R.I.	91	333	21	-	1	-
" attached.	8	8	8	-	-	-
Total.	104.	347.	31.	1	1	-

26-4-1915
LA COUTURE.

Fine morning. No parades owing to the working parties having returned so late the previous night. All Company Commanders went up to inspect the 1/4th Seaforth's trenches during the morning.

Heavy firing, gun and rifle, heard in front line trenches between 6.30 and 7 p.m.

27-4-1915.
LA COUTURE.

Fine day; weather warm. Received orders to relieve 1/4th Seaforths in the trenches E. of NEUVE CHAPELLE to night.

The Battalion marched from billets at 7.30 p.m. marching a round about way via CROIX BARBEE. On arrival at the main ESTAIRES-LA BASSEE road guides of the Seaforths were met who conducted Companies to their trenches. From this former junction to this Companies marched to the trenches at 5 minutes interval, on account of possible shell fire.

No.2 Company and 3 Company were in the

27-4-1915
(continued)

the firing trenches; 2 platoons of No.1 Company in the CHURCH REDOUBT and 2 in support; No.4 Company in reserve.

Reliefs were complete by 11 p.m. During the reliefs there was a considerable amount of rifle fire, and this continued most of the night.

Work was at once commenced in the trenches, improving and thickening parapet both in front and rear and improving traverses.

Casualties; Indian Ranks, Wounded 1. (2/39 G.)

Total to date.

	2/39th G.			1/39th G.		
	K.	W.	M.	K.	W.	M.
B.O's.	2	-	1	-	-	-
" attached.	-	1	-	-	-	-
I.O's.	3	5	1	1	-	-
" attached.	-	-	-	-	-	-
O.R.I.	91	333	21	-	1	-
" attached:-						
Dogras.	8	8	8	-	-	-
" Burma Police.	-	1	-	-	-	-
Total.	104	348	31	1	1	-

28-4-1915
Trenches.
NEUVE CHAPELLE.

Fine warm day. Fairly quiet morning, not much firing A few shells were fired at support and reserve trenches about midday, but no casualties resulted. Captain Harbord and Lieut. Rogers rejoined from leave today. Not much firing by enemy to night.

Casualties; Indian Ranks, Wounded 1. (1/39 G.)

Total to date.

	2/39th G.			1/39th G.		
	K.	W.	M.	K.	W.	M.
B.O's.	2	-	1	-	-	-
" attached.	-	1	-	-	-	-
I.O's.	3	5	1	1	-	-
" attached.	-	-	-	-	-	-
O.R.I.	91	333	21	-	2	-
" attached:-						
Dogras.	8	8	8	-	-	-
" Burma Police.	-	1	-	-	-	-
Total.	104	348	31	1	2	-

29-4-1915
Trenches
NEUVE CHAPELLE.

Fine warm day. Heavy cannonading was heard about 4.a.m. towards the north. A quiet day on our front: very little rifle fire, but the enemy fired a few shells at our support trenches about midday and struck the parapet 3 times but no casualties occurred.

The C.O. visited front line trenches at 6.30.a.m.

Two German aeroplanes were observed flying over our lines during the forenoon, but they flew off on being fired at by our anti-aircraft guns and the approach of our aircraft.

During the day a machine gun was located in a house on the edge of the BOIS de BIEZ; the gunners fired 2 shells into the house and set it on fire.

The C.O. and Company Commanders of the 1/3rd London Regiment came up to Battalion Head Quarters at 10.30 p.m. to see the breast work they would have to occupy in case of attack.

During the day news was received that the following awards had been granted by the C.-in-C. the British Army in the field.

Indian Order of Merit 2nd Class.
1/39th G. Jemadar Prem Sing Negi.
No. 2480 Rifn. Banchu Negi.

2/39th G. 762 Havr. Buthar Sing Negi.
463 Naik Bakhtwar Sing Bisht.
1283 "   Jaman Sing Bisht.

Indian Distinguished Service Medal.
1/39th G. Jemadar Kedar Sing Rawat.
Jemadar Guman Sing Negi.
No.1321 L.Nk. Dangwa Ramola.

2/39th G. No.1598 Rifn. Chandar Sing Pawar.
" 1465 " Gopal Sing Pharswan.

News was also received that the King had awarded the VICTORIA CROSS to No.1685 Rifn. Gobar Sing Patwal, for conspicuous gallantry at NEUVE CHAPELLE; and the Military Cross to Lieut. A.H. Mankelow (1/39th G.) and Jemadar Pancham Sing Mahar (2/39th G.).

30-4-1915
(continued)

Casualties. Indian Ranks, Wounded 1. (1/39 G)
Total to date.

	2/39th G.			1/39th G.		
	K.	W.	M.	K.	W.	M.
B.O's.	2	-	1	-	-	-
" Attached.	-	1	-	-	-	-
I.O's.	3	5	1	1	-	-
" attached.	-	-	-	-	-	-
O.R.I.	91	333	21	-	3	-
" attached						
Dogras.	8	8	8	-	-	-
" " Burma Police.	-	1	-	-	-	-
Total.	104	348	31	1	3	-

30-4-1915
Trenches
NEUVE CHAPELLE.

Misty morning, but afterwards a fine warm day. The G.O.C. Garhwal Brigade visited the front line trenches at 10.30.a.m. and made a careful inspection of them. The Germans fired a few shells during the day at the gunner observation posts and houses in NEUVE CHAPELLE, but no casualties occurred from this. The gunner observation officer ~~heaxxdxax~~ had a narrow escape.

Casualties during day. Indian Ranks Killed 1 (Burma Police)
Wounded 1. (2/39 G)
Total to date.

	2/39th G.			1/39th G.		
	K.	W.	M.	K.	W.	M.
B.O's.	2	-	1	-	-	-
" attached.	-	1	-	-	-	-
I.O's.	3	5	1	1	-	-
" attached.	-	-	-	-	-	-
O.R.I.	91	334	21	-	3	-
" attached						
Dogras.	8	8	8	-	-	-
" " Burma Police.	1	1	-	-	-	-
Total.	105	349	31	1	3	-

Serial No 96. Garhwal Reserve.

12/5799

WAR DIARY
OF
Garhwal Rifles.

From 1st May 1915 TO 31st May 1915

1-5-1915
Trenches
NEUVE CHAPELLE.

A quiet night. The Germans suddenly started a heavy bombardment of the trenches in vicinity of NEUVE CHAPELLE at 4.30.a.m., most of the fire was directed to the right of our trenches, and on the houses in rear. The bombardment lasted till 5.25.a.m., and died away 10 minutes later. A few shells fell near Battalion Head Quarters, and the ground over which supports would have had to advance in case of necessity was covered by shrapnel. Our guns replied to the German fire.

No casualties occurred from this bombardment in this Battalion, though a few were sustained by other regiments of the Brigade holding the front line trenches.

German aeroplanes were active after the bombardment, one being seen over our lines at 7.7.50, 8.45.and 9 a.m., being driven off each time by anto aircraft guns.

A quiet afternoon and evening. Weather fine and warm.

Reconnaissance was made to find the best route for supports and reserve to come up in case of necessity.

Casualties Indian Ranks Killed 2 (one 1/39 and one 2/39) Wounded 1 (Burma Police.

	2/39th			1/39th		
	K.	W.	M.	K.	W.	M.
B.O's.	2	-	1	-	-	-
" attached.	-	1	-	-	-	-
I.O's.	3	5	1	1	-	-
" attached.	-	-	-	-	-	-
O.R.I.	92	334	21	1	3	-
" attached						
Dogras.	8	8	8			
" = Burma Police	1	2	-			
	106	350	31	2	3	-

2-5-1915.
Trenches
NEUVE CHAPELLE.

A quiet night. Cloudy morning but weather mild. C.O. went round front line trenches at 6.30.a.m.

2-5-1915
(continued)

A quiet day with very shell fire. Slight rain commenced at 3 p.m. and weather became cloudy and cold.
Sound of very heavy cannonading heard towards North at 4 p.m.
Casualties Indian Ranks Wounded 4 (one 1/39 three 2/39).

Total to date.

	2/39			1/39		
	K.	W.	M.	K.	W.	M.
B.O's.	2	-	1	-	-	-
" attached.	-	1	-	-	-	-
I.O's.	3	5	1	1	-	-
" attached.	-	-	-	-	-	-
O.R.I.	92	337	21	1	4	-
attached Dogras.	8	8	8			
" Burma Police.	1	2	-			
	106	353	31	2	4	-

3-5-1915
Trenches
NEUVE CHAPELLE.

Fine morning, and warm day. A quiet day on the whole. The enemy shelled the gunner observation house in rear of trenches during the morning and dropped a few shells in the vicinity of some unoccupied reserve trenches in rear of our line in the afternoon, but no damage was done. Arrangements were made to establish visual signalling in case the telephone wires should be broken by shell fire etc., at any time.
Heavy guns bombarded the enemys trenches opposite our lines at 6.30 p.m. for about an hour.
Some rain fell during the night and weather was colder.
Casualties Indian Ranks Wounded 2 (one 1/39 one 2/39).(while on working party in support trenches)
News was also received of the death in hospital on 1st May from wounds received in action of No.445 Naik. Kedar Sing Rawat, Burma Police.

WAR DIARY
or
INTELLIGENCE SUMMARY.
(Erase heading not required.)

Army Form C. 2118.

Hour, Date, Place	Summary of Events and Information	Remarks and references to Appendices

Tatx 3-5-1915
(continued)

Total to date.

	2/39th G.			1/39th G.		
	K.	W.	M.	K.	W.	M.
B.O's.	3	1	-	4	-	-
" attached.	-	1	-	-	-	-
I.O's.	3	5	1	1	-	-
" attached.	-	-	-	1	-	-
O.R.I.	93	338	31	-	1	5
" attached Dogras.	8	8	8	-	-	-
" Burma Police.	1	3	-	-	-	-
	106	354	31	1	1 G	-

add 1.
Burma Police
died of wounds.
a subtract /m ~ recovered ~
107 353 31.

4-5-1915
Trenches
NEUVE CHAPELLE.

Cloudy morning, weather muggy. O.C. went round front line trenches during the morning. A quiet day. Rain commenced about 3 p.m., but not heavy; some rain also fell during the night. A fair amount of rifle fire during the night.

Casualties Indian Ranks Wounded 1. (Burma Police).

Total to date.

	2/39th G.			1/39th G.		
	K.	W.	M.	K.	W.	M.
B.O's.	3	1	-	-	-	-
" attached.	-	1	-	-	-	-
I.O's.	3	5	1	-	-	-
" attached.	-	-	-	1	-	-
O.R.I.	93	338	31	1	-	5
attached Dogras.	8	8	8	-	-	-
" Burma Police.	3	2	-	-	-	-
	107	354	31	2	5	-

Instructions regarding War Diaries and Intelligence Summaries are contained in F.S. Regs., Part II. and the Staff Manual respectively. Title pages will be prepared in manuscript.

5-5-1915
Trenches
NEUVE CHAPELLE.

Cloudy morning, weather muggy. Orders were received for the 59th Scinde Rifles to relieve the Southern Section (No.3 Coy.) of C Subsection, and the Manchester Regiment to relieve the Northern Section (No.3 Coy.). The C.O's of there regiments arrived at Battalion Head-Quarters at 10 a.m., to look round trenches. The C.O. was summoned to Brigade Headquarters at 11 a.m.

Rain commenced at midday, but was not very heavy. The enemy fired a few big shells about midday at gunner observation Station in NEUVE CHAPELLE; and again at 3.50.p.m. at houses in the village in vicinity of 2/3rd G.R., Headquarters.

Guides were sent to POINT LOGY to direct the Manchester Regiment and 59th Rifles to the trenches from POINT LOGY.

The guide was to meet the Manchesters at 8.p.m., but they did not arrive till after 10 o'clock, delays having occurred en route from block of transport etc., The 59th Scinde Rifles were due at 10.45 p.m., but did not arrive till about 1 a.m., after considerable delay the relief was effected and the last Company to be relieved left the trenches at 2.15 a.m.

The Regiment was billetted in two large farms in the LORETTO road, the last Company reaching there at 3.30.a.m.

Casualties Wounded Indian Ranks 1 (2/39thG.)
Total to date.

	2/39th G.			1/39th G.		
	K.	W.	M.	K.	W.	M.
B.O's.	3	-	1	-	-	-
" attached.	-	1	-	-	-	-
I.O's.	3	5	1	1	-	-
" attached.	-	-	-	-	-	-
O.R.I.	92	339	31	1	5	-
attached Dogras.	8	8	8	-	-	-
" Burma Police.	2	2	-	-	-	-
	107	355	31	2	5	-

6-5-1915
Billets.
LORETTO ROAD.

Muggy day. All B.O's went up to RUE du BOIS during the day to reconnoitre the ground and trenches in vicinity.

H.R.H. The Prince of Wales paid an informal visit to the Battalion during the afternoon. He just came in and was introduced to the British Officers and a few Native Officers. He asked the C.O. several questions concerning the regiment, and asked the C.O. to tell the Native Officers that he was very pleased to come and see them and congratulated them on the way the regiment had worked.

7-5-1915
Billets
LORETTO ROAD.

Fine dull morning, with rain in the evening.
Nothing special to record.
Operation Orders were received but subsequently cancelled.

8-5-1915
Billets
LORETTO ROAD.

Dull misty morning. Sounds of French bombardment near ARRAS heard by, it was rumoured 14 Divisions and 2000 guns on a front of 7 miles.

Commanding Officer accompanied the G.O.C. Brigade in a motor to Divisional Head quarters to attend a conference regarding the operations pending and regarding the special Detachment he was to command for the attack on the BOIS du BIEZ,

Operation orders received for operations next day.

8-5-1915
Trenches.

Regiment left billets at Farm in Loretto Road and passed X roads at Sq.M 27D at 10 p.m. Thence to PONT LOGY and via communication trench into position at G.I. North of RUE DE BOIS, where we arrived at 12.30 a.m. See General and special Ideas. Casualties Indian Ranks

	2/39th			1/39th G.		
	K.	W.	M.	K.	W.	M.
B.O's.	2	-	1	-	-	-
" attached.	-	1	-	-	-	-
I.O's.	3	5	1	1	-	-
" attached.	-	-	-	-	-	-
O.R.I.	92	340	21	1	5	-
attached Dogras.	8	8	8	-	-	-
" Burma Police.	2	2	-	-	-	-
	107	356	31	2	5	-

9-5-1915
Trenches.

Bombardment started at 5 a.m. 1st attack by Dehra Dun Brigade was held up, 2nd attack by Brigade was held up, this being launched at 7 a.m. A second bombardment was then ordered for 3 p.m. till 3.40 and an attack was then made by the Bareilly Brigade. This was also held up owing to the number of machine guns the enemy brought into play. Heavy shells fire was directed on to our line and the trenches occupied by the battalion for continuous period of 13 hours. Shelling by both sides ceased at 6 p.m. After which slight intermittent fire supervened. Battalion remained in its present trenches this night.

All available stretcher bearers were sent up to bring in wounded from main fire trench.

Casualties. 1.B.O.Killed (Major Woods.I.M.S.) 2 B.O.wounded, Capt.Berryman, 2nd Lieut.Saunders.I.A.R., G.O's. Wounded Subr.Gopi Sing Rawat, Jemadar Pancham Sing Mahar, Teg Sing Kaphola, Jura Sing Negi, and Kashi Sing Negi (Tehri Coy.) and O.R.I.2 Killed and 94 Wounded.

9-5-1915
(continued)

Total to date.

	2/39th.			1/39th.		
	K.	W.	M.	K.	W.	M.
B.O's.	3	1	1	-	-	-
" attached.	-	2	-	-	-	-
I.O's.	3	9	1	1	-	-
" attached.	-	1	-	-	-	-
O.R.I.	93	394	21	2	36	-
" attached Dogras.	8	8	8	-	-	-
" Burma Police.	2	9	-	-	-	-
" Tehri S.M.	-	2	-	-	-	-
	109	426	31	3	36	-

10-5-1915.
Trenches.

Fine clear day. Battalion was ordered to move into front line trenches on left of 2/Leicesters and to cover the orchard frontage with a view to making up attack at 3 p.m. on V.6., the enemy's redoubt in our front. This attack was to be preceded by a bombardment from 11 a.m. - 3 p.m. Operations were cancelled and night attack arranged for. This was also cancelled at 4 p.m., and battalion was withdrawn from front line and put in the ORCHARD redoubt in support of the 3rd London. Casualties OR/men wounded. 11

Enemy shelled orchard in evening at 5 - 6.p.
Total Casualties to date.

	2/39th			1/39th		
	K.	W.	M.	K.	W.	M.
B.O's.	3	1	1	-	-	-
" attached.	-	2	-	-	-	-
I.O's.	3	9	1	1	-	-
" attached.	-	1	-	-	-	-
O.R.I.	93	399	21	2	41	-
" attached Dogras.	8	8	8	-	-	-
" Burma Police.	2	10	-	-	-	-
" Tehri S.M.	-	2	-	-	-	-
	109	432	31	3	41	-

11-5-1915
Trenches.

Fine spring day. Slight firing during day. Battalion remained in support in trenches in rear of 3rd Londons. Wounded 4 Riflemen, by shell fire.

Total Casualties up to date.

	2/39th			1/39th G.		
	K.	W.	M.	K.	W.	M.
B.O's.	3	1	1	-	-	-
" attached.	-	2	-	-	-	-
I.O's.	3	9	1	1	-	-
" attached.	-	1	-	-	-	-
O.R.T.	93	402	21	2	42	-
" attached Dogras.	8	8	8	-	-	-
" Burma Police.	2	10	-	-	-	-
" Tehri S+M		2				
	109	435	31	3	42	-

12-5-1915.
Trenches.

Fine day. Quiet night. Captain Gatherer and 4 men reconnoitred ditch in front of main fire trench with a view to bridging same in attack. Enemy was seen repairing his wire entanglement; Maxim Gun fire opened on enemy. Enemy shelled as usual, RUE DE BOIS and our orchard between 10 and 11 a.m. Captain Wilcox and 1 man killed 15 men wounded. C.O. and Adjutant in accordance with G.O.C's orders observed effect of 100 high explosive howitzer shells on enemy's parapet. The object being to break same. Resultant effect practically nil. Certain points were also bombarded by 9.2.guns result of which was not seen by us.

Casualties. Killed B.O.1, O.R.1. wounded 15

Total to date.

	2/39th.			1/39th.		
	K.	W.	M.	K.	W.	M.
B.O's.	4	1	1	-	-	-
" attached.	-	2	-	-	-	-
I.O's.	3	9	1	1	1	-
" attached.	-	1	-	-	-	-
O.R.I.	94	410	21	3	43	-
" attached Dogras.	8	8	8	-	-	-
" Burma Police.	2	12	-	-	-	-
" Tehri S+M.		6				
	111	449	31	4	44	-

13-5-1915
Trenches.

Rainy to day with heavy clouds. Attack on V.6., redoubt, preceded by bombardment for 36 hours, was ordered for night of 14/15 May. In afternoon battalion was withdrawn from ORCHARD and put into trenches in rear of R.E. Depot with a view to resting it a little after the continuous shelling of the last 6 days. Enemy shelled intermittently through out the day whilst our guns concentrated steadily on V.6 to break parapet there and destroy obstacles.

Battalions Headquarters were in dug out on RUE DE BOIS.

Casualties to day 1 G.O. Wounded, 4 O.R.I. Killed and 10 Wounded.

	2/39th			1/39th		
	K.	W.	M.	K.	W.	M.
B.O's.	4	1	1	-	-	-
" attached	-	2	-	-	-	-
I.O's.	3	10	1	1	1	-
" attached.	-	1	-	-	-	-
O.R.I.	95	415	21	3	48	-
" attached Dogras.	8	8	8	-	-	-
" Burma Police.	2	12	-	-	-	-
" Tehri S+M.						
	112.	455.	31.	4.	49.	-

14-5-1915
Trenches.

Weather fine and rainy. Contemplated attack on V.6. was postponed for 24 hours and orders were received that it would be made at 11.30. p.m. the night of 15th instant. The artillery bombardment which had been normal, but continuous was to cease at 11.25 p.m. At 3 p.m. orders were received for battalion to move down into trenches between Windy Corner and Lansdowne Post for a day's rest. Arrived these at 5 p.m., the distance there to from the firing line being about 1400', Lieut. A.H. Mankelow was killed to day by a shell which exploded near bomb guns. Captain R.G.T. Gatherer (attached from 2/10th G.R.) slightly wounded by shrapnel in leg. 1 G.O. 4 O.R.I. Wounded.

Total Casualties to date.

14-5-1915.
(continued)

	2/39th.			1/39th.		
	K.	W.	M.	K.	W.	M.
B.O's.	4	1	1	1	-	-
" attached.	-	3	-	-	-	-
I.O's.	3	10	1	1	2	-
" attached.	-	1	-	-	-	-
O.R.I.	95	435	21	5	64	1
" attached Dogras.	8	8	8			
" Burma Police.	5	15	-			
" Tehri S&M		7				
	115	480	31	7	66	1

15-5-1915.
Trenches.

Remained till 7.30 p.m., in trenches by WINDY CORNER. Enemy shelled us and the vicinity vicinity intermittently all day, one of which struck the house where Battalion Headquarters were located. Several premature burst occurred over these trenches and Headquarters from our own guns of which there was a battery 400 - 500 in rear of us. Two of these shells burst in the small courtyard of Headquarters house.

Battalion moved by Companies at 7.50 p.m. This throgh CRESCENT communication trench and took up position in accordance with Brigade operation orders received at noon to day. The Garhwal Rifles were on the left with a x frontage of about 60ˣ, the 2/Leicesters on the right with a frontage of about 100ˣ, supported by 3rd Londons, and 2/3rd G.R., respectively. C. and D.Coys. under Lieut. Rogers were in the front line by platoons and filed out thro' the outlets made the previous night by the S.& M. They crossed the stream (average width 8') by 8' bridges which had been previously placed in position. E. and F.Coys. under Lieut.Fox, were formed into platoons and E.Coy. filed out so as to take post between the parapet and the stream an average distance of 5ˣ F.Coy. remaining ready in fire trench to advance over the parapet, G.H.A.B.Coys. were formed up in the open ground in rear of the rear parapet, ready to advance in support.

Captain Etherton acting Adjutant was detailed by the C.O. to place the bridges over the stream and owing to the lateness in arram arriving of the Company from which

15-5-1915
(continued)

4 men had been detailed to assist, one man was asked for from the 3rd Londons to help Captain Etherton. Whilst moving up the communication trench a shell exploded amongest the bomb boxes carriers of "A" Coy., all of whom were killed or wounded. At 11.30.p.m the attack was launched but owing to heavy rifle fire and to the enemy bringing up 2 machine guns it could not be pressed. The attack proceded, F.Coy., was launched over the parapet and ½ H.Coy. Eventually. However as the attack quite failed it was not pressed further in force of such heavy fire, and so no more Companies were sent out, as the enemy too employed a search light which lit up the whole line of our fire trench and line of our advance.

Previously to the attack a considerable amount of firing was heard on our extreme left by the LAHORE DIVISION, who were occupying the trenches E of NEUVE CHAPELLE. What they were firing at was not apparent, but it was a great nuisance as it caused the Germans to reply and send up innumerable flares which lit up the surroundings and made the placing out of the bridges a matter of greater danger and difficulty. A request was made by the Brigade to Division to have it stopped which was eventually done, as being fire abnormal to what was of nightly occurrence, was absolutely of no use and caused the Germans to be on the greater "qui vive."

After the failure of the 1st attack, orders were received for the 3rd Londons to relieve the Garhwal Rifles in fire trench and for them to make another attack which was to be preceded by an artillery bombardment, at 3.15 a.m. The Battalion was accordingly withdrawn to the orchard and Companies reorganised which was a matter of some difficulty as a certain amount of admixture of Companies had occurred during the operations and owing to the remnants of C.D.E. and F Coys., being withdrawn back to the fire trench and the enemy shelling the orchard very heavily. The Battalion was ordered to support the 3rd London attack. This attack however when launched was no more successful than the first one. In combination with the 3rd London attack, the 2/3rd Gurkhas were to cooperate and advance in place of the 2/Leicesters to the attack with the London regiment. It was quite light now and nothing more could be done. The Battalion was withdrawn in the early

~~morning to the assembly~~

15-5-1915
(continued)

morning to the assembly trenches near the RUE DE BOIS where it remained till 8.15.p.m., when in accordance with orders it withdrawn and marched to bivouc in trenches near CROIX BARBEE.
    Casualties during the day were Lieut. G.S.Rogers, wounded, Jemadar Padam Sing Rawat, and Tilok Sing Sauntiyal wounded, 4 men Killed 136 Wounded, and 11 Missing.

Total *to date*:

	2/39th.			1/39th G.		
	K.	W.	M.	K.	W.	M.
B.O's.	4	1	1	1	1	-
" attached.	-	3	-	-	-	-
I.O's.	3	10.	1	1	2	-
" attached.	-	1	-	-	-	-
O.R.I.	99	499	26	5	115	6
" attached Dogras.	8	8	8	-	-	-
" Burma Police.	5	23	-	-	-	-
" Tehri S.& M.	-	20	1	-	-	-
	119.	565	37	7.	118	6

16-5-1915
Bivouac Trenches B2.
~~Croix Barbee~~ RUE du BOIS

    Battalion moved into B 2., assembly trenches. Moderate shelling. Left assembly trenches N. of RUE DE BOIS at 8.15.p.m. and arrived in above bivouac at 8.50.p.m. Only leaky shelters. Captain Burton rejoined Battalion. Also 147 reinforcements of chiefly Burma Police.
    Casualties. 2 G.Os + 10. O.R.9 wounded.

Total Casualties to date:-

	2/39th.			1/39th.		
	K.	W.	M.	K.	W.	M.
B.O's.	4	1	1	1	1	-
" attached.	-	3	-	-	-	-
I.O's.	3	11.	1	1	3	-
" attached.	-	1	-	-	-	-
O.R.I.	99	503	26	5	121.	6
" attached Dogras.	8	8	8	-	-	-
" Burma Police.	5	23	-	-	-	-
" Tehri S.& M.	-	20	1	-	-	-
	119.	570	37	7.	125.	6

17-5-1915
Bivouac, CROIX BARBEE.

Dull rainy day with mud everywhere. Remained in bivouac till 5.15.p.m., when battalion moved into billets close by.

18-5-1915
Billets
CROIX BARBEE.

Very heavy rain during the night and roads very muddy. A few shells dropped rather near Battalion Head Quarters.

19-5-1915
Billets
CROIX BARBEE.

Dull and rainy day. Quiet and nothing doing. Rest of Brigade went into the trenches and occupied the line from ORCHARD inclusive to CINDER TRACK inclusive S. of RUE DE BOIS and RICHEBOURG L' AVOUE. 2/8th G.R., being withdrawn to billets as Brigade reserve and the battalion acting as Divisional Reserve. Captain Kunhardt, 74th Punjabis, and 2nd Lieut. Lamb, I.A.R. joined as reinforcements.

20-5-1915.
Billets
CROIX BARBEE.

Fine day. Battalion still in Divisional Reserve, nothing special to record. Heavy artillery firing during afternoon. Guards Brigade attacking.
A Coy., went out to clear the battle field S. of RUE DU BOIS. Owing to heavy casualties among Garhwali officers and Non-Commissioned Officers, great difficulty is experienced is filling up the vacancies by suitable men. This was represented to Divisional & Corps Commanders.

20-5-1915
(continued)

To ease the difficulty the C.O. formed the number of men present into 3 Companies only dividing up No.2 Company being the smallest among the others, making each a strength of 182 - 185 - 190 respectively, strength of the amalgamated Battalion being 11 British Officers, 6 Garhwali officers, and 554 O.R. I. 2nd Lieut. Tibbs. I.A.R., was taken to acting as Brigade Bomb Gun Officer vice Lieut. Mankelow, 1/39th G. Killed in action on 14-5-15.

21-5-1915
Billets
CROIX BARBEE.

A dull cloudy day; Heavy rain later and consequently much mud. Lieut. Collins from 9th G.R. arrived today, to be attached to the Battalion as a Platoon Commander and was posted to No.3 Company.

22-5-1915
Billets.
CROIX BARBEE.

Fine dull day, somewhat muggy and warm.
Sounds of much firing during the night.
Companies went for route march and paraded for such work as could be done near billets.
Captain Etherton, 1/39th G., was transferred to B.F.A., with a slight attack of measles.
Captain Burton was lent to a Brigade of the Highland Division for instructional purposes temporarily and left Battalion to join.
Heavy thunder storm during the night.

23-5-1915.
Billets CROIX BARBEE.

Fine day and clearer after the thunderstorm but hot. Country dries up after rain.
Companies paraded under Company Commanders. Signallers under senior N.C.O.
Lieut. F.N.Fox joined Battalion Head Quaretrs to act as Adjutant vice Captain Etherton, and Captain Harbord took over Command of No.1 Company vice Captain Burton temporarily lent to Highland Division.
Enemy shelled Batteries near Battn Head Quaretrs a bit during f renoon.
2 Companies proceeded at 8 p.m. to clear up battlefield and bury the dead.

24-5-1915.
Billets CROIX BARBEE.

Fine day. Sounds of firing in the night. 3 shells fell very close to Battn Head Quarers about 7 p.m. in the orchard.
Batteries by Battn Head Quarters shelled in the morning some falling rather close.
Day turned out very hot. Ground drying up quickly.
Major Battine Intelligence Corps I.A.Corps Head Qrs, called to ask for details regarding the numbers of Burma Military Police, Tehri Sappers, etc the Regiment was now composed of, also for a short narrative account of Rif. Gobar Sing Negi V.C. 2nd Battalion and Naik Darwan sing Negi V.C. 1st Battalion, which were sent him.
Received orders to relieve the 2nd Leicester, tomorrow evening in A sub section from Cinder Track exclusive to the Copse inclusive S.of RUE DU BOIS.
Sounds of heavy artillery firing about 9.p.m.

25-5-1915.
Billets
CROIX BARBEE.

Fine hot day. C.O. went out to see O.C.Lecisters to arrange details of taking over A subsection to night British Officers Commanding Companies, also went out and saw the

25-5-1915
(Continued)

portion of fire trench they each had to takeover. A certain amount of shelling was going on. Aid post was established at WINDY CORNER. 2 Companies were in fire line trench and supports 1 Company in Reserve by Bn. Head quarters with 1 Coy. Leicesters. Battalion Head Quarters was in a sandbag dug out behind a small ruined house near and N.of RUE DU BOIS. 2/3rd G.R., were on our left in B.Sub-section with 1 Company 3rd Londons in the ORCHARD. The relief was completed in an hour and a half very expeditiously, and would have been even quicker if Companies, which started at 10 minutes interval, the first at 5.p.m.,had not been blocked by troops of another Brigade and transport. If seemed as if every other Brigade was being relieved too judging by the block.

Two attacks were made one at 6.30 p.m.and one at 9 p.m.by the 47th London Division and Canadian Division opposite FESTUBERT and some advance made.

26-5-1915.
Trenches
RUE DU BOIS.

Fine morning. Rather cool in the early morning 47th London Division gained 3 points in the German Trenches only of artillery firing in the night.
At 4.30 a.m. a German aeroplane came over and was fired at by Anti Air-craft guns., some of ours went up and were fired at by Germans with rifles. The engine of one stopped, and would appear to have been hit for it turned and came down in our lines.
Slight shelling during morning and Bn Hd Qrs was hit by a howitzer shell and only saved by remains of a roof which still remained near dug out. One orderly slightly struck while under cover but not returned as wounded.

Hour, Date, Place	Summary of Events and Information

27-5-1915
Trenches
RUE DU BOIS
—
RICHEBOURG
L'AVOUE.
	Cloudy morning with signs of rain. Heavy Artillery fire heard to the S.towards ARRAS at 3.a.m. C.O. went round the trenches in the early morning. Shelling began about 8 a.m., at the usual objects of the Factory and houses on the RUE DU BOIS, all of which now present a sorry spectacle being shelled to ruins. Information was sent to Brigade and our heavy guns were turned on and they ceased firing, but commenced again later at 2.p.m., and put a few on our left on RUE DU BOIS, and the rest in direction of RUE des BERGEAUX. Portion of our parapet in front line was damaged by shell fire.
	    Heavy firing again heard in direction of ARRAS from 2.p.m.onwards.
	    Weather cleared up later, but a coldish wind blew. Italy it was announced had declared war on Austria. Captain BURTON rejoined from his temporary duty with 124th Brigade.

28-5-1915
Trenches
RUE DU BOIS
RICHEBOURG.L'AVOUE.
	Dull cold day with wind. Quiet night, little or no firing. Rumour received that enemy were massing in front of P.10 away on our right towards in front of the Orchard near INDIAN VILLAGE to E. and all were cautioned. Owing to the late successes our line from FESTUBERT northwards has advanced a good deal, only got hung R - up by one or two strong points as fortified farms of FERME du BOIS and FERME du COUR D'AVOUE.
	    Still sounds of heavy artillery fire head in direction of ARRAS.
	    Received instructions regarding wearing and care of respirators for use against xxxxxxxxxx Poision gas.
	    C.O. went round fire trenches during the night, all quiet. Work was continued on the communication trench which had been knocked in.

29-5-1915
Trenches
RUE DU BOIS.

Fine day and much warmer. The wind having died down.

G.O.C. came round trenches in forenoon. Enemy started shelling, so information was sent to Brigade who arranged for our guns to fire no other incidents to record, absolutely no rifle fire during the day and little during the night. German front trench in our immediate front does not appear to be held or if held only by very few men in the day. Perhaps owing to the western portion of their fire trench near V.1. having been taken by us, they may have retired to their second line, only holding their front line just here very lightly. In front of the Bois de Biez, they are very strongly entrenched with 2 rows of trenches and wire entanglements and much more sniping and firing goes on in that front as we found when the Battalion was holding the trenches there.

Work was continued on strengthening the fire parapet and improving the communication trenches, aided by 2 parties from 2/Leicesters to carry on work on the other two and repair of guards trench. 2 (1 ³/39 & 1 B.M.P.) Wounded

Casualties O.R.I. Killed one (Rifle fire)(²/³⁹)
Total casualties to date.

	2/39th.			1/39th.		
	K.	W.	M.	K.	W.	M.
B.O's.	4	1	1	1	1	-
" attached.	-	3	-	-	-	-
I.O's.	3	11	1	1	3	-
attached.	-	1	-	-	-	-
O.R.I.	100	504	26	5	121	6
" attached Dogras.	8	8	8	-	-	-
" " Burma Police.	6	23	-	-	-	-
" " Tehri S.& M.	-	20	1	-	-	-
	121.	571	37	7	125.	6

30-5-1915
Trenches
RUE DU BOIS.

Dull morning but cleared up later with a cold W wind. Quiet night though the enemy sent up a few more flares and sniped a bit more than usual.
Recommended that Guards trench being so knocked about and insanitary be abandoned and a fresh one as 2nd Line be dug 30 or so ahead with a better field of fire. Enemy appear to be strengthening their line very much opposite V.2, making a sort of redoubt there.
Received instruction to be ready for relief to night as though no definite had there been received, it was probable we might be relieved. Our Artillery shelled certain points in enemy's line as usual.
Sounds of heavy artillery fire towards ARRAS during the day.
Received further intimation that the Battalion would be relieved tomorrow night.
Casualties O.R.I. Wounded 3 (Shell fire)(1/39$)
Total casualties to date.

	2/39th.			1/39th.		
	K.	W.	M.	K.	W.	M.
B.O's.	4	1	1	1	1	-
" attached.	-	3	-	-	-	-
I.O's.	3	11	1	1	3	10
" attached.	-	1	-	-	-	-
O.R.I.	100	504	26	5	124	6
" attached Dogras.	8	8	8	-	-	-
" " Burma Police.	6	23	-	-	-	-
" " Tehri S.&.M.	-	20	1	-	-	-
	121	571	37	7	128	6

31-5-1915
Trenches
RUE DU BOIS
RICHEBOURG
L'AVOUE

Fine day though very cold at night and for the time of the year.
Sounds of heavy artillery fire towards ARRAS at 3.a.m.

31-5-1915
(continued)

German aeroplane came towards our lines at 4.45.a.m. but was driven off by anti aircraft guns.
Orders came for us to be relieved by the 57 (Wildes) Rifles to night. Enemy shelled our trenches during the night. We shelled theirs in the hope of catching working parties out, which they have nightly working on a new strong line they are making from V.2 to FERME DU BOIS.
Orders regarding relief were changed to 4th London Regiment relieving us instead of 57th Rifles and later still after all arrangements had been made regarding taking over orders were again changed and our front ordered to be taken over by 4 different units. The 57th Rifles, 4th Londons, 129th Baluchies, and Connaught Rangers, and this order only came 9.30.p.m. In consequence delay was experienced and owing to so many reliefs going on at the same time, 4/London arrived 2 hours late and relief was not funished till 1.30.a.m. A good deal of shelling and shipping occurred owing to the noise which always seems to occur when we are relieved by a British unit and the enemy sent a lot of Howitzer and shrapnel shell over to WINDY CORNER.
Last Company reached billets at VIELLE CHAPELLE 2.30.a.m.

Serial No. 98.

121/6128

WAR DIARY
OF
1/39th Garhwal Rifles.

From 1st June 1915. To 30th June 1915.

2/39- Garhwal Rifle

WAR DIARY or INTELLIGENCE SUMMARY.
(Erase heading not required.)

Army Form C. 2118.

1-6-1915
Billets
VIELLE CHAPELLE.

Fine day, warm and dusty, though cool in the wind and shade. Remained all day here and received orders to go to our new billets near cross road Square M.28.d., which were vacated by the 2nd Black Watch and very much better. Left at 7.p.m., and marched the short distance there, about 1 mile. Billets a bit scattered along the road, which is unavoidable.

The French have made further progress south and captured ABLAIN.

2-6-1915
Billets
RUE MARSY
VIELLE CHAPELLE.

Fine hot day. C.O's. went in to Brigade Headquarters at 9.45.a.m., to meet the L.G.C.Division at LES LOBES. As Colonel Drake Brockman was not well Captain Burton, Offg.2nd-in-Command went instead. Parades were held under Officers Commpanding Companies near billets and men settled down into their billets.

3-6-1915.
Billets
RUE MARSY
VIELLE CHAPELLE.

Fine hot day, and somewhat cloudy.
Birth day of His Majesty's King George.
Companies went for bathing at ZELOBES in turns and in the evening for a route march muster parade and inspection of Companies inturn by C.O.during the day.

Running drill every morning for 15 minutes under Platoon Commanders and ordinary parade afterwards under Coy. Commanders were held. Some shelling during the night was heard.

Captain Etherton rejoined from Hospital today.

Jemr. Balbhadar Sing Gusain rejoined with a few men.

4-6-1915
Billets
RUE DU MARYS
VIEILLE CHAPELLE.

Dull cloudy day with signs of rain, 200 men went out last night as a working party under Lieut. Lamb, and Rana Jodha Jang Bahadur, got back 3.a.m.

5-6-1915
Billets
RUE DU MARYS
VIEILLE CHAPELLE.

Fine day and hot and dusty.
Companies paraded as usual, and went for a route march.
A German aeroplane came over today 11.a.m., at a great height, and another earlier in the morning which was fired at.
Orders received for Garhwal Brigade to go into the trenches on night of 7/8th June.

6-6-1915
Billets
RUE DU MARYS
VIEILLE CHAPELLE.

Fine hot day.
British Officers went out to see Support trenches where the Battalion is to be located tomorrow night, in support of 2/Leicesters and 2/3rd G.R., in firing line.
Companies practised with proper bombs, French pattern, jam pot, and hair brush pattern in the afternoon.

7-6-1915
Billets
RUE DU MARYS
VIELLE CHAPELLE.

Fine hot day.
Sent 1st Line off to new billets in VIELLE CHAPELLE, 2nd Line Wagons came at 10.a.m., were loaded up and went off.
Very heavy artillery fire audible all yesterday and to day to the South.
Left billets 9.p.m.and arrived Headquarters 6th Jats at 10.p.m. Relief was completed by 10.25.p.m. Very expeditiously a fair amount of sniping going on, chiefly on the left.

8-6-1915
Bivouac
Trenches,
near
RUE DES BERCEAUX.

Fine hot day. Clouded over later with thunderstorms and heavy rain which cooled the atmosphere, which was getting very hot and oppressive.
Some shelling with field guns was commenced at 6.30.a.m., apparently searching for the battery in rear of us. The first few shells fell quite close to Battalion Headquarters, just the other side of the road. Whole Battalion ordered out on digging a communication trench during the night.
Later on about 2.p.m., orders were received to take over the front held by the H.L.I., of Sirhind Brigade and 3rd Londons to relieve us and C.O. went over to arrange matters. This was subsequently cancelled at 4.p.m.and orders for the fatigue party, half in each subsection were received to complete 2 communication trenches, one in each subsection.
Some heavy artillery fire on our part took place in the afternoon which quieted down by 6.p.m.
Casualties O.R.I. Wounded 1 (Burma Police)
Total casualties to date.

	2/39th G.			1/39th G.		
	K.	W.	M.	K.	W.	M.
B.O's.	4	1	1	1	1	-
" attached.	-	3	-	-	-	-
I.O's.	3	11	1	1	3	-
" attached.	-	1	-	-	-	-
O.R.I.	100	504	26	5	124	6
" " Dogras.	8	8	8			
" " B.M.P.	6	34	-			
" " Tehri S.& M.	-	20	1			
	121	572	37.	7	128	6.

9-6-1915
Bivouac
Trenches.
Near RUE DES
BERCEAUX.

Fine day, a bit cloudy and considerably cooler after the thunderstorm of yesterday.

The flies are getting very bad. This is not to be wondered at considering every French farm is built in the form of a square with a pit in the centre into which is thrown all their measure and filth. Orders have been issued to clear these out and to cover them over with earth much to disgust of the owners where they are present as this "midden" is a great asset to them for their fields. Also the water supply is a great problem. There are only pumps in each farm and as there are situated close to and the "midden" and sometimes to the water closet, it is not to be wondered at that the water supply is nearly in all cases Contaminated. Some houses do not even have pumps but get their water from the road side ditch. All water is treated with chloride of lime.

The Battalion has only had one case of enteric to date, which speaks bolumes for the sanitation and health of the men.

There have been some cases of measles and mumps at times.

Another problem which is getting acute is sanitation in the trenches. As these are held now for a considerable time, the area in the immediate vicinity is getting somewhat insanitary owing to the number of latrines that have been dug rather close, as you can not get very far back behind fire trench as you would have no cover. This is due in a great many cases thro' some regiments when occupying the trenches in not sappering out properly a short distance methodically and digging a deep hole and filling up when necessary and sappering out again a bit further.

The removal system with salt, iron, buckets is not under consideration, but this is a great difficulty with Indian troops unless you have the regimental sweepers up in the fire trenches to do the job. They are however followers, and would be in the way there and their presence not altogether desirable. They could of course be sent up each evening but that might not be enough. Moreover they are scarerly enlisted or paid to go into the firing line. Again Medical Officers seen divided in their opinion as to the soundness of the plan. And moreover to be made cover, a sap must run out to the pit where the night soil has to be thrown.

9-6-1915
(continued)

C.O. went in to Brigade Head Quarters to see G.O.C., with other C.O's., talked on points noted at Divisional confrence. Chiefly sanitation and use of gas helmets.
Enemy again shelled WINDY CORNER with heavy howitzer probably 8 inch ones., and shrapnel towards RICHEBOURG in the afternoon.
Thunder in the evening and rain set in about 5.30.p.m.
Battalion ordered out digging again in two parties as last night, on the 2 communication trenches.

10-6-1915
Bivouac
Trenches
Near RUE DES BERCEAUX.

Dull rainy day and misty, rather like a day in the rains in India.
Very quiet day. Little shelling one or two falling near Battalion Head Quarters in the morning and evening. Major Battine of Army Corps Intelligence Corps came round to see Colonel Drake Brockman on one or two points concerning the Battalion.
Whole Battalion ordered out on digging in D.Sub-Section to night. Officers incharge went to Headquarters 2/Leicesters to see place and arrange.
Casualties O.R.I. Wounded 2 (1. BMP.
1 Tehri).

Total casualties to date.

	2/39th G.			1/39th G.		
	K.	W.	M.	K.	W.	M.
B.O's.	4	1	1	1	1	-
" attached.	-	3	-	-	-	-
I.O's.	3	11	1	1	3	-
" attached.	-	1	-	-	-	-
O.R.I.	100	504	36	5	124	6
" " Dogras.	8	8	8			
" " B.M.P.	6	26	1			
" " Tehri S.&.M.	-	21	1			
	121	574	37	7	128	6

11-6-1915
Bivouac
Trenches
Near RUE DES BERCEAUX.

Dull misty and rainy day.
Companies out digging last night had a rotten time. Mud stickly clay and water in communication trenches and rainny the greater part of the time. G.O.C. Brigade was present a portion of the time.

C.O. went over to see O.C.2/3rd G.R., regarding taking over their sub section of the Line on monday next 14th June.

A good deal of sniping last night and a maxim was particularly lively the greater part of the night, bullets passing over Battalion Head quarters. Very little shelling by enemy, due probably to bad weather for observation.

Casualties O.R.I. Wounded 1 (Burma Mily.P.).
Total casualties to date.

	2/39th G.			1/39th G.		
	K.	W.	M.	K.	W.	M.
B.O's.	4	1	1	1	1	-
" attached.	-	3	-			
I.O's.	3	11	1	1	3	-
" attached.	-	1	-			
O.R.I.	100	504	26	5	124	6
" attached Dogras.	8	8	8			
" " B.M.P.	6	26	-			
" " Tehri.	-	21	1			
	121	575	37	7	128	6

12-6-1915
Bivouac. Trenches.
Near RUE DU BERCEAUX.

Dull cloudy day. Mud and water in the communication trenches owing to the late heavy rain, is very bad and makes going very heavy. Cleared up later. C.O. went in to see G.O.C., at Head quarters at 2.30.p.m. 3 shells shrapnell hit Headquarters house while there necessitating retiring to the dug out to carry on the conversation.

Considerable shelling of our front line trenches during the day with heavy howitzers, but a good number were belived. A certain amount of damage was done to

12-6-1915
(continued)

to ~~xxxxx~~ Leicesters trench. One or two shells fell between Leicesters reserve trench and our trenches. Whole Battalion ordered out on work on communication trenches in D.Sub-Section. Shelling still continued up to 9 p.m. Though sniping was less than last night.

13-6-1915
Bivouac
Trenches
Near RUE DES
BERCEAUX.

Fine day with a cool wind.
Enemy burst 3 shells at 4.45.a.m.over Ex Battalion Head Quarters doing no damage.
British officers taking over trenches went out 3 a.m., to see 'C' Sub-Section trenches at present by 2/3rd G.R., with a view to relief on 15th possibly.
Enemy again shelled orchard to South of Battalion Head Quarters at 4.45.p.m., with shrapnel. Also small Howitzer shells at 7.p.m., on road junction N. of Battalion Head Quarters and again at 9 p.m.,
Lieut. A.E.Clarke rejoined from Sick List today.

14-6-1915
Bivouac
Trenches near
RUE DES BERCEAUX.

Fine though cloudy day with a cold East wind. Sunny later on.
Usual "hate" started in the shape of a few shrapnel shells at 5.a.m., in the same place by Battalion Head Quarters.
Bombardment of enemy's line occurred during the day.
C.O. went up with O.C.Leicesters to his Reserve trenches and after to Gunner observation post. Met G.O.C. on return at Leicesters Head Quarters.

15-6-1915.
Bivouac
Trenches
Near
RUE DES BERCEAUX.

Beautiful fine day, with cool North wind.
Sounds of heavy artillery fire still continues to the South.
Bombardment by our artillery with 9.2 howitzer of V.1., to be attacked by H.L.I., who were to work up to V.3., if possible by bombing.
Battalion ordered to stand by to fall in and move at a moments notice. Enemy put some heavy howitzer shells close to road junction 150 N. of our Head quarters, where ration carts come down to, which appears to have caused them to retreat up the road at more than 16   , juding by the noise.
Casualties. O.R.I. Wounded 1 (Shrapnell)(2/39 G.)
Total Casualties to date.

	2/39 G.			1/39 G.		
	K.	W.	M.	K.	W.	M.
B.Os.	4	1	1	1	1	-
" attached.	-	3	-			
I.O's.	3	11	1	1	3	-
" attached.	-	1	-			
O.R.I.	100	505	26	5	124	6
" attached Dogras.	8	8	8			
" " D.M.P.	6	26	-			
" " Tehri S.&.M.	-	21	1			
	121	576	37	7	128	6

16-6-1915.
Bivouac
Trenches, near
RUE DES BERCEAUX.

Beautiful fine day.
Still sounds of heavy Artillery fire to the South towards ARRAS.
Attacks on V.1.V.3. yesterday evening by Highland Light Infantry of Sirhind Brigade, Indian Army Corps, a failure. The attack further South by 2nd Canadian Brigade and 7th Division successful in parts in capturing German 1st Line Trench towards RUE D'OUVERT.
The 9.2.Howitzer apparently did not get a direct hit on the German barricade opposite our barricade at V.1., and behind their barricade, was a Machine Gun which held up

16-6-1915
(Continued)

up the bombing party.
    Very heavy artillery duel heard towards ARRAS again between 11 and 12 noon.
    4th Corps resumed its operations opposite LA BASSEE. Meerut Division artillery co-operated same as yesterday.
    9 of our aeroplanes were up in the evening reconnoitring all at one time.
    Casualties O.R.I. Wounded 1 (1/39 G.)
    Total Casualties to date.

	2/39 G.			1/39 G.		
	K.	W.	M.	K.	W.	M.
B.O's.	4	1	1	1	1	-
" attached.	-	3	-			
I.O's.	3	11	1	1	3	-
" attached.	-	1	-			
O.R.I.	100	506	26	5	125	6
" attached Dogras.	8	8	8			
" " B.M.P.	6	26	-			
" " Tehri. S.& M.	-	21	1			
	121	576	37	7	129	6

17-6-1915
Bivouac
Trenches
Near
RUE DES BERCEAUX.

    Beautiful fine day. Cool N.E, breeze. News received of some success near YRES by 2nd Army and capture of 157 Prisoners, On our right here also some first line trenches have been captured on RUE D'OUVERT.
    A German biplane came over at 8.a.m.
    Orders received to be ready for relief of 2/3rd in "C" Sub-Section. They to come here in these trenches occupied by us after relief. Londons and 2.Companies, 2/8th Gurkhas relieving the Leicesters in "D" Sub-Section.

Hour, Date, Place	Summary of Events and Information
18-6-1915 Bivouac Trenches Near Rue des Berceaux.	Fine day with strong cool breeze. Quiet night. Germans were reported massing opposite RUE DU BOIS, at 7.30.p.m., last night. No attack on our front. Attack by 4th Corps at 3.5.a.m., after a bombardment of 20 minutes. Assisted by the Meerut Divisional artillery. Subsequently intimation received that operations had been postponed for 24 hours. Received orders to relieve 2/3rd and Companies left at 9.p.m., at 5 minutes interval across country to RUE DU BOIS where guides met each and took them up. Relief was completed by 10.45.p.m.
19-6-1915 Trenches C. Sub-Section.	Fine morning though very cold for the time of the year owing to a cold N.E.Wind blowing. Work was continued on the trenches and in digging the new bit extending to the left to FARM CORNER to connect up with LONDONS on our left. Our communication trench and old British Line where our local reserve is located was shelled during the day and about 100 heavy howitzer shells were fired, but fortunately no damage done except a little to communication trench. A party of 2/8th G.R., came to work on this trench to repair and deepen etc., where necessary.
20-6-1915 Trenches.	A fine day. Cold wind. But hot and sultry later. German aeroplane came over 5.30.a.m.and cleared off when fired at. 3 sausage baloons visible today; generally only one. C.O.went round trenches and made a careful

Army Form C. 2118.

WAR DIARY or INTELLIGENCE SUMMARY.

(Erase heading not required.)

Army Form C. 2118.

Hour, Date, Place	Summary of Events and Information	Remarks and references to Appendices
20-6-1915 (continued)	careful inspection of new work going on. Discovered an orange insulated cable in a portion of new trench dug which may have been attached to a mine. It was cut as a precaution. It can easily be joined up if necessary to try and see by tapping if it is a telephone line. Very heavy artillery firing to the South during the early part of the night. Work was continued during the night on the main communication trench by a party of 2/8th G.R., and also by our supports on the new bit leading up to new fire trench. Casualties O.R.I. Wounded 2 (1/39 G.) Total casualties to date.	
21-6-1915 Trenches.	Fine cloudy day. New fire trench completed last night and occupied. It requires improving which will be done nightly. German patrols very active here in our front from Farm COUR D'AVOUE. There is a small undulation between our respective trenches which hides us from each other, aided now by the tall grass up which they and we can creep unseen. We have in addition to scouts 3 Standing Patrols out day and night. At 11.a.m. our left Standing Patrol saw a German patrol coming up a ditch or may be an old communication trench along a line of trees from the FERME DU BOIS. They fired on them and they returned the fire wounding the L.Naik., in charge. It could not be ascertained then if any of the German were hit. Their being able to come along	

Casualty table:

	2/39 G. K.	2/39 G. W.	2/39 G. M.	1/39 G. K.	1/39 G. W.	1/39 G. M.
B.O's.	4	1	1	1	1	-
" attached.	-	3	-			
I.O's.	3	11	1	1	3	-
" attached.	-	1	-			
O.R.I.	100	505	26	5	127	6
" attached Dogras	8	8	8			
" " Tehri S.& M.	-	21	1			
" " B.M.P.	6	26	-			
	121	576	37	7	131	6

21-6-1915
(continued)

in day light is due to there being such tall grass in addition to old trenches and ditches. Work continued on main communication trench.

Casualties O.R.I.1 (B.M.P.). Wounded.
Total casualties to date.

	2/39 G.			1/39 G.		
	K.	W.	M.	K.	W.	M.
B.O's.	4	1	1	1	1	-
" attached.	-	3	-			
I.O's.	3	11	1	1	3	-
" attached.	-	1	-			
O.R.I.	100	505	26	5	127	6
" attached Dogras.	8	8	8			
" " B.M.P.	6	27	-			
" , Tehri S.&.M.	-	31	1			
	121	577	37	7	131	6

22-6-1915
Trenches.

Beautiful fine day.
Germans were reported massing near Q.15, by the FERME DU BOIS, and adjacent communication trenches. Some few rounds of shrapnel were fired at them. Patrols were cautioned to be more on the a-lert and men in trenches remained ready during the night as a precaution. ½ local reserve was pushed up to support trench ready.
The Germans continued firing shrapnel every ten minutes during the night which rather interfered with the work on the main communication trench and caused 5 Casualties amongst 2/8th G.R., party working on it.
Besides our standing patrols and night picquets, 2 parties of Battalion Scouts are out nightly and Lieut. Clarke went out with one and reconnoitred vicinity of FERME COUR D'AVOUE. German patrols were encountered one and with bomb ax throwers who threw a bomb or two. Our party fired on them, and they returned the fire.
C.O. with Adjutant made a long turn of inspection of front line trenches.
Casualties O.R.I. Wounded 1.(B.M.P.)

22-6-1915.
(continued)

Total Casualties to date.

	2/39th G.			1/39th G.		
	K.	W.	M.	K.	W.	M.
B.O's.	4	1	1	1	1	0
" attached.	-	3	-			
I.O's.	3	11	1	1	3	-
" attached.	0	1	-			
O.R.I.	100	505	26	5	127	6
" attached Dogras.	8	8	8			
" " B.M.P.	6	28	-			
" " Tehri S.& M.	-	21	1			
	121	578	37	7	131	6

23-6-1915
Trenches.

Dull cloudy and rainy. It rained slightly during the night and day and cleared later.

A quiet night. Yesterday evening the Germans were heard cheering in their trenches with what object one could not make out. Perhaps to get our men to took over the parapet in curiosity and then to fire on them as they did fire along our parapet at the time.

Work was continued on the main communication trench by 2/8th, and on our new one linking up fire trench with support in revetting the same.

Special report was called for regarding a long ditch in our front, so Lieut. Clarke with scouts, was deputed to reconnoitre and report which was sent in to the Brigade in original. German patrols are pretty active in our front some with bomb throwers having been met.

Sudden orders received 4 p.m., that we were to be relieved by 2nd Gurkhas and the whole Brigade to be over a new line from R.5., to V.1. 2/8th thence to HAZARA communication trench and 3rd Londons thence to ORCHARD.

Relief was completed by 12.p.m. Sudden change meant lengthening out our line and the Indian Corps holding more and so releaving other troops for another portion of the front.

24-6-1915
Trenches
RUE DU BOIS.

Dull thundery day with rain later on.
New section was taken over. Not a nice bit. Very smelly with corpses lightly covered. Portion by V.1., opposite German barricade especially so.
This is a specially nasty bit. C.O. went round whole line carefully. Met L.G.C. Division Sir Charles Anderson and accompanied him. Also G.O.C. Brigade on return to Battalion Head quarters. Arranged for new support trench to be dug 50ˣ, in rear of our fire trench.
Casualties O.R.I. Killed 2 (1.1/39th G. and 1 Tehri S.&.M.).

Total casualties to date.

	2/39th G.			1/39th G.		
	K.	W.	M.	K.	W.	M.
B.O's.	4	1	1	1	1	
" attached.	-	3	-			
I.O's.	3	11	1	1	3	-
" attached.	-	1	-			
O.R.I.	100	505	26	6	127	6
" attached Dogras.	8	8	8			
" " B.M.P.	6	28	-			
" " Tehri S.& M.	1	21	1			
	122	578	37	8	131	6

25-6-1915
Trenches.

Dull misty day. Thunder storm and heavy rain later and in evening.
The Commanding Officer received the congratulation of the G.O.C., and Brigade on his being mentioned in dispatches and being awarded the C.M.G. Also Captain Burton, received the D.S.O. Captain Blair mentioned in dispatches and Subedar Sangram Sing Negi, 2nd Battalion, Jemadar Bishan Sing Rawat, 1st Battalion were awarded the Military Cross. Jemadar Pancham Sing Mahar, 2nd Battalion was also awarded the Military Cross, by the Field Marshal Commanding-in-Chief before. All were for NEUVE CHAPELLE battle.
Major Stewart, 2nd Battalion, Brigade Major, Garhwal Brigade was also mentioned in dispatches *and received the D.S.O.*

25-6-1915 (continued)

C.O., went round the trenches with G.O.C. Brigade and made a good inspection accompanied by C.R.E., and decided on various things to be done.

Rain set in during the evening.

Enemy shelled small orchard 100x South of Battalion Head Quarters, with howitzers about 5.30.p.m.

Casualties O.R.I. Wounded 1.(2/39th G.).

Total Casualties to date:-

	2/39th G.			1/39th G.		
	K.	W.	M.	K.	W.	M.
B.O's.	4	1	1	1	1	-
" attached.	-	3	-			
I.O's.	3	11	1	1	3	-
" attached.	-	1	-			
O.R.I.	100	506	36	6	127	6
" attached Dogras.	8	8	8			
" " B.M.P.	6	28	-			
" " Tehri S.& M.	1	21	1			
	122	579	37	8	131	6

26-6-1915
Trenches.

Fine clear day after the heavy storm & rain. Battalion Head Quarters leaked like a sieve owing to so many tiles being broken by shrapnel.

Enemy shelled FARM CORNER continuation of our section, heavily today breaking in the parapet.

Received intimation of being relieved shortly by 1/4th Black Watch. O.C. with some of his Coy Commanders came round at 9 a.m. to see Section.

German biplane came over between 10 & 11 a.m. In the evening 5 of our aeroplanes were up.

Working party of 2/3rd G.R. who are in reserve came for work on support and communication trench and did good work.

Casualties O.R.I. Killed 1 (2/39th G.).

Total casualties to date.

	2/39th G.			1/39th G.		
	K.	W.	M.	K.	W.	M.
B.O's.	4	1	1	1	1	-
" attached.	-	3	-			
I.O's.	3	11	1	1	3	-
" attached.	-	1	-			
O.R.I.	101	506	36	6	127	6
" attached Dogras.	8	8	8			
" " B.M.P.	6	28	-			
" " Tehri S.& M.	1	21	1			
	123	579	37	8	131	6

27.6.1915.
Trenches.

Dull cloudy day with rain in the evening. Quiet night.

Enemy put a dozen 4" howitzer shells in vicinity of orchard 100 yards S.of Battalion Head Quaretrs about 9 a.m. also about 12.30 p.m. Some heavy shells at chocolate menier corner and old gunner observation Post.

Commanding Officer went round trenches to see work done, and met some officers 1/4 Black Watch at Head Quaretrs, before leaving and took them round to see state of trenches, work to be done and the situation.

Notice received 5 p.m. that all orders cancelled and we would not be relieved now for 4 or more days which will make nearly a month.

Casualties O.R.I. Wounded 2 (1 1/39G. & 1 Tehri).
Total casualties to date:-

	2/39th G.			1/39th G.		
	K.	W.	M.	K.	W.	M.
B.O's	4	-	-	1	1	-
B.O's attached	-	3	-			
I.O's	3	11	1	1	1	-
" attached	-	1	-			
O.R.I.	101	506	36	6	133	6
" attached Dogras.	8	8	-			
" " B.M.P.	6	38	-			
" " Tehri S.M.	1	23	1			
	123	580	37	8	135	6

28.6.1915.
Trenches.

Dull cloudy rainy day.

Commanding Officer went round trenches and made an exhaustive inspection. From tonight in accordance with new orders the front is altered to from R5 inclusive to BOND street Communication trench, with 2 Coys 2/8G.R. holding the left bit in continuation of the Garhwal Rifles, with 2 Coys in Section Reserve in rear of Battalion Head Quarters where the 2/3rd G.R. were, the whole under Lieut.Colonel D.H.Drake Brockman C.M.G.

A lot of work is necessary on all trenches, especially fire trench. Some regiments doing absolutely

28.6.1915. (Continued)
Trenches.

absolutely nothing especially most British Regiments not even for their own comfort, safety and sanitation.
2/3rd G.R. working party of 200 men helped in new support trench last night.
Very little firing and no casualties.

29.6.1915.
Trenches.
Dull cloudy day. Cleared up in the evening but rained at night.
Received intimation that the G.O.C. had been granted leave and that the O.C. Lt.Col D.H.Drake-Brockman C.M.G. would take over command of the Brigade and Lt.Col Morris 2/8 G.R. the command of the section.
About 9.30a.m. enemy shelled orchard just N. of Battalion Head Head Quarters where now 1/2 Battalion 2/8th G.R. is located in Section reserve. 2 shrapnell shells caught some men together killing 2 and wounding 6.
Officer Commanding went in see the G.O.C. before he left on leave.
Casualties O.R.; Wounded 1.(Tehri).
Total Casualties to date:-

	2/39th G.			1/39th G.		
	K.	W.	M.	K.	W.	M.
B.O's	4	1	1	1	1	-
" attached	-	3	-			
I.O's	3	11	1	1	3	-
" attached	-	1	-			
O.R.I.	101	506	26	6	128	6
" attached Dogras.	8	8	8			
" " B.M.P.	6	28	N			
" " Tehri S.M.	1	23	1			
	123.	581.	37	8.	135.	6.

30-6-1915
Trenches.

Cloudy day with heavy rain on morning.
Working parties out last night on PALL MALL communication trench were shelled and 14 Casualties occurred among the Leicesters.
The party of 200 men of the Leicesters was unable to work on the new support trench owing to shelling by the Germans in this area from 9.p.m.to 11 p.m.
The party of S.& M.,with 30 men of No.1 Coy., worked on the bridge and trench just South of old British Line.
The supporting points off PALL MALL communication trench South of old British Line were improved by No.1 Company.
Nothing unusual to report.Slight sniping all night of 30 - 1st,day very quiet.
Casualties O.R.I.Wounded 1 (1/39th G.)
Total Casualties to date.

	2/39th G.			1/39th G.		
	K.	W.	M.	K.	W.	M.
B.O's.	4	1	1	1	1	-
" attached.	-	3	-			
I.O's.	3	11	1	1	3	-
" attached.	-	1	-			
O.R.I.	101	506	26	6	129	6
" attached Dogras.	8	8	8			
" " B.M.P.	6	28	-			
" " Tehri S.& M.	1	23	1			
	123	581	37.	8	133	6
Died of Wounds. +	3	- 3	-	+ 4	- 4	-
	126	578	37	12	129	6
	-	+ 1	-3	-	- 8	-
	126	579	34	12	121	6

Died of Wounds.
2/39th ... 1
B. M. P. ... 1
Tehri. ... 1
1/39th ... 4

Serial No. 98

12/6502.

WAR DIARY
OF
Garhwal Rifles.

From 1st July 1915. To 31st July 1915.

1-7-1915
Trenches.

Quiet day very few shots fired.
Some shelling by field guns about V.1., between 7 a.m. and 8 a.m. C.O., went round trenches from 11.a.m., till 3.p.m. New support trench going on well. There appears to be a Machine Gun or Gun emplacement 50 S.W., of V.3, as a large steel should can be seen here.
Cloudy day no rain.
Casualties O.R.I. Wounded 2 (1.1/39th G.1.B.M.P.)
Total casualties to-date:-

	2/39th G.			1/39th G.		
	K.	W.	M.	K.	W.	M.
B.O's.	4	1	1	1	1	-
" attached.	-	3	-			
I.O's.	3	11	1	1	3	-
" attached.	-	1				
O.R.I.	102	506	23	10	125	6
" attached Dogras.	8	8	8			
" " B.M.P.	7	28				
" " Tehri S.&M.	2	22	1			
	126	580	34	12	129	6

2-7-1915
Trenches.

Party of 100 Leicesters worked on new support trench and 100 Leicesters on RITZ communication trench on night of 1st-2nd. Of 44 traverses in new support trench, 17 are complete 12 almost so and 17 dug 2 feet deep and revetted 2 rows sandbags. No.4 Company shelled with heavy howitzers about 7.30.a.m. 4 men wounded and 2 hurt by falling parapet.
The working party was shelled with .77. Machine Guns intermittently from 12.30.a.m. but no casualties occurred.
At 7.30.a.m., the Junior Duck's Bill was shelled with about 40 heavy shells and 6 casualties occurred.
At 3.p.m., our right trenches were shelled with .77.M. Field Guns but no damage was done.
Enemy's snipers busy during the night of 1st-2nd.

2-7-1915
(continued)

The enemy was busy working during night on portion of his new trench S.W., of V.2.
Orders for relief by 2/3rd received in afternoon.
Casualties O.R.I.5 O.H.I.wounded (2.1/39th G., 1., 2/39th G.,2., Tehri S.&.M.)
Total casualties todate:-

	2/39th G.			1/39th G.		
	K.	W.	M.	K.	W.	M.
B.O's.	4	1	1	1	1	-
" attached.	-	3	-	-	-	-
I.O's.	3	11	1	1	3	-
" attached.	-	1	-	-	-	-
O.R.I.	102	507	23	10	120	6
" attached Dogras.	8	8	8	-	-	-
" " B.M.P.	7	28	-	-	-	-
" " Tehri S.& M.	2	24	1	-	-	-
	126	583	34	12	124	6

3-7-1915
Trenches.

Party of 2/3rd G.R., worked on PALL MALL continuation and support trench during night of 2nd-3rd.
Patrols went out as usual & located 2 German picquets, one where an old German trench cuts into the ditch at R.7., the other at junction of ditch running from R.3. towards FERME DE BOIS, and ditch from R.7., towards FERME DE BOIS. Enemy were improving their wire opposite right of No.4 Coy.
A Machine Gun was located 50' W., of V.2., this gun fires across the gap between ours and German barricades.Slight shelling only during previous 24 hours. The projection at V.1., was somewhat straightened to enable the M.G., to have a clear field of fire for 30.
C.O., went round trenches in morning. A hot day,occasionally cloudy no rain.
Casualties O.R.I.1 Killed (1/39th G.)

3-7-1915
(continued)

Total casualties todate:-

	2/39th G.			1/39th G.		
	K.	W.	M.	K.	W.	M.
B.O's.	4	1	1	1	1	-
" attached.	-	3	-			
I.O's.	3	11	1	1	3	-
" attached.	-	1	-			
O.R.I.	102	507	33	11	120	6
" attached Dogras.	8	6	8			
" " B.M.P.	7	28	-			
" " Tehri S.& M.	2	34	1			
	126	583	34	13	124	6

4-7-1915
Trenches.

Bright sunny day no rain.
Party of 300 Leicesters worked on PALL MALL continuation and new support trench. State of these now as under:-

PALL MALL revetted on East side as far as GUARDS trench, 2' to 2½' trench deep thence through RUE DE BOIS. No parados on West side anywhere.

NEW SUPPORT TRENCH. Between old British and old German lines front parapet 4½ high but needs thickening as it approaches old German line. No parados at all. 2 bays of sample supervision trench ready for Sappers to erect dug outs. South of old German line has been dug to depth of 1 foot only to within 40 yards of DEHRA DUN Brigade line.

Germans shelled our right and communication trenches in rear with 20 - 25 heavy shells about 10 of which were blind from 7 a.m., to 8 a.m. Hostile aeroplane was over at same time.

The enemy were reported by our scouts to have been working along their whole front during the night and to have been wiring the old communication trench as far as their own piquet reported yesterday at Q.7. Their new trench S.of V.2., previously reported is almost completed. Work continued as usual during night of 3rd-4th on dismantling Junior Duck's bill straightening our projection at V.1, and

4-7-1915.
Continued.

thickening parapet generally. An enemy's working party was dispersed by our fire at 11.p.m. Officers 2/3rd G.R., visited the line from 6.a.m.

The Battalion was relieved by 2/3rd G.R., in the evening and marched to billets in VIELLE CHAPELLE. Reliefs were completed by 11.p.m.

Casualties O.R.I. Wounded 1 (1/39th G.)
Total Casualties todate :-

	2/39th G.			1/39th G.		
	K.	W.	M.	K.	W.	M.
B.O's.	4	1	1	1	1	-
" attached.	-	3	-			
I.O's.	3	11	1	1	3	-
" attached.	-	1	-			
O.R.I.	102	507	23	11	121	6
" attached Dogras.	8	8	8			
" " B.M.P.	7	28	-			
" " Tehri S. & M.	2	24	1			
	126	583	34	13	125	6

5-7-1915
VIELLE CHAPELLE.

Dull cloudy day. No rain.

Bathing for Nos.1 and 3 Companies 50 men at a time, from 8 a.m., to 12 noon and 2 p.m. to 5 p.m.

Distribution of new clothing and inspection of kits by Company Commanders.

Casualties O.R.I. Wounded 1. (B.M.P.).
Total casualties to date.

	2/39th G.			1/39th G.		
	K.	W.	M.	K.	W.	M.
B.O's.	4	1	1	1	1	-
" attached.	-	1	-			
I.O's.	3	11	1	1	3	-
" attached.	-	1	-			
O.R.I.	102	507	23	11	121	6
" attached Dogras.	8	8	8			
" " B.M.P.	7	29	-			
" " S. & M.	2	24	1			
	126	584	34	13	125	6

6-7-1915
VIELLE CHAPELLE.

Bright sunny day, slight shower in evening.
Parades. 15 Minutes running drill in morning under C.O's.
Morning. Squad Drill without arms under Company Commanders.
Evening. Squad Drill with arms and Rifle Exercises under Company Commanders.
A fatigue of 120 men under Lieut.Clarke, was furnished at X orchard S.8.C.8.1., at 9 p.m. As a carrying party.
Casualties Killed O.R.I.1.(1/39th G.)
Casualties to date.

	2/39th G.			1/39th G.		
	K.	W.	M.	K.	W.	M.
B.O's.	4	1	1	1	1	-
" attached.		1				
I.O's.	3	11	1	1	3	-
" attached.	-	1	-			
O.R.I.	102	507	23	12	121	6
" attached Dogras.	8	8	8			
" " B.M.P.	7	29	-			
" " Tehri S.&M.	2	4	1			
	126	582	34	14	125	6

7-7-1915
VIELLE CHAPELLE.

Cloudy day, varied by sunshine.
Parades. Running Drill in morning under C.O's.
11.a.m. Medical Inspection. Names of 13 unfits and 13 fit for duty on Lines of Communication submitted to Brigade. Usual afternoon parade under Company Commanders except for Nos.3 and 4 Company of which 200 men under Captain Blair and 2nd Lieut. Rana Jodha Jang Bahadur, were detailed for fatigue at 9.p.m., at 2/3rd Head quarters in ALBERT ROAD for work on support trench in rear of 2/3rd front. This party returned to billets about 2 a.m.

8-7-1915
VIELLE CHAPELLE.

Bright sunny day.
Inspection by Lord Kitchener at ZELOBES at

8.7.1915
(continued)

at 11.45.a.m. The Battalion left billets at 9.45.a.m., and returned to billets at 12.45.p.m., after the departure of Lord Kitchener, Sir James Willcocks accompanied by Sir Charles Anderson walked down the ranks.

Usual afternoon parade by No.1 Coy. Those of Nos.3 and 4 Companies, who were on fatigue on night of 7th - 8th were excused parade in the afternoon.

Orders received from Brigade to be prepared to march to HAVERSKERQUE on 9th July.

9-7-1915
VIELLE CHAPELLE.

Bright sunny day.
15 minutes running drill under G.O's., as usual in morning.

Companies had just fallen in for morning parade when orders were received to be in readiness to march to HAVERSKERQUE at 15 minutes notice. In accordance with operation orders attached.

The Battalion on relief by the Royal Scots Fusiliers marched at 11.30.p.m., and arrived at billets at 5.15.a.m., on 10th July. The night was fine through somewhat misty. The road was a good condition.

10-7-1915.
HAVERSKERQUE.

The men were very tired after the long march of the previous night and no parades were held.
Day was fine.

11-7-1915
HAVERSKERQUE.

Day fine and clear.
Usual parades of 15 minutes double under G.O's and morning and afternoon parades were held.

12-7-1915
HAVERSKERQUE.

Slight showers in morning from 7.a.m. Remainder of day fine.

Parades.   7.30 to 9 a.m., under Company Commanders.
11.30 to 1.p.m. "   "   "

Only men selected by Company Commanders as being slack paraded in the afternoon.

13-7-1915
HAVERSKERQUE.

Fine day some clouds.
Parades as usual.

Colonel D.H.Drake Brockman.C.M.G., Captain P.T.Etherton, and Captain R.L.Duncan, I.M.S., returned from leave.

14-7-1915
HAVERSKERQUE

Fine day with strong wind. Clouded over later.
Companies paraded as usual.

Captain Burton.D.S.O., Captain Blair and 2nd Lieut.Rana Jodha Jang Bahadur, went on leave today.

The numbers of the Battalion are now as follows:-

GARHWAL RIFLES.	2/39th G.	1/39th G.	Total.
Garhwali officers.	4	4	8
Rank and File.			
Original men.	174	139	313
Reservists.	32	21	53
Attested Recruits.	13	41	54
Burma Mly.Police.	98	23	121
Tehri S. & M.		51	51
Grand Total.	317	275	592.

15-7-1915.
HAVERSKERQUE.

Fine morning with slight rain.
Companies paraded as usual.
Received orders to send Officer to see new billets, it being the intention to move the Battalion further up the road nearer Brigade Head-Quarters.
2nd Lieut. Shaw (Interpreter), Lieut. Collins rejoined from leave today.

16-7-1915.
HAVERSKERQUE.

Fine morning. Cool breeze. Slight rain later.
Received orders to move into new billets and be clear of old billets by 12 noon.
Early morning and afternoon parades as usual.

17-7-1915.
HAVERSKERQUE.

Rainy windy day.
Parades as usual.
Captain G.R.Mainwaring, 1st Battalion reported his arrival today, from Hospital and Base Depot Boulogne.

18-7-1915
HAVERSKERQUE.

Fine morning, less wind.
Muster ordered by Division held today 11.a.m. Other parades as usual.
Captain Mainwaring 1st Bn., took over duties of Adjutant from Captain Etherton 1st Bn., who was acting.
Sir John Hewett, late Lieut. Governor of the U.P. India called to see the Officer Commanding and congratulated him on the conduct of the Battalion, during the war, and asked that it might be promulgated to all ranks, and it was published in Battalion Orders.

19-7-1915.
HAVERSKERQUE.

Fine day and warm.
Parades as usual.
Orders received for all reinforcements received since last inspection by Corps Commander, to parade for his inspection at 11.45.a.m., tomorrow, including B.O's. and I.O's.

20-7-1915
HAVERSKERQUE.

Fine day. Cloudy at times.
Bomb throwers practised with live bombs in trench near the school at St VENANT.
Reinforcements received since 4.1.15, date of last inspection by Corps Commander paraded for his inspection at 11.45.a.m., together with those other units of the both Lahore and Meerut Division.
Parades as usual.
Bt.Colonel E.R.R.Swiney,who had rejoined from Hospital and Boulogne was appointed to Command of all details convalescent and others from Marseilles as a sort of Reserve Battalion.
The Command of the Battalion remaining on Colonel Drake Brockman.
10 sick men from Hospital rejoined the Battalion today (one 1/39 G.and nine 2/39th G.)

21-7-1915.
Billets
HAVERSKERQUE.

Fine day and hot.
C.O. and officers went out to see Right Sub Section with a view to taking over tomorrow night. Remained in ESTAIRES as distance 10 miles was too far to get back in time to march with regiment, which came on with 2/8th G.R., under the senior officer. 2/8th G.R., are not go into the trenches but to remain in Reserve. Both Battalions marched 4.45.p.m., and reached billets near LAVENTIE at 9.30.p.m.

WAR DIARY or INTELLIGENCE SUMMARY.

Army Form C. 2118.

Hour, Date, Place	Summary of Events and Information	Remarks and references to Appendices

22-7-1915
Billets
near
LAVENTIE.

Fine day. C.O.with Captain Etherton and Interpreter went on by motor to St.OMER.
Captain Burton and 2nd Lieut.Rana Jodha Jang returned from leave.
Captain Blair missed train and did not come
Companies marched 9.30.p.m. at 5 minutes interval to relieve Black Watch in D.Sub Section. Relief completed 12.30.a.m.

23-7-1915
Trenches
near N of
NEUVE CHAPELLE.

Dull morning cleared up later with cool breeze. Some showers in afternoon. Some shelling with 4"2 inch howitzers by enemy at 8.30.a.m.and 1 p.m.1 direct hit on TILLELOY South Post.which caused no casualties. Also Battalion Head Quarters at 5 p.m..Captain Blair arrived 3.p.m.from leave.

Casualties.O.R.I.Killed 1 (B.M.P.)wounded 4, (2.2/39th G.1.1/39th G.and 1 Tehri S.& M.).
Total casualties todate.

	2/39th G.			1/39th G.		
	K.	W.	M.	K.	W.	M.
B.O's.	4	1	1	1	1	-
" attached.	-	1	-			
I.O's.	3	11	1	1	3	-
" attached.	-	1	-			
O.R.I.	102	509	23	12	122	6
" Attached Dogras.	8	8	8			
" " B.M.P.	8	29	-			
" " Tehri S.& M.	2	25	1			
	127	585	34	14	126	6

24-7-1915
Trenches
near N of
NEUVE CHAPELLE.

Fine cloudy morning with cool wind blowing. Captain Etherton with Scouts patrolled front last night.

24-7-1915
(continued)

G.O.C. Brigade called at Battalion Head Quarters and C.O. accompanied him round front line.

Points 197 - 206 trench map were bombarded by our howitzer at 4 p.m. Enemy replied with a good number more shells both howitzers and field guns, fortunately causing no casualties.

Casualties. Killed O.R.I. One (Tehri S.&M.) Wounded one (B.M.P.)

Total casualties to date:-

	2/39thG.			1/39th G.		
	K.	W.	M.	K.	W.	M.
B.O's.	4	1	1	1	1	-
" attached.	-	1	-			
I.O's.	6	11	1	1	3	-
" attached.	-	1				
O.R.I.	102	502	23	12	122	6
" attached Dogras.	6	8	8			
" " B.M.P.	8	30				
" " Tehri S.& M.	3	25	1			
	128	566	34	14	126	6

25-7-1915
Trenches Near/of NEUVE CHAPELLE.

Fine day with clouds and nice breeze.

C.O. 84th Battery who is responsible for covering our front came to see the C.O., this morning and went up to front line afterwards.

Two hostile biplanes observed one at 6.30.a.m., and one 6 p.m., being a beautiful fine evening. Our aeroplanes were also active.

Enemy shelled vicinity of Battalion Head Quarters with 4.2 inch howitzers at 6.30.p.m.

Orders received for the relief of the Battalion by 2/8th G.R., tomorrow night. The Battalion going that night into billets near LAVENTIE and the next day back to MERVILLE.

26-7-1915
Trenches
N. of
NEUVE CHAPELLE.

Fine day with small showers occassionally.
Orders for relief by 2/8th G.R., cancelled last night 11.p.m. C.O. met F.O.C., at junction of MOATED GRANGE trench with RUE de TILLELOY to see about trench for Local Reserves. It was dicided to use Line B., north of RUE de TILLELOY for this purpose when it was completed.
Enemy shelled our local Reserve Coy., with 4.2 inch howitzers and knocked in the parapet.
Casualties. Wounded O.R. I.3 (one 1/39th G., one 2/39th G., one Tehri).
Total casualties todate.

	2/39th G.			1/39th G.		
	K.	W.	M.	K.	W.	M.
B.O's.	4	1	1	1	1	-
" attached.	-	1	-	-	-	-
I.O's.	3	11	1	1	3	-
" attached.	-	1	-	-	-	-
O.R.I.	102	510	23	12	123	6
" attached Dogras.	8	8	8			
" " B.M.P.	8	30	-			
" " Tehri S.& M.	3	26	1			
	128	588	34	14	127	6

27.7.1915
Trenches
N. of
NEUVE CHAPELLE.

Dull cloudy morning with heavy showers. Fine later and showery in afternoon.
Enemy rather cheerful apparently last night playing cornets, shouting and whistling. Scouts were out patrolling as usual and tried to get some wire to try with our wire cutters as it is said they wont cut German wire. Scouts apparently made some noise and were spotted and one L.Naik.Killed. Captain Etherton was out on the left and went out on the right with one Rifleman when moon was observed a bit and fire had died down and brought his body in. Our proper Battalion trained scouts are dwindling rapidly.
25 unfits went as for inspection by L.G.C.

27-7-1915.
(continued)

Division. Captain Etherton went in at a moments notice from the Brigade.

Casualties Killed O.R.I. One (1/39th G.)
Total Casualties todate.

	2/39th G.			1/39th G.		
	K.	W.	M.	K.	W.	M.
B.O's.	4	1	1	1	1	-
" attached.	-	1	-	-	-	-
I.O's.	3	11	1	1	3	-
" attached.	-	1	-	-	-	-
O.R.I.	102	510	23	13	123	6
" attached Dogras.	8	8	8	-	-	-
" " B.M.P.	8	30	-	-	-	-
" " Tehri S.& M.	3	26	1	-	-	-
	128	588	34	15	127	6

28-7-1915.
Trenches
N. of
NEUVE CHAPELLE.

Windy and cloudy and showering. Fine afternoon and evening.

C.O. with Captain Burton and Medical Officer inspected fire trenches during the monring. Considerable improvements done.

Our 1st Line Depot was shelled with shrapnel this morning at 11.30 a.m., and 3 followers wounded.

Information received that the Battalion would be relieved on night of 30-31st.

Enemy's aeroplane seen 4.30.p.m. flying E., to W., which cleared off or being fired at by our anti aircraft guns.

Enemy's machine gun was active in firing at our aeroplane.

Casualties Wounded O.R.I. 2 (one 1/39th G., one B.M.P.).

Total Casualties todate.

	2/39th G.			1/39th G.		
	K.	W.	M.	K.	W.	M.
B.O's.	4	1	1	1	1	-
" attached.	-	1	-	-	-	-
I.O's.	3	11	1	1	3	-
" attached.	-	1	-	-	-	-
O.R.I.	102	510	23	13	124	6
" attached Dogras.	8	8	8	-	-	-
" " B.M.P.	8	31	-	-	-	-
" " Tehri S.& M.	3	26	1	-	-	-
	128	589	34	15	128	6

29-7-1915
Trenches
N. of
NEUVE CHAPELLE.

Beautiful fine day. Cloudy later.
German aeroplane up over our lines 5 a.m., and 7 a.m.
Enemy shelled orchard by Battalion Head Quarters and MIN FARM the other side of the road from 2 to 2.30.p.m., with 4.2.inch howitzers.
Orders for relief cancelled. Only the Left and Left centre Sections being relieved., that is 3/Londons and 2/8th G.R. The Sirhind Brigade going out to billets CROIX MARMUSE and xxxxxxx Bareilly Brigade coming up. The admixture of units will I presume soon be made straight. For the last 8 days we have been under Sirhind Brigade., and now come under Bareilly Brigade, and we still nominally are under Garhwal Brigade As we gets correspondence, orders documents and memos from both Brigades.
Casualties to Wounded O.R.I. one (1/39th G.).
Total casualties todate:-

	2/39th G.			1/39th G.		
	K.	W.	M.	K.	W.	M.
B.O's.	4	1	1	1	1	-
" attached.	-	1	-			
I.O's.	3	11	1	1	3	-
" attached.	-	1	-			
O.R.I.	103	509	23	13	125	6
" attached Dogras.	8	8	8			
" " B.M.P.	8	31	-			
" " Tehri S. & M.	3	26	1			
(Died of Wound One 2/39th G.).	129	588	34	15	129	6

30-7-1915
Trenches
N. of
NEUVE CHAPELLE.

Fine misty morning.
Recieved Garhwal Brigade orders giving our new front. i.e., from SIGN POST LANE (inclusive) which is at N. End of NEUVE CHAPELLE up to WINCHESTER ROAD inclusive. We are to be relieved by the 2/8th G.R., on night 1st August.
G.O.C. Sirhind Brigade Br. General Walker V.C., C.B.

30-7-1915
(continued)

over charge of this front to night, came round to see O.C. He said how please he was to have had us under him. C.O. went over to Leicesters to arrange details regarding exchange of fronts on 1st August.

Casualties. Killed O.R.I. One (2/39th G.)
Total Casualties todate:-

	2/39th G.			1/39th G.		
	K.	W.	M.	K.	W.	M.
B.O's.	4	1	1	1	1	-
" attached.	-	1	-			
I.O's.	3	11	1	1	3	-
" attached.	-	1	-			
O.R.I.	104	509	23	13	125	6
" attached Dogras.	8	8	8			
" " B.M.P.	8	31	-			
" " Tehri S.& M.	3	26	1			
	130	588	34	15	129	6

31-7-1915
Trenches N. of NEUVE CHAPELLE.

Fine day. Cloudy hot.
German biplane came over 8.30.a.m. Also at 6.p.m.
Enemy bombed our right front, wounding 2 men, but ceased on our Field Battery firing at them. Some pipes were seen on the enemy's parapet in front of next Section which were fired at by our 9.2 howitzers at 6 p.m. On the chance of their being for gas. They were quickly withdrawn.
German Machine Guns very active as usual from 8 to 8.45.p.m., about the time ration parties are moving about and coming down.

Casualties. Wounded O.R.I. 2 (one 1/39 G. and one B.M.P.).
Total casualties todate:-

	2/39th G.			1/39th G.		
	K.	W.	M.	K.	W.	M.
B.O's.	4	1	1	1	1	-
~~" attached.~~	~~-~~	~~1~~	~~-~~			
I.O's.	3	11	1	1	3	-
" attached.	-	1	-			
O.R.I.	104	509	23	13	126	6
" attached Dogras.	8	8	8			
" " B.M.P.	8	32	-			
" " Tehri S.& M.	3	26	1			
	130	589	34	15	130	6

Serial No. 98.

121/6948.

WAR DIARY
OF
The Garhwal Rifles.

FROM 1st August 1915 TO 31st August 1915

2/39 Garhwal Rifles

1-8-1915
Trenches
N. of
NEUVE CHAPELLE.

Fine warm day with strong Southerly breeze.
Enemy shelled vicinity of Battalion Head-
Quarters for 3/4 of an hour with 4.2 inch howitzers from
8.a.m., getting one direct hit on the ruined farm opposite
our dug outs where we had the Mess and ruining a lot of
Mess Kit. Fortunately no one was in the actual room at the
time.
G.O.C. and Brigade Major came round to inspect
trenches at 10.30.a.m., and went up with Captain Burton. The
C.O., remained for O.C.2/8th G.R., to arrange details of relief
this evening.
The Battalion took over Leciester front i.e.,
Left Sub Section this afternoon at 2.p.m.
Two German Sausage balloons up during the
day.
On the whole a very quiet day.
Relief by 2/8th G.R., whose first Company
arrived 9.20.p.m., was completed by 11 p.m.
Casualties O.R.I. Wounded One.(B.M.P.)
Total Casualties todate:-

	2/39th G.			1/39th G.		
	K.	W.	M.	K.	W.	M.
B.O's.	4	1	1	1	1	-
" attached.	-	1	-			
I.O's.	3	11	1	1	3	-
" attached.	-	1	-			
O.R.I.	104	509	23	13	126	6
" attached Dogras.	8	8	8			
" " B.M.P.	8	33	-			
" " Tehri S.& M.	3	26	1			
	130	590	34.	15	130	6.

2-8-1915
Billets
PONT DU HEM.

Fine day. Cool breeze.
Billets very bad and flies awful.
Battalion ordered to make up wire balls for
the front line to be put out with the wire entanglement.

2-8-1915
(continued)

Sharp rain storm at 5 p.m., which nicely cooled the temperature as it was getting very dusty.

G.O.C., came to Head Quarters/billet when passing back from trenches.

3-8-1915.
Billets
PONT DU HEM.

Cloudy, showery day with strong cool breeze.

Captain KUNHARDT, attached to the Battalion was appointed Brigade Grenade Officer. He and Lieut. Clarke, and 1 N.C.O., proceeded to the School near ESTAIRES for instruction in grenade throwing etc.

Information received that the Official Photographer to the Government of India would visit us for the purpose of taking several photos.

No.3 Company portion of which had to sleep out in the open the first night and went into a billet the next night. Were again turned out for a Company of British Pioneers and had to squeeze in with the other 2 Companies of the Battalion.

One Division the 19th of Kitchener's Army has been attached to the Indian Army Corps.

The whole Battalion went out 8.30 p.m., on fatigue, digging a communication trench near front line.

4-8-1915.
Billets
PONT DU HEM.

Dull rainy morning. Fine later.

Enemy dropped a few 5.9. howitzers in vicinity of cross roads and Battalion Head Quarters at 8.30.a.m., and again at 1.p.m., owing to too much traffic coming down the roads.

The Official Photographer to the Government of India came in the afternoon and took some cinematograph photos of the Battalion marching, manning trenches.

Also,

4-8-1915
(continued)

Also groups of British Officers and Garhwali officers and 4 men typical of the Garhwali.
The Battalion paraded as usual. ½ of each Company parading whole the other ½ Battalion made up wire balls to put outside the parapet in addition to the wire entanglement.

5-8-1915
Billets
PONT DU HEM.

Fine though cloudy morning.
Parades and making of wire balls as usual.
Whole Battalion out digging a new support trench at night. Crops are being cut and harvesting has begun.

6-8-15
Billets
PONT DU HEM.

Dull cloudy day, threatening rain.
Parades as usual in the afternoon.
Orders received for relief by Dehra Dun Brigade, on night 8th-9th August. The Battalion going into billets at LA GORGUE on relief by 1st Seaforths.

7-8-1915.
Billets
PONT DU HEM.

Dull cloudy day, but no rain.
Parades as usual.
Whole Battalion out digging and revetting support trenches at night, on our sub-section.

8-8-1915
Billets
PONT DU HEM.

Dull cloudy day.
Companies packed up kits.
1st Seaforths arrived 9.55.p.m., and the Battalion marched at once to billets near RIEZ BAILLEUL.
Our billets reported by O.C.1/Seaforths as the ~~element~~ *cleanest* he had even taken over.

9-8-1915.
Billets
near
RIEZ BAILLEUL.

Cloudy stuffy day.
Parades 3 times a day.
Billets fair, no house for mess so cover made by tarpaulins. Intimation received that the trenches at Hooge had been recaptured from the Germans and some more in addition, which accounted for the heavy cannonade early this morning.

10.8.1915.
Billets
near
RIEZ BAILLEUL.

Fine, hot day.
Companies paraded as usual.
Men went in fifties to the Corps baths at LESTREM for bathing.
150 men out digging during the night.
Casualties Wounded O.R.I.1.(1/39th G.)
Total Casualties todate.

	2/39th G.			1/39th G.		
	K.	W.	M.	K.	W.	M.
B.O's.	4	1	1	1	1	-
" attached.	-	3	-			
I.O's.	3	11	1	1	3	-
" attached.	-	1	-			
O.R.I.	104	504	23	13	127	6
" attached Dogras.	8	8	8			
" " B.M.P.	8	33	1			
" " Tehri S.& M.	3	27	1			
	130	593	34	15	131	6
Died of Wounds, O.R.I.1, 2/39th G.	1	1				
	131	592	34.	15	131	6

11-8-1915
Billets
Near
RIEZ BAILLEUL.

Cloudy cool morning.
Companies paraded as usual.
Men for inoculation went in to 128 I.F.A., at 10.30.a.m.including half the British Officers.
Remainder of men in bathes of 50 went to Corps bathes at LESTREM.

12.8.1915
Billets
near
RIEZ BAILLEUL.

Dull day - hot but with Cool breeze.
Party of 100 men with one British Officer went down LA BASSEE road to help farmers cut their crops.
Remainder of men with British Officers went for inoculation (enteric) to No.128 I.F.A.at ESTAIRES.

13-8-1915
Billets, near
RIEZ BAILLEUL.

Fine morning, cloudy later and rain.
100 men under Lieut.Collins, went again today for helping farmers in harvesting.
Orders received for the Brigade to take over C.Sub-Section from WINCHESTER ROAD to FAUQUISSART on night of 16th-17th next.
A Brigade Grenadier Company has been formed from today. 30 men from each Battalion.

14-8-1915
Billets, near
RIEZ BAILLEUL.

Fine morning changing to smart and almost tropical shower and later.
Some details of 2nd Gurkhas and 6th Jats were attached as being in the resting Brigade before
joining

14-8-1915
(continued)

joining their own units.
Heard that 6th Jats and 41st Dogras were off to
Marseilles. Both these Battalions especially the 41st Dogras
are very weak and the former composed of 9 different units.
41st Dogras and 6th Jats details sent to rejoin
their 1st Line Depots during the afternoon.
Information received that both Subedars
NAIN SING CHINWARH, and MAKAR SING KUNWAR, had been awarded
the Order of British India 2nd Class, published in Gazette
of India Extraordinary of 4th August 1915.

15-8-1915
Billets
near
RIEZ BAILLEUL.

Cloudy day, thunderstorm and rain.
Parades as usual.
Nothing special to record.

16-8-1915
Billets, near RIEZ BAILLEUL
and TRENCHES FAUQUISSART.

Cloudy day and cool after the thunderstorm. Heavy rain in the afternoon and thunderstorm which made moving down communication trenches difficult.

The Battalion left billets 7.15.p.m., and arrived punctually at 9.10.p.m., at cross roads. Relief finished by 11.30.p.m. Fortunately no rain occurred during relief.

17-8-1915
Trenches FAUQUISSART.

Misty morning with a little rain and thunder mid-day, fine later.

Enemy shelled BEDFORD ROAD leading to FAUQUISSART with heavy 8 inch Howitzers at 10.30.a.m., dropping 6 shells, evidently having seen Salvage Corps men collecting material in a house there and at Artillery observer Posts.

Two Staff Officers 19th Division came round trenches in the afternoon.

A German sniper very persistent all day, especially in one spot in prolongation of a ditch which runs from our parapet to theirs.

18.8.1915
Trenches FAUQUISSART.

Dull day cloudy but no rain.

Quiet on our front except for the usual sniping.

Work continued all day on parapet; parados and dug outs and general improvements made.

C.O. went round trenches and posts making thorough inspection.

C.O. Called in to Brigade Head Quarters in the evening to see G.O.C.

Casualties. Killed O.R. One (Tehri S.& M.)

Total casualties to-date:-

	2/39th G.			1/39th G.		
	K.	W.	M.	K.	W.	M.
B.O's.	4	1	1	1	1	-
" attached.	-	3	-			
I.O's.	3	11	1	1	3	-
" attached.	-	1	-			
O.R.I.	105	503	23	13	127	6
" attached Dogras.	8	8	8			
" " B.M.P.	8	38	1			
" " Tehri S.& M.	4	27	-			
	132	592	34.	15	131	6

19-8-1915.
Trenches
FAUQUISSART.

Dull cloudy and inclement rain. Clearing up later morning passed quietly.
G.O.C. came round 2 p.m., to see the Line.
4.15 p.m., the enemy commenced shelling our fire trench with 5.9.inch howitzers and at 4.35.p.m., fired their large Minenwerfer in combination, firing one 5.9.inch and immediately a large Minenwerfer. The idea being presumably to disguise the noise of discharge also prevent location of the Minenwerfer. The latter shell could be easily seen coming through the air and the explosion was terrific. This went on till 7.15.p.m., Our Batteries replied both Field and Howitzer, which did not at put stop their firing. Our parapet was damaged in one place and a traverse knocked down. ########### 6 men only fortunately slightly wounded and 6 rifles damaged, 3 badly and some accoutrements. Some 80 shells were fired at night the enemy opened heavy bursts of rifle and Machine Gun fire on the damaged parts to prevent our repairing. But we repaired all damaged parts during the night. ######
Strength of Battalion in the front line being now :-

Firing Line. ... ... 145.
Supports. ... ... 60.
Local Reserve. ... ... 191.
Total. 396.

Casualties. Wounded O.R.I.3.(2.1/39 G.)
(1.B.M.P.).

Total casualties to-date:-

	2/39th G.			1/39th G.		
	K.	W.	M.	K.	W.	M.
B.O's.	4	1	1	1	1	-
" attached.	-	3	-	-	-	-
I.O's.	3	11	1	1	3	-
" attached.	-	1	-	-	-	-
O.R.I.	105	503	23	13	129	6
" attached Dogras.	8	8	8			
" " B.M.P.	8	39	1			
" " Tehri S.&.M.	4	27	-			
	132	593	34.	15	133	6

20.8.1915
Trenches
FAUQUISSART.

Fine morning. Cloudy later.
Enemy sent some 4.2.inch howitzers in orchard to our left, with one or two Field Gun shrapnel.
Day passed quietly till the enemy when a few 5.9.inch howitzer shells were placed near cross road W., of Battalion Head Quarters some hit over parapet.
Enemy's Machine Guns opened on our aeroplane in the evening.
Two emplacements have been made for Machine Guns near Battalion Head Quarters for firing at German aeroplanes.
4 Officers of 6th Wilts Regiment Kitcheners Army arrived today to be attached for 48 hours for instruction.
Enemy commenced a heavy bombardment of our trenches at 10.30.p.m., with 4.2.inch, 5.9.inch howitzers and Field Guns on our front line but chiefly on our support and Communication trenches., where our working parties were. Also again at mid-night. In the intervals they opened bursts of rifle and Machine Gun fire. This may have been due to an apprehension that we were going to attack or may have been intentional to harass our working parties which they may have seen working during the day from their Sausage Balloons to the S., of the AUBERS RIDGE.
Casualties fortunately not heavy. Killed O.R.I. 4.(3.2/39th G.) (1.B.M.P.) Wounded O.R.I.4 (2.1/39th G. and 2.B.M.P.). Total Casualties todate:-

	2/39th G.			1/39th G.		
	K.	W.	M.	K.	W.	M.
B.O's.	4	1	1	1	1	-
" attached.	-	3	-			
I.O's.	3	11	1	1	3	-
" attached.	-	1	-			
O.R.I.	108	503	23	13	131	6
" attached Dogras.	8	8	8			
" " B.M.P.	9	41	1			
	4	27	-			
	136	595	34.	15	135	6

21-8-1915.
Trenches
FAUQUISSART.

Rainy morning, clearing up later.
Damaged done last night not very much fortunately and easily repaired. One shell went straight in to a dug out, half completed, in which a man was sitting and exploded without killing the man, only severely bruising him.
General Anderson, with his G.S.O.(1) and A.D.C., came round to Head-Quarters at 3.p.m., and shortly afterwards G.O.C. Garhwal Brigade.
Received news that we the Garhwal Brigade had to give up this portion of the front to 3rd Corps. Again we are being changed out and have to go to another portion.
Enemy's sniper appears to have spotted our snipers post, as it was hit time after time this morning. Beside usual sniping, day and night passed quietly.
Captain Harbord went into Head Quarters and was attached to the 1/4th Gurkhas going to the Dardanelles.
Casualties. Killed O.R.I.1.(1.2/39th G.).
Total Casualties todate.

	2/39th G.			1/39th G.		
	K.	W.	M.	K.	W.	M.
B.O's.	4	1	1	1	1	-
" attached.	-	3	-			
I.O's.	3	11	1	1	3	-
" attached.	-	1	-			
O.R.I.	109	503	23	13	131	6
" attached Dogras.	8	8	8			
" " B.M.P.	9	41	1			
" " Tehri S.& M.	4	27	-			
	137	595	34.	15	135	6.

22-8-1915
Trenches
FAUQUISSART.

Fine morning, with cold N. wind and clouds.
A German aeroplane L.V.G. Biplane was up at 7.45.a.m., and 8.45.a.m., over our line and lower down than usual. Our anti-aircraft and M.Guns placed in position for firing at them, opened fire on it, with result.
Lieut. Collins went in to the Brigade Machine Gun

22-8-1915
(continued)

Gun Officer for instruction prior to going to a course at the Machine Gun School.

Captain Lyell was granted an extension of sick leave. The 4 Officers of the Wiltshires who were attached for 48 hours left this morning and 4 more Officers of L.N. Lancashire Regiment came to be attached to the Battalion for instruction for the sametime.

Germans did a lot of firing at our aeroplanes in the evening with anti air craft guns and brought one of ours down which fell in German lines, one of theirs came over at 7.p.m., and was fired at by our guns and Machine Guns without result. The shooting of the anti air craft guns was very wide.

Sent up a green rocket for practice from ~~xxxxx~~ Head Quarters in accordance with orders received.

The Battalion is disposed as follows on this dated:-

Firing Line.	... ...	152
Support.	... ...	146
Local Reserve.	... ...	88
	Total.	386.

23-8-1915
Trenches.
FAUQUISSART.

Dull cloudy inclined to rain. Fine later night passed quietly. Very cold at night for the time of year.

Enemy fired 8.a.m., ½ dozen Field Gun shells on our right near FAUQUISSART cross roads.

A German aeroplane came near 7.45.a.m., but kept over their own lines chiefly. It was fired at by our firing line on the right.

Received instructions that the 6.D.x.L.I. would relieve us on night of the 27/28th.

Our guns fired a few rounds as usual on their barbed wire entanglement.

Received the good news that the Russian had sunk in the Baltic 1 Superdreadnought 2 Cruisers and 7 Destroyers of the German Fleet, and repulsed a landing at PERNAU in the Gulf of RIGA, in which the German lost all their boats.

23-8-1915
(continued)

The 2/Leicesters on our right sent up a white rocket at 9.30.p.m., in accordance with orders for practice and at the same time cheered, which our men took up, in honours of the Russian Naval Victory.

Casualties. Wounded O.R.I. One (2/39th G.).
Total Casualties to date.

	2/39th G.			1/39th G.		
	K.	W.	M.	K.	W.	M.
B.O's.	4	1	1	1	1	-
" attached.	-	3	-			
I.O's.	3	11	1	1	3	-
" attached.	-	1	-			
O.R.I.	109	504	23	13	131	6
" attached Dogras.	8	8	8			
" " B.M.P.	9	41	1			
" " Tehri S.& M.	4	27	-			
	137	596	34.	15	135	6.

24-8-1915
Trenches
FAUQUISSART.

Fine morning.
Night quiet. We bombed a German listening post and opened a rapid fire with rifles and Machine Gun on receiving a report from our patrols that the enemy were working outside his parapet. They sent over 3 bombs which fell short.

Captain D.A.Blair was attached to the Meerut Divisional Train for duty with the Salvage Company.(Meerut Division No.Q.A.453/1, dated 23.8.15., and Garhwal Brigade No.S.C.125/17, of 23.8.15).

C.O. and Officers of 6th Ox.L.I., came round preparatory to taking over. Also 4 more Officers attached of South Lancashire Regiment for instructions.

G.O.C.58th and 60th Brigades came round inspecting our line which they are taking over.

Casualties Wounded O.R.I.2.(1.1/39th G.) (1.2/39th G.)

24-8-1915.
(continued)

Total Casualties todate.

	2/39th G.			1/39th G.		
	K.	W.	M.	K.	W.	M.
B.O's.	4	1	1	1	1	-
" attached.	-	3	-			
I.O's.	3	11	1	1	3	-
" attached.	-	1	-			
O.R.I.	109	505	23	13	132	6
" attached Dogras.	8	8	8			
" " B.M.P.	9	41	1			
" " Tehri S.& M.	4	27	-			
	137	597	34	15	136	6.

25-8-1915.
Trenches
FAUQUISSART.

Fine day.
Night passed quietly.
Work on parapet, parados dug-outs and communication trenches continued and the line is now getting in excellent condition.

Operation orders for relief received. We go out tomorrow night to billets near LA GORGUE for one night.

Went over to see new section we have to take over on night of 28th instant. Along way round via ROUGE CROIX; EUSTIN communication trench to Battalion Head Quarters near S.of NEUVE CHAPELLE. We and the 3/Londons take it over, a large front for our strength.

26-8-1915
Trenches
FAUQUISSART.

Lovely fine and hot day. Quiet night but usual sniping.

Heavy dews at night and quite cold.
Put out by our scouts, "Life" an American paper, like Punch and a letter C.O. wrote in German telling them of the naval victory of the Russians as they probably never get full

26-8-1915
(continued)

full and correct news.
New Batteries of Kitchener's Army coming in relief of our Corps batteries were registering all day.
Relief were very punctual and completed by 9.45.p.m.
A long march to Billets. Battalion arriving 1.a.m. men rather tired.

27-8-1915.
Billets
near
LA GORGUE.

Fine hot summer's day.
Men had a good rest and clean up after night march.
Company Commanders went round new Line we are taking over tomorrow night from the 1st Gurkhas and to take over Trench Stores.
C.O. went to see 3/Londons at their Head-Quarters on RUE DU BACQUEROT, about the location of local reserve as they hold the line with us, all under the Command of Lieut.Colonel D.H.Drake Brockman., C.M.G.,
M.Bree our French Interpreter left us today having been ordered back to Paris and London and finally to Madagascar to see after the affairs of a large firm of which he is head.
Strength of the Bn. is now:-
10.B.O's., 10.G.O's., and O.R.I.545, trench strength is 417. i.e. A.Coy.72., B.Coy.70., E.Coy.70., F.Coy.68., G.Coy.70., H.Coy.67.

28-8-1915
Billets
near
LA GORGUE.

Fine hot sommer day.
Battalion rested till time to march men having a good wash and clean up.
Battalion fall in 4.p.m., and with 3/Londons march to vicinity of PONT DU HEM and waited in an orchard till time to march down the LA BASSEE road in relief of 1st Gurkhas.
Guides were to meet us at junction of LORETTO road and the Companies marched in single file down to the POINT LOGY road where we found the guides who should have been further up as arranged.
As usual at cross road undescribable confusion and lack of arrangement. From post going both ways and lots of troops coming out apparently before actually relieved. Always the way, appear to be in such a having to get out.
Companies got in all right and eventually reliefs were completed by 10.45.p.m., would have been earlier but for the block. Night passed quietly.
Heavy clouds rolled up and a few drops of rain fell during relief.

29-8-1915
Trenches
NEUVE CHAPELLE.

Dull rainy morning. Eventually turning cloudier and rainier and windy with a N.Wind.
C.O. went round whole line with C.O. Londons met the G.O.C., in our Section and went on round 2/8th G.R., Section with him and out by PORT ARTHUR, back to Section Head Quarters.
Enemy were shelling orchard on our right with field guns from 11.a.m.to 1.p.m.
Our guns shelled enemy's line in front of our old section on front of MOATED GRANGE with field guns and howitzers for 3 hours and a mine was also exploded.
A deserter who came in gave the information that the Germans were bringing up gas and liquied fire arrangements in the vicinity.
The trenches are very bad and for all this time

29-8-1915
Trenches
NEUVE CHAPELLE.

time the regiments of Lahore Division who have occupied them did not appear to have done a hand's turn on them. Some more communication trenches have been made and B.Line dug and partially funished by working parties from Reserve and Sappers.

30-8-1915.
Trenches
NEUVE CHAPELLE.

Fine morning, cold N.wind. Cloudy later and threatening rain.
C.O. went round trenches. They require a very great deal of work on them. Enemy did no shelling today. Our guns again shelled the same piece of line as yesterday. 2 German aeroplanes were of this morning at 9.a.m.
Received information that 1/9th G.R., would relieved us on night of the 1st and that we would go to PONT DU HEM in reserve and furnish garrisons for 3 posts in RUE DU PUITS.
Message came 10.p.m., cancelling relief.
Enemy's snipers fairly active last night.
Casualties wounded. O.R.I.1.(2/39 G.)
Total casualties todate.:-

	2/39th G.			1/39th G.		
	K.	W.	M.	K.	W.	M.
B.O's.	4	1	1	1	1	-
" attached.	-	3	-			
I.O's.	3	11	1	1	3	-
" attached.	-	1				
O.R.I.	109	506	23	13	132	6
" attached Dogras.	8	8	8			
" " B.M.P.	9	41	1			
" " Tehri S.& M.	4	27	-			
	137	598	34.	15	136	6.

31-8-1915
Trenches
NEUVE CHAPELLE.

Fine day, cloudy and at one time threatening rain

31-8-1915
(continued)

rain with thunder.
C.O. went round trenches chiefly the communication ones and conected map.
A memo came saying relief would be made on the night of 1st - 2nd September by the Jullender Brigade. The 47th Sikhs taking over this line held by us and up to OXFORD street as well. Met C.O. and officers of 47th Sikhs and came down to our Head Quarters with them and arranged details of relief some anxiety about possible attack with gas by the Germans so new pattern helmet was issued to the men. A deserter of the 13th Bavarian regiment said that a lot of gas cylinders had been brought up and issued to his regiment and the 15th Regiment too. on our front.
Casualties. Killed O.R.I. 1 (Tehri).
Total Casualties todate:-

	2/39th G.			1/39th G.		
	K.	W.	M.	K.	W.	M.
B.O's.	4	1	1		1	-
" attached.	-	3				
I.O's.	3	11	1	1	3	-
" attached.	-	1	-			
O.R.I.	109	506	23	13	132	6
" attached Dogras.	8	8	8			
" " B.M.P.	9	41	1			
" " Tehri S. & M.	5	27	-			
	138	598	34.	15	136	6.

Serial No 98.

121/7286

WAR DIARY
OF
Garhwal Rifles.

From 1st September 1915 to 30th September 1915

1-9-1915
Trenches
NEUVE CHAPELLE.

Cloudy windy morning.
Hostile biplane observed 8.15.a.m., flying over our lines to the South. Operation Orders for relief by Jullender Brigade came. The Battalion goes to billets beyond LA GORGUE which we occupied on the 27th-28th August.15.
Quiet day. Rain set in at 2 p.m., Sounds of heavy guns heard down S., at 2.30.p.m.
47th Sikhs in relief arrived fairly punctually but were delayed by the usual congestion at the cross roads and not enough time being allowed for each regiment to file off the road down the communication trenches which commence from the main road. 15 minutes is not quite enough, result block and delay.
Relief was completed once under way, by 11.p.m., and we got to billets beyond LA GORGUE at 2.a.m.
Rain set in shortly after arrival and the Companies just came in for it.

2-9-1915
Billets
near
LA GORGUE.

Dull cold cloudy day. Getting decidedly cold a nights now.
Men had a good rest and clean up during the day.
Heavy rain at night.

3-9-1915
Billets, near
LA GORGUE.

Dull cold rainy day.
C.O.went in to Brigade Head Quarters called in by G.O.C., with all other C.O's.
Received 558 birthday cards of H.M.Queen Alexandra and the late King Edward VII, for distribution to the Officers and men.
A working party of 300 men under Captain. Etherton, went

3-9-1915
(continued)

went out at 6 p.m., for working all night. Got back 3.30.a.m.
Very wet and work very hard in consequence. Men wet through,
men had to march 6 miles before commencing work.

4-9-1915
Billets
near
LA GORGUE.

Fine morning. Cloudy and rain threatening later.
Men has a quiet day after their soaking and
fatigue last night.
Jemadar Balbahadur Sing Gusain, promoted Subedar
vide Gazette of India No.712, of 30.7.15.
Machine guns are to be supplied with limbered
wagons in lieu of mules and pack saddles.

5-9-1915
Billets
Near
LA GORGUE.

Cloudy rainy morning. Fine later.
Companies paraded as usual. Paid out advances
after afternoon. And sent off mens' money orders.
Went and saw aero drome A-- near by and all
machines coming and going.

6-9-1915
Billets near
LA GORGUE.

Fine day. Cool N. wind.
C.O. went as to see G.O.C. Brigade.
Parades as usual, nothing special to record.
200 men on working digging last night.
Casualties Wounded O.R. I.2 (1/39 G.)
Total Casualties todate.

6-9-1915
(continued)

	2/39th G.			1/39th G.		
	K.	W.	M.	K.	W.	M.
B.O's.	4	1	1	1	1	-
" attached.	-	3	-			
I.O's.	3	11	1	1	3	-
" attached.	-	1	-			
O.R.I.	109	506	23	13	134	6
" attached Dogras.	8	8	8			
" " B.M.P.	9	41	1			
" " Tehri S. & M.	5	27	-			
	138	598	34.	15	138	6

7-9-1915
Billets near LA GORGUE.

Fine autumn day.
C.O. went up to front line held by Dehra Dun Brigade. Also Company Commanders to reconnoitre lines if approach etc.

Companies paraded as usual., nothing special to report.

8.9.1915
Billets near LA GORGUE.

Fine autumn day.
Companies paraded as usual.
Inspection of emergency rations, smoke helmets and sand-bags.
Whole Battalion (300 men) on working digging communication trenches at night.
2nd Lieut. Shaw Interpreter met with an accident yesterday falling from his horse which necessitated his going to hospital.

WAR DIARY or INTELLIGENCE SUMMARY.

Army Form C. 2118.

9-9-1915
Billets
near
LA GORGUE.

Fine day.
Company Commanders went out reconnoitering communication trenches and front line.
Parades as usual.

10-9-1915
Billets
Near
LA GORGUE.

Fine day. S.E. wind.
C.O. went round front line with Captain Etherton reconnoitering front line and communication trenches.
All G.O's and N.C.O's with 2nd Lieut. Rana Jodha Jang Bahadur, went to see experiment with gas and its effect on men with gas helmets on.
Bomb throwers went to Grenadier School to practice bomb throwing.
Parades as usual.

11-9-1915
Billets
near
LA GORGUE.

Fine day, cool N.E. wind.
Parades as usual.
Nothing special to record.
Orders received for going into trenches tomarrow night.

12-9-1915.
Billets
Near
LA GORGUE.

Fine day. Cool wind.
Weather just now is beautiful autumn weather.

12-9-1915
(continued)

Operation Order came for relief of Dehra Dun Brigade by Garhwal Brigade to night, taking the line from SIGN POST Lane to S.MOATED GRANGE St. 3/Londons and Garhwalis in front line and support with 1 Company 2/Leicesters. 2/3rd and 2/8th G.R., in local reserve all under Command of Lieut.Colonel. D.H.Drake Brockman.C.M.G. 2/8th (less 1 Coy) in B.line in Brigade reserve, to be called on of necessary by O.C.Section. Battalion marched 5.10.p.m. for the junction of communication trench and RUE DU BACQVEROT at 7.20.p.m. Relief was completed by 10.p.m.

13-9-1915
Trenches
MAUQUISSART.

Fine day.
C.O.made exhaustive inspection of front line trenches.

G.O.C.came round. Also in the afternoon.
Quiet night.
Casualties Killed O.R.I.1 (2/39 G.)
Total Casualties todate:-

	2/39 G.			1/39th G.		
	K.	W.	M.	K.	W.	M.
B.O's.	4	1	1	1	1	-
" attached	-	3	-			
I.O's.	3	11	1	1	3	-
" attached.	-	1	-			
O.R.I.	110	506	23	13	132	6
" attached Dogras.	8	8	8			
" " B.M.P.	9	41	1			
" " Trhri S.& M.	5	27	-			
	139	598	34	15	136	6

14-9-1915
Trenches
MAUQUISSART.

Dull cloudy day, with some rain.
C.O.went round whole line arranging work and in

14-9-1915
(continued)

inspecting front.
Our guns shelled German Line in the afternoon.

15-9-1915
Trenches
MAUQUISSART.

Dull cloudy day, inclined to rain.
Quiet night, little sniping or Machine Gun fire.
C.O. went round from line to see work being done in conjunction with other units.
Enemy shelled a little during the forenoon.
Our guns were active during the day.

16-9-1915
Trenches
MAUQUISSART.

Dull tho' fine day. quiet night.
Work continued at high pressnre on front line, support line and the communication trenches. 3/Londons also hard - at it doing good work, *quite transforming the Duck's Bill*.
C.O. went round inspecting as usual.
Our Artillery active during the day, and cut wire opposite M.36.a.4.8. Rifle and M.G.fire kept on the place to prevent Germans repairing it. 3/Leicesters, *and Londons*, specially doing good work on trenches. This regiment always does well.

Casualties Killed O.R.I. 1 (Tehri S.& M.)
Total Casualties todate:-

	2/39 G.			1/39 G.		
	K.	W.	M.	K.	W.	M.
B.O's.	4	1	1	1	1	-
" attached.	-	3	-			
I.O's.	3	11	1	1	3	-
" attached.	-	1	-			
O.R.I.	110	506	23	13	132	6
" attached Dogras.	8	8	8			
" " B.M.P.	9	41	1			
" " Tehri S.& M.	6	27				
	140	598	34	15	136	6

17-9-1915
Trenches
MAUQUISSART.

Dull morning. No rain, hot and thundering. Quiet night, little sniping.

Work continued all night on various parts of line and new combined Aid Post.

Work all day hard on parapet, parados, dug-outs and parados for gun emplacement.

G.O.C. came round in the afternoon and C.O. accompanied him round. Orders came for relief tomorrow 18th by 4/Seaforths.

Casualties Killed O.R.I.2 (1.1/39 G. 1.2/39 G.) Wounded 1 (1/39th G.) Accidentally wounded by a bomb exploding when being dug up. O.R.I.1. (2/39 G.).

Total Casualties todate:-

	2/39 G.			1/39 G.		
	K.	W.	M.	K.	W.	M.
B.O's.	4	1	1	1	1	-
" attached.	-	3	-			
I.O's.	3	11	231	1	3	-
" attached.	-	1	-			
O.R.I.	111	507	23	14	133	6
" attached Dogras.	8	8	8			
" " B.M.P.	9	41	1			
" " Tehri S.& M.	6	27	-			
	141	599	34	16	137	6
(Died of wounds O.R.I.1.				1	1	-
1/39th G.).				17	136	6

18-9-1915
Trenches
MAUQUISSART.

Fine day.

German aeroplane up at 9.15.a.m.

2.B.O's.(I.A.R.Officers) ~~1xxxyxandy2x~~ Lieut.E.A.Courthope.I.A.R., 2nd Lieut.S.Angelo.I.A.R., 1.G.O., and 218.O.R.I., arrived yesterday as reinforcements for the Battalion. To be inspected by the G.O.C.Corps tomorrow.

Placed up cross for the chaplin on Major Becher,(of 2nd Gurkhas) grave who was killed in November last year.

4/Seaforths arrived punctually and relief completed 9.45.p.m. Got home rather late as distance to billets

18-9-1915
(continued)

billets near LA GORGUE, same place as last time, is about 6 miles, and filing out of 2000 yards of narrow trench in single file takes time.

19-9-1915
Billets near LA GORGUE.

Fine hot day. Freeze N.E., breeze blowing.
Reinforcements were inspected by Corps Commander at 10.45.a.m., very young lot, all lads of 8 months service.
Men rested and cleaned up accoutrements, and had renewals of clothing and boots issued them.
Orders received for inspection of Brigade by Lord Kitchener tomorrow morning at 10.30.a.m.
A number of our aeroplanes went off this evening together evidently on a raid.

20-9-1915
Billets, near LA GORGUE.

Fine day. Cold wind.
Battalion marched 9.a.m., to rendezvous near PONT ROUCHON for inspection by Lord Kitchener at 10.30.a.m. His Lordship did not arrive till 11.50.a.m., being late driving from St OMER or BOULOGNE.
He walked down the whole Brigade which was drawn up in line of Battalions, each Battalion in having Companies in line of quarter colum of Platoons.
On arrival of the Battalion he was very complimentary and said "The Garhwalis have made a great name for themselves" and done very well better than the others."
General Sir Douglas added at the same time,"
"Yes all through the campaign!"
This was very gratifying and being high praise from one in such high authority and I trust it may lead to something for the regiment.
All British Officers, Garhwali Officers, and
N.C.O's,

20-9-1915
(continued)

N.C.O's, rendezvoused at appointed place for a rehearsal of future work to be done.
Getting back to billets at 1.a.m.

21-9-1915
Billets, near.
LA GORGUE.

Fine cold day.
Battalion practised formation rehearsed last night i.e., filing up communication trenches into Reserve trench and getting up into the Firing and Support trenches in proper order.
Heavy Artillery fire all day on our front and to the South.

22-9-1915
Billets. Near
LA GORGUE.

Fine cold day.
Parades as usual practising parades of yesterday.
C.O. went in to Brigade Head Quarters.
Heavy Artillery firing continued.
Operation orders for move to concentration area received.

23-9-1915
Bivouac
BOUT DE VILLE.

Fine day cloudy.
Battalion marched 5.45.p.m., to new bivouac in concentraction area. Baggage Wagons accompanied the Battalion.
Heavy Artillery fire continued all day. Our own and hostile aeroplanes active. Sent up jars of Anti gas solution, vermorel sprayers to trenches.
C.O. and Captain Burton went into Brigade Head-Quarters to see G.O.C. at 5.p.m., conference.
Heavy rain and thunderstorm set in about 7.p.m., and drenched the Battalion, which arrived at bivouac at 7.45.p.m., Bivouack very muddy and men spent a miserable night out in the open.

24-9-1915.
Bivouac near POUT DE VILLE.

Dull miserable rainy morning and day.
Men very *cheerful* considering the wretched night spent in the rain.
The Battalion marched 7.p.m., to take up its position of assembly in the trenches as Brigade Reserve for the attack on 25th September, getting into position, by 10.30.p.m., which was very good going as the distance from the RUE DU BACQUEROT to the HOME COUNTIES trench by SUNKEN road communication trench/was 1500 yards long all in single file and trench a bit sticky.

25-9-1915
Trenches.

Dull cloudy morning inclined to rain.
The Battalion occupied HOME COUNTIES TRENCH all night., At 5.48.p.m., the mine was sprung under the German salient on WINCHESTER Road and 2 minutes later the signal for the gas to be turned on (white rockets) went up. The attack by 2/3rd, 2/Leicesters, 2/8th Gurkha Rifles was launched in the order named from right to left.
The gas however turned out a failure and instead of going on and asphyxiating the Germans, it advanced a little, rose and if any thing came back, with the result that our own men were affected by it; also one of the cylinders on the right in the DUCKS bill leaked and affected the 3/Londons occupying this place.
The attack was unsuccessful on the right and centre; only a few so reported as having got in on the 2/Leicesters left. But on the left the 2/8th got in to the Germans firing and support lines.
The Bareilly Brigade on our left also got in and as far as the MOULIN DU PIETRE cross roads but apparently, not getting support the Germans got round their rear into the trenches again and so they were cut off.
Meanwhile, the crush in our own trenches was terrific. The Battalion being in Brigade Reserve was to hold the whole front from SUNKEN ROAD to S.MOATED GRANGE St., and had on the mine going off commenced filing up by 3 communication trenches to get into the firing line to occupy it. On arrival at the head of these communication trenches, it was found impossible to get on for the time any further, as wounded men of both

(our front parapet was being heavily shelled all the time - also support trenches.)

25-9-1915
(continued)

both 2/3rd and Leicesters and "gassed" men had crowded back and blocked the whole place. The 2/3rd had not sent on the whole of their reserve and still had a Company blocking up the trench and these with the 2/Leicesters simply made moving impossible.

The 2/8th G.R. had all gone on and our left Company (No.4) was able at last to get into the fire trench.

The situation was reported to the G.O.C. by telephone and a M.S. was sent to the O.C. to organise 2 attacks of a Battalion each, with 2 bombing parties to reinforce 2/3rd on right and Leicesters on left. Owing to the crowded state of the trenches movement was impossible, it taking a single man an hour to get 50X, the trenches were so narrow.

As the Battalion was spread out over 600 yards of front it was a Herculean task to get into touch with the Company Commanders and the 2.Head Quarters dug-outs with telephone which it was anticipated would be vacated by the O.C.2/3rd and Leicesters were still occupied and not available. Shortly after this the Dehra Dun Brigade who had been ordered to attack and advance on HAUT POMMEREAU and LA CLIQUETERIE began to arrive and made the congestion worse. Fortunately the O.C. met the G.O.C. Dehra Dun Brigade and pointed out that he had been ordered to organise an attack with 2 bombing parties but that until the trenches were cleared of his Brigade, progress was impossible. The O.C.2/Leicesters was asked to clear his men out who were crowding all over the place round his Head Quarters.

The G.O.C. Dehra Dun Brigade arranged to clear his troops down to the left and leave our area clear, but it was not until 2.30.p.m., that the Companies were in position.

By this time the golden opportunity had been lost.

The Germans had recovered their trenches from the 2/8th G.R., and the C.O. reconnoitering with a periscope could see that a small German flag was flying on their parapet and their fire rifle and Machine Gun was now beginning to be heard, bullets striking all along the parapet.

It was a foregone conclusion that with only 2 Companies and the Dehra Dun Brigade only sending forward 1 Company that the attack would fail, as it was impossible now

25-9-1915
(continued)

now the trench was held to get over 150%., of ground without Artillery preparation.

The Companies advanced however in accordance with orders on a signal from O.C.and got about 40%., when they had to lie down under cover of the grass and folds in the ground and crawl up.

The Leading Company was under 2nd Lieut.Rana Jodha Jang who led it very well. The 2nd Company was not however sent on as it was seen to be hopeless and only a needless sacrifice of life. So those that had advanced were withdrawn under cover of darkness.

Heavy rain set in about 6.p.m., and drenched everyone to the skin and made the trenches knee deep in mud and water and going up or down a heavy labour.

The Battalion was reorganised at last and held the line from SUNKEN St., to S.MOATED GRANGE St., for the night, the other 3 Regiments or what remained of them going into support.

A miserable night was spent. Rations came up with great difficulty.

Casualties:- O.R.I. Killed 4.(3.2/39.,1.Tehri S.& M.) Wounded 1.B.O.,2.G.O's., and 40.O.R.I.(1/39.G.2.G.O's.,and 11.O.R.I.,2/39 G.20., B.M.P.5., Tehri 4),Missing O.R.I.26. (1/39 G.13.,2/39 G.8., B.M.P.5.).

Total Casualties todate:-

	2/39th G.			1/39th G.		
	K.	W.	M.	K.	W.	M.
B.O's.	4	1	1	1	1	-
" attached.	-	4	-			
I.O's.	3	11	1	1	5	-
" attached.	-	1				
O.R.I.	114	527	31	15	143	19
" attached Dogras.	8	8	8			
" " B.M.P.	9	46	6			
" "Tehri/S.& M.	7	31				
	145	629	47.	17	149	19.

26-9-1915.

Dull miserable day. Trenches shelled by "Minen wes" as in the
morning. 45 coming over altogether.
The trenches were in a terrible state of liquid   This .... son
mud up to the knees in parts. Orders were received for   ceased in
our relief by 2/Gurkhas, which which was completed by 4.30.p.m., our trench
the last Company reached billets by 6.30.p.m., in HARROW Road.   mortar replying
Casualties:- Killed O.R.I.1.(2/39th G.)
Total Casualties todate.

	2/39th G.			1/39th G.		
	K.	W.	M.	K.	W.	M.
B.O's.	4	1	1	1	1	-
" attached.	-	4	-			
I.O's.	3	11	1	1	5	-
" attached.	-	1	-			
O.R.I.	115	527	31	15	143	19
" attached Dogras.	8	8	8			
" " B.M.P.	9	46	6			
" " Tehri S.& M.	7	31	-			
	146	629	47	17	149	19.

27-9-1915.
Billets
HARROW ROAD.

Dull rainy day, with heavy rain in the night.
Roads very heavy and muddy.
Men rested and cleaned up.
Reports still favourable of our advance S. of LA
BASSE and French advance in CHAMPHGNE.

28-9-1915
Billers
HARROW ROAD.

Dull cloudy day.
C.O. went to Brigade Head Quarters to see G.O.C.
Men rested and went on cleaning up accoutrements
etc.   Intimation received to be ready to move tomorrow.
French reported still progressing and guns captured now amount
to 46, and 20000 prisoners.

29-9-1915
Billets
HARROW ROAD.

Dull miserable day with cold N.wind and squalls.

G.O.C.Brigade moved to CALONNE this afternoon. No news of our moving come yet.

Dehra Dun Brigade evidently relieved last night by the 20th Division. Some of the 93rd Punjabis passed our billets from trenches, having missed their way early this morning, to PONT DU HEM.

They looked a most woe begone lot. Certainly this their first experience of the trenches was not a very propitious one.

Some sick and wounded men rejoined today.

Heavy rain continued in the evening and night.

Rumours that the French advance was continued and German Line really pierced, 2 Divisions having pressed through.

The 1.B.O., 1.I.O. and 20 men sent to Garrison MIN POST rejoined last night on relief by 6th K.S.L.I.

30-9-1915
Billets
HARROW ROAD.

A fine day thank Heaven for a change, with a cold N.wind blowing but clouded over later and rained heavily in the night.

Battalion received orders to march 3.p.m. via PONTRIQUEUIL and MERVILLE to new billets at REGNIER L'ECLERE near CALONNE, where it arrived after a cool march of 9 miles at 5.15.p.m.

Billets very nice and people most king and obliging.

News received that the French had made further progress in CHAMPAGNE and had to date taken 100 Guns and 26000 prisoners.

Serial No. 98

Confidential

121/7601

War Diary

of

Garhwal Rifles

FROM 1st October 1915. TO 31st October 1915.

THE GARHWAL RIFLES

1st October.1915.
Billets
REGNIER L'ECLERQ

Fine morning.
Lieut.Clarke taken to Command the Brigade Grenadier Company. These extra regimental appointments always are filled from and so deplete regiments of their Officers. The worst is too how that when a senior or fairly senior officer is wounded or goes sick, you get a 2nd Lieut. I.A.R.Officer in exchange, a very unequal one. So now 2nd Lieut.Rana Jodha Jang has to command a Double Company, and I have only 3 Captains, one 2nd-in-Command, one Commanding a Company and one Adjutant, all the rest are 2nd Lieuts. and I.A.R.Officers.

Some of our good old men returned after a long absence varying from 9 months and under, away at Boulogne and Marseilles. Some of whom were very slightly wounded. From this it is to be inferred that Marseilles is the BELEM of the Penunsular war. The rest of reinforcements from India are absolute boys, and if weather like the present is going to continue they will not stand a winter.

It is getting very cold now at night especially.

G.O.C.Division came round and saw all Officers British and Garhwali at their billets.

Operation orders for move to LEHAMEL on 3rd instant received.

2-10-1915.
Billets
REGNIER LECLERQ

Fine day.
Companies paraded under Company Commanders. Some men from each Company under a Garhwali officer visited MERVILLE close by during the afternoon.

3-10-1915
Billets
MESPLAUX.

Fine day.
Battalion marched at 11.30.a.m., and passed the starting

3-10-1915
(continued)

starting point at 12 noon and took its place in the line of march in Brigade which marched as a whole via PARADIS and LOCON to present billets.
    Regiments are much scattered.
    Billets good but left very dirty by the late occupants who were gunners the wagon pack of a Battery.

4-10-1915
Billets
MESPLAUX.

Dull rainy morning fine later
Companies paraded as usual.
2 B.O's, 1 G.O., and 22 O.R.I., arrived as reinforcements today. All recruits with 13 old men convalescants from Marseilles.
    Sounds of Artillery and rifle fire during the night.

5-10-1915
Billets
MESPLAUX.

Dull cloudy rainy day.
No parades on account of weather.
Fitted rucksacks received.
G.O.C. Brigade came round visiting and saw latest drafts of reinforcements.

6-10-1915
Billets
MESPLAUX.

Dull cold misty morning. It cleared a bit later on.
Companies paraded as usual.
The newly joined recruits paraded for trench digging with all new Officers under 2nd Lieut. Rana Jodha Jang in the afternoon.

7-10-1915
Billets
MESPLAUX

Dull misty day.
Companies paraded. Recruits continued digging trench and filled in the same in the evening.
C.O. went into Brigade Head quarters to see G.O.C., concerning the new bit of the line to be taken up on 11th instant.
Received orders on account of the amalgamation of the 2/8th and 2/3rd G.R., to exchange billets with 2/8th, so that they could be near 2/3rd G.R.

8-10-1915
Billets near
ESSARS.

Dull cloudy day.
Marched 11.a.m. to new billet arriving 12.noon.
2 N.C.O's and 18 men of No.1 Company went to Brigade Grenade Company for instruction at 2.p.m.
Very heavy cannonading all the afternoon and evening to the South showing a battle to be in progress.
Battalion ordered to remain a state of constant readiness.

9-10-1915
Billets. near
ESSARS.

Dull misty day.
C.O. and Company Commanders went out to see new line N. of Canal. The result of yesterday's battle was satisfactory, the Germans who attacked us S. of LA BASSEE Canal, being repulsed and losing heavily.
Companies paraded as usual.

10-10-1915
Billets, near
ESSARS.

Dull misty day clearing up later.
2nd Squad of bomb throwers went for instruction to the Grenadier Company.
Major Lumb rejoined the Battalion from duty at MARSEILLES.
Sounds of heavy bombardment to the S.Midday.

11-10-1915
Trenches
GIVENCHY.

Dull cloudy day but fine till 6 p.m., when it got cloudier and rain fell.
Battalion marched 9.45.a.m.and arrived punctually at 12 noon at VAUXHALL Bridge on canal behind GIVENCHY where guides met us and Companies went up to their respective places.
Relief completed by 1.30.p.m.
C.O.went over to Head Quarters of 1st Seaforths to see G.O.C.,at 4.p.m.
Heavy bombardment to the south all day by the French who were attacking. Our Artillery also bombarded evening S.of canal.
Desultory artillery fire by our guns all night.
No.of rifles in Firing Line, Support and Local Reserve as follows.
    Firing Line.   ...   369.
    Support.   106
    Local Reserve.   ...   314
    Total trench   :   589.
        Strength.   :
Casualties O.R.I.Wounded 1 (2/39th G.)
Total Casualties to date:-

	2/39th G.			1/39th G.		
	K.	W.	M.	K.	W.	M.
B.O,s.,	4	1	1	1	1	-
" attached	-	4	-			
I.O,s.	3	11	1	1	5	-
" attached	-	1	-			
O.R.I.	112	526	29	15	145	15
" Dogras	2	8	8			
" B.M.P.	10	45	6			
" Tehri S &m	7	31	-			
	151	627	45	17	151	15

12.10.15.
Trenches
GIVENCHY.

Fine but very misty morning. C.O. went round trenches arranging about repair of which a lot is needed, so little appears to have been done by last Division.

A little shelling this morning which unfortunately took effect, killing Captain G.W. Burton D.S.O. one of my best officers.

There is a very persistant sniper in our front who is hard to spot. appears to be on the embankment on edge of the canal.

Heavy bombardment during after-noon and evening to S. of the canal.

Casualties Killed B.O. 1. Captain G.W. Burton., D.S.O. 2nd Battalion. O.R.I. One (1/39th G.) Wounded O.R.I.4.(2.1/39 G.) (2.2/39th G.).

Total Casualties todate:-

	2/39th G.			1/39th G.		
	K.	W.	M.	K.	W.	M.
B.O's.	5	1	1	1	1	-
" attached.	-	4	-			
I.O's.	3	11	1	1	5	-
" attached.	-	1	-	16	147	15
O.R.I.	119	528	29			
" attached Dogras.	8	8	8			
" " B.M.P.	10	45	6			
" " Tehri S.& M.	7	31	-			
Total.	152	629	45	18	153	15.

13.10.15.
Trenches
GIVENCHY

Dull misty day with a little rain and fine though cloudy evening. Attack took place S of Canal n direction of LOOS and HULLUCH, the Indian Corps cooperating by sending over Phosphorous smoke bombs. The wind which was favourable at first slightly changed and so smoke rather hung and came back in some parts of the trenches. It is was of course harmless.

Our batteries bombarded the whole day enfilading the German support trenches and 2nd line to the S of Canal. The nearest attack being made by us was on Fosse No.8 again.

Our throwing of bombs elicitated rifle and Machine Gun fire from the enemy but little artillery fire, which did little or no damage. Some minenwerfer bombs were thrown over and breached the parapet in six places but caused no casualties. 2nd Lieut Rana JODHA JANG was very slightly wounded last night in the arm, while making a loophole and came in and was dressed and went out again this morning to supervise the Coy during their smoke attack, and unfortunately wounded again rather more severely in the neck by shrapnel and so has been evacuated to the Field Ambulance. He did very well.

The enemy also let up fires all along the parapet to disperse the gas and smoke.

Heavy bombardment started to the south about 5.30 p.m which sounded like German counter attacks. In their last counter attack they suffered very heavily leaving 7 to 8000 dead on the field in front of our trenches.

Casualties. Wounded B.O.1.O.R.I.4.(2.1/39th G., 2.2/39th G.)

Total Casualties to date:-

	2/39th G.			1/39th G.		
	K.	W.	M.	K.	W.	M.
B.O's.	5	1	1	1	1	-
" attached.	-	5	-			
I.O's.	3	11	1	1	5	-
" attached.	-	1	-			
O.R.I.	119	530	29	16	149	15
" attached Dogras	8	8	8			
" B.M.P.	10	45	6			
" Tehri S.& M.	7	31	-			
	152	632	45	18	155	15

14.10.15.
Trenches
GIVENCHY

Dull misty day, inclined to rain, fine evening.

The smoke from our bombs hung about a bit on the damp night as the wind seemed to have changed shortly after we commenced throwing them, and it came back.

Result of yesterdays battle satisfactory.

HOHENZOLLERN redoubt captured also the quarries and the battle went on during the night and commenced again this morning.

A captured letter found on an officer of the German General Staff recently killed in action and written by a senior officer of the German G.H.Q. is of interest:-

"An army corps Commander writes:-

" Please give instructions that a large number of proclamations be issued to the Prussian soldier. I rely upon the secret order of the Emperor William on this subject being executed. It is necessary to do everything possible to weaken the Russian Army which is escaping from our grasp and withdrawing to an unknown destination. Time is not far distant when our situation will become intolerable and it is possible that we may be compelled to sign a peace treaty, of which the terms may be dictated by our enemies. Men who formerly had dreams of the world no longer think today of taking London Paris, Petrograd, this task will be reserved for our grandsons and not for the heroic German Warriors who are now sacrificing their lives on the endless field of Russia."

The G.C.O. Bde came round trenches and the C.O. accompanied him. They require a lot of repair especially on our right.   Casualties Killed O.R.I.1 (2/39) Wounded O.R.I.1(1/39)

Total Casualties to date:-

	2/39th G.			1/39th G.		
	K.	W.	M.	K.	W.	M.
B.O's.	5	1	1	1	1	-
" attached.	-	5	-			
I.O's.	3	11	1	1	5	-
" attached.	-	1	-			
O.R.I.	120	530	29	16	150	15
" attached Dogras.	8	8	8			
" " B.M.P.	10	45	6			
" " Tehri S.& M.	7	31	-			
	153	632	45	18	156	15.

15-10-1915
Trenches
GIVENCHY.

Dull and very misty damp morning.
Very quiet on our front. Very little fire, artillery or other by us or enemy.
Some little rifle grenade fire by us and by enemy, the latter unfortunately taking effect and killing Captain Bald, 2/3rd G.R., Brigade M.G.Officer, and badly wounding 2/Leicesters M.G.Officer Lieut.Rolfe, who subsequently died.
Work on parapet and reserve dug-outs pushed on.
3/Londons relieved the 4th Cavalry in the 2 posts in our subsection today.
Casualties. Wounded O.R.I.1., (1/39th G.).
Total Casualties to date:-

	2/39th G.			1/39th G.		
	K.	W.	M.	K.	W.	M.
B.O's.	5	1	1	1	1	-
" attached.	-	5	-			
I.O's.	3	11	1	1	5	-
" attached.	-	1				
O.R.I.	120	530	29	16	151	15
" attached Dogras.	8	8	8			
" " B.M.P.	10	45	6			
" " Tehri S.& M.	7	31	-			15
	153	632	45	18	157	15

16-10-1915
Trenches
GIVENCHY.

Dull and mist day. Everything *weeping* wet.
A quiet day and night except for a few rifle grenades being fired.
C.O. went in to see G.O.C. at 1/Seaforths Headquarters at 4.30.p.m., regarding measures for counter attack.
C.O. went round both posts and reserve line and arranged for and inspected work done.
Casualties Killed O.R.I.1 (2/39th G.).
Total Casualties to date:-

	2/39th G.			1/39th G.		
	K.	W.	M.	K.	W.	M.
B.O's.	5	1	1	1	1	-
" Attached.	-	5	-			
I.O's.	3	11	1	1	5	-
" attached.	-	1				
O.R.I.	121	530	29	16	151	15
" attached Dogras.	8	8	8			
" " B.M.P.	10	45	6			
" " Tehri S.& M.	7	31	-			
	154	632	45	18	157	15

17-10-1915
Trenches
GIVENCHY.

Dull damp and very misty and inclined to rain.
Quiet night, the usual sniping and M.G. fire in the early part of the night.
Artillery fire on our part commenced at 5.a.m.
Impossible in this dense must to see anything or do any sniping to try and catch that sniper.
It cleared up a bit about 2.p.m., and C.O. observing with a telescope periscope of Major Samuel, 3/Londons, managed to spot the sniper. First a periscope just over the parapet was visible, and as he fired, a slight faint puff of smoke was visible each time, distinctly showing his position which was behind a sandbagged loophole plate right at the edge of their trench where it rank up slightly to the canal bank. Major Samuel, having observed the place went to try and find a suitable spot to fire from with his telescope rifle.
Afternoon quiet. A working party of the 2/8th I suppose showing themselves, were fired on by shrapnel, on our left.
C.O. had a good inspection of the line the work on which is going on well and the local reserve line getting on well and quickly.
Casualties. Wounded O.R.I.1 (1/39th G.).
Total Casualties todate:-

	2/39th G.			1/39th G.		
	K.	W.	M.	K.	W.	M.
B.O's.	5	1	1	1	1	-
" attached.	-	5	-			
I.O's.	3	11	1	1	5	-
" attached.	-	1				
O.R.I.	121	530	29	16	152	15
" attached Dogras.	8	8	8			
" " B.M.P.	10	45	6			
" " Tehri S.& M.	7	31	-			
	154	632	45	18	158	15

18-10-1915
Trenches
GIVENCHY.

Dull misty damp morning as usual finer afternoon. Quiet day and night on the whole.

18-10-1915
(continued)

In the morning enemy started sending over minenwerfer bombs which making said luckly did no damage. Our howitzers were put on to them which stopped them.

Heard we are to be relieved in this section tomorrow must be a very sudden resolve and to go back to our old spot in RUE DU BOIS, poor old shaltered RUE DU BOIS where we started our trench life first one year ago, Excxxxxx C.O. of the Buffs and Officers came to Head quarters and C.O. took them round.

Casualties Wounded O.R.I.1 (1/39th G.)
Total Casualties todate.

	2/39th G.			1/39th G.		
	K.	W.	M.	K.	W.	M.
B.O's.	5	1	1	1	1	-
" attached.	-	5	-			
I.O's.	3	11	1	1	5	-
" attached.	-	1	-			
O.R.I.	121	530	29	16	153	15
"attached Dogras.	8	8	8			
" " B.M.P.	10	45	6			
" " Tehri S.& M.	7	31	-			
	154	632	45	18	159	15

19-10-1915
Billets
LOCON.

Misty morning, fine later.

The Buffs arrived punctually at the bridge 9.a.m., and relief was completed by 11.a.m.

Companies on relief marched via LA BASSEE Canal to old billets near LOCON.

Very cold wind blowing.

Battalion returns tomorrow to its old line in the trenches opposite RUE DU BOIS, which it went into just a year ago, relieving the 8th Gloucesters of 19th Division.

Very heavy artillery fire to the south at 5.30.p.m., lasting first hour and intermittently a bit later.

Casualties Wounded O.R.I.1(1/39th G.)
Total casualties todate:-

19-10-1915
(continued)

	2/39th G.			1/39th G.		
	K.	W.	M.	K.	W.	M.
B.O's.	5	1	1	1	1	-
" attached.	-	5	-			
I.O's.	3	11	1	1	5	-
" attached.	-	1	-			
O.R.I.	121	530	29	16	154	15
" attached Dogras.	8	8	8			
" " B.M.P.	10	45	6			
" " Tehri S.& M.	7	31	-			
	154	633	45	18	160	15

20-10-1915
Trenches
RUE DU BOIS.

Dull misty day.

C.O. and Company Commanders went to RUE DU BOIS to see and take over new line held by 8/Gloucesters. Got back 2.p.m., Battalion marched 3.45.p.m. and arrived WINDY CORNER 6.p.m., where guides met Companies and took them up. Distribution 2 Companies in firing and support. One in Local Reserve.

Quiet night and little firing during relief.

21-10-1915
Trenches
RUE DU BOIS.

Dull misty morning a bit, Finer later then rain in the evening.

C.O. went round the line which as usual requires a lot of work on it. Parapet had been breached badly in 2 places by Minenwerfer.

G.O.C. came round and arranged work to be done with C.O.

The "Glory Hole" now styled the Boars' Head is as bad as ever; the point is only 15 yards from the German trench, as this was an old bit of German trench that was captured in May last.

21-10-1915.
(Continued)

Their Machine Guns are always active at dusk, tap tapping along the top of our parapet, and just when a certain amount of movement always takes place with men going for rations and water down communication trenches to the RUE DU BOIS.

22-10-1915
Trenches
RUE DU BOIS.

Fine though misty morning, trenches very stictky and sloppy after the rain.
Preparations are being made for the winter, by building up trenches and putting down boards along them on up so that the water can run underneath.
Enemy fired a few shrapnel at 2/3rd on our right and some howitzers on our left. We replied by howitzers and field guns.
2 German aeroplanes seen up. One about 11.a.m., and one 2.30.p.m. The latter sent out 2 rockets, which gave out a shower of stars and the resualt was some shells sent for away in direction of LA COUTURE.
Enemy also shelled RUE DU BOIS at 5.p.m., again and our front trenches with bomb guns to which our bomb guns and trench howitzers replied.
Casualties O.R.I. Killed 1.(1/39th G.) Wounded 1, (1/39th G.).
Total casualties to date:-

	2/39th G.			1/39th G.		
	K.	W.	M.	K.	W.	M.
B.O's.	5	1	1	1	1	-
" attached.	-	5	-			
I.O's.	3	11	1	1	5	-
" attached.	-	1	-			
O.R.I.	121	530	29	17	155	15
" attached Dogras.	8	8	8			
" " B.M.P.	10	45	6			
" " Tehri S.& M.	7	31	-			
	154	632	45	19	161	15.

23-10-1915
Trenches
RUE DU BOIS.

Dull misty morning. Land low lying round about which I suppose accounts for the heavy Drenching mists daily.

C.O. went round front line in the morning and communication trenches. Sappers are doing some work on fire trenches.

Our howitzer Battery put one shell plumpy into our support trench on our right, knocking it all in, but no casualties fortunately no one was just at that part at the time.

German aeroplanes rather busier today 3 being seen, 1 in forenoon and 2 in the afternoon.

Our own Divisional artillery have taking over our front now from 19th Division and have been registering all day.

Casualties O.R.I. Wounded 2. (1/39th G.)
Total casualties to date:-

	2/39th.			1/39th G.		
	K.	W.	M.	K.	W.	M.
B.O's.	5	1	1	1	1	-
" attached.	-	5	-			
I.O's.	3	11	1	1	5	-
" attached.	-	1				
O.R.I.	121	530	30	17	157	15
" attached Dogras/	8	8	8			
" " B.M.P.	10	45	6			
" " Tehri S.& M.	7	39	-			
	154	639	46	19	163	15.

24-10-1915
Trenches
RUE DU BOIS.

Dull misty morning, damp and raw. Rain in the evening. I do not remember such mornings last year in this month.

Our Battery covering our front had a premature burst just over our fire trench and wounded 2 Havildars and 1 Tehri man working nearby.

Names have been called for by Division for 2 Names of Indian Officers to be submitted, it being the intention to send 2 Parties one of Mussalmans and 1 of Hindus, to England to see the country, sent sent in Subadar Balbhadur Sing Gusain and Jemadar Dhirat Sing Pundir's names.

24-10-1915
(continued)

C.O., went round fire, support and communication trenches and met C.R.A., and G.S.O.(1).

Our artillery dropped 2 shrapnel right behind out fire trench, hitting the ground. No excuse for this. Our howitzers shelled Germans salient opposite our BOAR's at 1.45.p.m., with 4.5"s¢

Germans shelled section on our left with 4.2"s and later 5.9" and during afternoon with 5.9"s, all along RUE DU BOIS up to 4.p.m., Several were blind.

Trench mortar Battery takes out today having fired all their rounds. No more at present available for them. Bomb guns also withdrawn to be replid so we have nothing to reply to the enemy with in that line.

Evening Enemy very raw and cold and very wet and damp.
Casualties O.R.I. Wounded 2.(2/39th G.)
Total casualties todate:-

	2/39th G.			1/39th G.		
	K.	W.	M.	K.	W.	M.
B.O's.	5	1	1	1	1	-
" attached.	-	5	-			
I.O's.	3	11	1	1	5	-
" attached.	-	1	-			
O.R.I.	121	532	29	17	157	15
" attached Dogras.	8	8	8			
" " B.M.P.	10	45	6			
" " Tehri S.& M.	7	31	-			
	154	634	45	19	163	15.

25-10-1915
Trenches
RUE DU BOIS.

Dull rainy raw miserable day with east wind. Trenches horribly messy and sticky.

Rations came up a bit later last night owing to road being blocked by Bareilly Brigade who were relieving the Dehra Dun Brigade on our left.

Altogether a most wretched and miserable day. Although the rain was not very heavy tho' presistent, the whole line of trenches got water logged and water begain to rise so men were turned out to drain it, which owing to the trench,

25-10-1915
(continued)

a trench on account of breastwork being a bit lower than ground level made it a difficult job. By digging a big hole the water was got off a bit but some permanent drainage scheme will be necessary for the winter, as water level there is only 1 foot below the surface.

Enemy shelled behind our reserve line and some fairly close to the line itself during the afternoon from 2.30.p.m., to 4.p.m. Our artillery responded vigorously and stopped it as they gave them more than they give us.

The communication trenches are very bad, all falling in because not revetted all the way up at a proper slope. The trenches also giving trouble. Pointed this out to Brigade. They will never stand the winter in their present condition.

26-10-1915
Trenches
RUE DU BOIS.

Fine day after the rain, with cold N.E. wind. Clouded over in the afternoon.

Men put on clearing up and repairing trenches.

German biplane passed over our lines 10.30. p.m., 1.p.m., and 3.p.m.

Enemy shelled vicinity of ORCHARD and PORTARTHUR from 10 a.m. to 3.p.m., with 5.9" Howitzers.

C.R.E., came round trenches., but C.O. do nothing to draw there would require an officer to do the levelling and he had more to spare other work on hand.

Operation orders for our relief on 28th came today, Leicesters to relieve us.

27-10-1915
Trenches
RUE DU BOIS.

Rain again in the night. Dull rainy miserable morning. Wind changed rounded to S.W. Afternoon finer tho' still cloudy about noon.

Enemy shelled section on our left with a few 5.9"howitzers and some shrapnel. Our guns retaliated. Some shells were also sent in to RUE DU BOIS near Factory Post and our Aid Post between 3 and 4.p.m.

Continued repairs to trenches necessary all day and night.

Casualties O.R.I. wounded 2. (1/39th G.)
Total casualties to date:-

	2/39th G.			1/39th G.		
	K.	W.	M.	K.	W.	M.
B.O's.	5	1	1	1	1	-
" attached.	-	5	-			
I.O's.	3	11	1	1	5	-
" attached.		1				
O.R.I.	121	532	39	17	159	15
" attached Dogras.	8	8	8			
" " B.M.P.	10	45	6			
" " Tehri S.& M.	7	31	-			
	154	634	45	19	165	15

28-10-1915
Trenches
RUE DU BOIS.

A dull miserable rainy day again.
Wind changed round to S.W.

The Germans were unusally quiet during the night, why cannot say unless the weather was the cause or relief taking place or what.

A few shells were fired by enemy about 9.30.p.m. towards the Factory and RUE DU BOIS an unusual thing for them to fire at night.

2/Leicesters began to arrive 5.15.p.m., but the relief was very slow as the trenches were nothing but mud and water and some of them seem to have lost their way. It was eventually finished by 9.p.m., and Companies filed out the last Company No.4.Company arriving in billets 11.30.p.m.

C.O.was called in during the afternoon to see G.O.C.Division at Brigade Head-Quarters.

Presistent rain the whole day and night trenches falling in on many places.

Today completes just one year of trench life, the Battalion entering the trenches on the night of 28th-29th October.1914.

29-10-1915
Billets
KING's ROAD.

Dull cloudy day. Billets bad.
Some men had to to bivouac outside in dug-outs and trenches, But as many as possible were crowded into barns so as to get them under cover.
150 men went out on working in CADBURY communication trench in the night, which is full of mud and water, getting back 12.30.a.m.
Enemy shelled road LA COUTURE, RICHEBOURG St VASST between 10.11.p.m.

Dyxx
30-10-1915
Billets
KING's ROAD.

Dull cloudy day.
Companies paraded under Company Commanders. Bomb platoons separately. Practice with Grenade Company as usual with live grenades during the day.

31-10-1915
Billets
KING's ROAD.

Dull rainy day. Cold E. wind blowing, mud everywhere.
Companies paraded as usual.
Bomb platoons went for practice to Grenade Company. Working and carrying parties out as usual.

From

        The Officer Commanding,

            The Garhwal Rifles.

To

        The Chief of the General Staff,

            Army Head-Quarters,

                I N D I A.

No. 766/W.A.   PORT SAID.   D/= 4th Decr.1915.

    Reference:- Field Service Regulations Part II, Chapter XVI., para 140.(2).

    I forward herewith the War Diary of the Battalion under my Command for the month of November.1915.

                                    Lieut.Colonel.

                    Commanding The Garhwal Rifles.

THE GARHWAL RIFLES.

1-11-1915
Billets
KING's ROAD.

Cold and dull with intermittent heavy rain.
Brigade Major's Message No.387, dated 31-10-15, intimating that Meerut Division will embark shortly at Marseilles for an unknown destination received last night.
3.a.m. to 4 a.m., heavy cannonading to South.
Company parades dismissed owing to rain., men employed cleaning accoutrements. Bomb Platoon went for practice to Grenade Company. Working and carrying parties out as usual.
Lieut.Colonel D.H.Drake-Brockman and Captain.P.T.Etherton proceeded on short leave to England.
Operation Order No.97 dated 1.11.15, received ordering Regiment to proceed to Billets at PARADIS.

2-11-1915
Billets
PARADIS.

Dull rainy weather, thick mud everywhere.
Marched to PARADIS 12.30.p.m., on relief by 4th Seaforths., arrived 3.p.m., Billets comfortable. Intimation received that the Garhwal Brigade will be the first to entrain for MARSEILLES.

3-11-1915
Billets
PECQUEUR.

Weather fine, some sunshine. Marched in Brigade to Billets about THIENNES. Left old billets at 7.30.a.m. Settled into new billets at 3.p.m., in village of PECQUEUR.
Captain G.R.Mainwaring, 2nd Lieut.C.W.Hayne and Lieut.R.T.Collins proceeded on short leave to England.

5-11-1915
Billets
PECQUEUR.

Weather fine in morning rain in afternoon.
Companies exercised in Route marching in morning and employed in cleaning equipment in afternoon.
Lieut. A.E. Clarke rejoined from Commanding the Grenadier Company. Lieutenant Colonel D.H. Drake Brockman, C.M.G., rejoined from short leave in England during the night 5th-6th.

6-11-1915.
Billets
PECQUEUR.

Fine cold frosty morning.
Companies went out route marching in the forenoon and practised entraining in the afternoon under C.O.
Intimation received that the Brigade would probably entrain tomorrow, Indian regiments first in following order.
Garhwal Rifles, 2/8th G.R., 2/3rd G.R., commencing at 2 p.m., and after at 2 hours interval.
All Officers on leave rejoined during the night.

7-11-1915
Billets
PECQUEUR.

Cold day and cloudy with sunny intervals.
Battalion received definite orders to entrain entrain at THIENNES at 16.25 p.m. Transport and baggage being loaded up at 1.p.m.
The Corps Commander Lt. Genl. Sir Charles Henderson K.C.B. and G.O.C. Brigade Br. Genl. Blackader, D.S.O., came down to see the Battalion off.
The train left punctually at 16.25.p.m., for Marseilles.
100 men and 2 B.O's of 2/Leicesters were entrained in the same train and left with the Battalion
A very complimentary message from the Field Marshal Commanding-in-Chief received thro' the Brigade. Congratulating the Brigade on its excellent work in France and wishing it success.

8-11-1915
Enroute
MARSEILLES.

Cold cloudy day.
Halts were made at VILLENEUVE ST.GEORGES and MONTARGIS.
No arrangements at all for men's latrines nor halts for British officers food. This had to be snatched as best one could.

9-11-1915
En-route
MARSEILLES.

Cold misty morning. Fine later.
A halt was made at PARAY LE MONIAL during the night at 4.a.m., tea distributed to the men. These arrangements by the French Government were very good, but officers had great difficulty in getting anything as there were most inconvenient halts and no cooking or heating arrangements on the train.

10-11-1915
MARSEILLES.

Dull day with some rain.   hours
Train arrived very late at 2 a.m., six behind time. Battalion was detrained at once and marched to the docks and embarked on S.S.ARONDA and S.S.COCONADA.
Battalion Head-quarters and ½ Battalion being on the former ship with the 107th Pioneers.
G.O.C.Garhwal Brigade also travelled by this ship.
No naval escort accompanied the ship.
S.S.COCONADA left 10.a.m.,and ARONDA 12.noon. S.S.ARONDA was very nice and clean and heaps of accomodation.
Lieut.Colonel D.H.Drake Brockman.,C.M.G., was O.C.Troops and Captain G.R.Mainwaring Ship's Adjutant and Lieut.F.N.Fox Ship's Quartermaster.

11-11-1915
En-route
EGYPT
S.S.ARONDA.

Fine day with strong breeze and somewhat rough sea
Usual morning inspection at 10.a.m. A good number of men sea sick.

12-11-1915
En-route
EGYPT
S.S.ARONDA.

Fine day, less wind and calmer.
All ranks consequently more cheery. Usual inspections 10.a.m.
Passed Sicily on the port side at 10.a.m. and Malta on the starboard side at 4.p.m.

13-11-1915
En-route
EGYPT
S.S.ARONDA.

Fine day, nice breeze and calmer.
Usual inspection 10.a.m.
Cleaning up off accoutrements and rifles.
Due to arrive Alexandria monday. 15th about 7.a.m.

14-11-1915.
En-route
EGYPT
S.S.ARONDA.

Fine calm day.
Usual parade and inspection.
Passed cruiser (British India vessel employed navy by nave and armed) at 4.p.m. who came up and informed us that an Enemy's submarine had been sighted off Rasel TYN on Thusday xxxxxxxxxxxxxxxxxxxxxxxxxxxx
xxxxxxx on African coast about 80 miles from where we met the cruiser.

15-11-1915
En route
EGYPT
S.S.ARONDA.

Fine day, calm cloudy.
Arrived Alexandria 9.a.m. and anchored in naibour. After some time a Staff officer came on board but he knew nothing about us and only could say he thought we should have gone on to Port Said.
A naval Staff officer also came later but he gave no news. An A.P.M., also turned up to arrest all civilians who had come on board. There consisted of 2 newspaper boys who were taken away.
Eventually orders came and we left for Port Said 4.30.p.m.

16-11-1915
PORT SAID.

Fine calm day. Arrived Port Said 5.a.m. Disembarked 10.a.m. and *march* to camp close to docks. Men were accomodated in temporary huts being built for British troops coming sometime. Officers had to occupy the cook houses. Battalion as far as orders stand is to relieve the 56th Rifles here. All guards were taken over and these are numerous and duties heavy. Their detachment across the harbour at salt works was not relieved yet.

Battalion appears to be split up a lot which is unavoidable.

The Coconada not having arrived and all mess kit and servants being on board her., Officers used the 56th Rifles mess by kindness of C.O. and Officers.

17-11-1915
PORT SAID.
CANAL DEFENCES. 3rd SECTION.

rather hot Fine day, cool in the morning and evening. still hottest in the day but getting better daily.

S.S.Coconada arrived 10.a.m.and No.3 Coy., under Captain Etherton was able to get off in time to relieve the 56th Rifles at the Salt Works during the day.

H.Coy., under Lieut.Clarke went off 12.50. p.m., by train to TINEH and RASELAISH to relieve detachments of 56th Rifles there. G.Coy.will follow tomorrow.

Br.Gen.Blackader, D.S.O., was informed verbally that we would return to France and the Brigade be handed over to Major Gen. Sir V.Cox., K.C.M.G., with 3 other regiments making 7 altogether, with Head Quarters at EL KANTARA.

C.O. met General Sir.V.Cox this morning at POST Commandant Office. He had served under him in the *Imperial* service troops in 1900.

18-11-1915
PORT SAID.
CANAL DEFENCES. 3rd SECTION.

Fine cloudy day., and cool.

G.Coy., left 8.20.a.m, with 56th Rifles for their post TINEH

C.O.went over to Salt Works to inspect and see if there was sufficient room to accomodate another Company.

18-11-1915
(continued)

when the British Division arrive here, necessitating the transfer of Battalion Head Quarters.
There was plenty of room and one hut empty which would accomodate half a Company.
Heard that the British Division which had left Marseilles for here, had also en route been directed to Salonika.
Information received that the S.S.URLANA with our 1st Line Transport Carts is due tomorrow. Our mess equipment was all put on board this ship, so we have been without any and had to hire.
Companies paraded under Company Commanders.

19-11-1915
PORT SAID.
CANAL DEFENCES. 3rd SECTION.

Fine day with clouds and strong breeze which makes so much dust owing to being en-camped on sand.
Companies paraded under Company Commanders for smartening and setting up drill. Youngsters of last batch of reinforcement under the Adjutant. These are very bad & cant handle a arm
All men went by turns to the sea and had a good wash which was badly needed.
General Sir George Younghusband handed over to General Sir Herbert Cox and left today.
S.S.URLANA arrived and our horses and Mess kit were got off.

20-11-1915
PORT SAID.
CANAL DEFENCES 3rd SECTION.

Fine day, strong breeze and very dusty.
C.O. and 2nd-in-Command went to post TINEH to inspect. Found it required a lot of repairing and so ordered O.B.Lieut.Clarke to commence pulling down and rebuilding the sand-bag parapets. Returned in the evening by an empty goods train as they would not stop the mail without sanction from G.O.C.ISMAILIA.
Companies paraded as usual under Company Commanders.

21-11-1915
PORT SAID
CANAL DEFENCES 3rd SECTION.

Fine warmer day and somewhat steamy after the strong wind. A nice breeze started later about midday.
C.O. called in the morning on General Sir H. Cox., K.C.M.G. prior to departure of the latter to EL KANTARA for a few days, where his Head quarters and greater portion of his command is.
Companies paraded as usual and young soldiers went for a bath.
2 British regiments came ashore and camped near us for a couple of days to get a bath and walk round while the ship H.M.S. "Terrible" was being coaled and cleaned up.

22-11-1915
PORT SAID
CANAL DEFENCES 3rd SECTION.

Fine day cool breeze.
Companies paraded under Company Commanders.
Some Garhwali officers, N.C.O's, and men were taken over H.M.S. IMPLACABLE today.

23-11-1915
PORT SAID.
CANAL DEFENCES 3rd SECTION.

Fine day tho' cloudy with cool breeze.
Companies paraded as usual under Company Commanders.
C.O. and 2nd-in-Command and quartermaster went over to SALTWORKS inspecting posts and defences returning to Camp 3. p.m.
Br. General Blackader., D.S.O., left today for France. The whole Brigade were very sorry to lose him having confidence in him as a man of decision and who knew his own mind. In wishing the C.O. good luck, which was heartily reciprocated he said how sorry he was not to be able to come and see us all before going but the regiment being split up so made this impossible.
Head that a small column had been sent out from KANTARA and had encountered some Turks some of whom were killed and some taken prisoners by us.

24-11-1915
PORT SAID
CANAL DEFENCES 3rd SECTION.

Cloudy morning clear later. Cool breeze.
Companies paraded as usual under Company Commanders.
Patrol on Railway Line caught one man who tried to bolt. He was handed over to Post Commandant Port Said.

25-11-1915
PORT SAID
CANAL DEFENCES 3rd SECTION.

Fine morning; strong wind all last night and all day raising a lot of dust, which made the night uncomfortable; and which blow the grass "Chappar" huts in which the Officers were about a good deal. It clouded over in the afternoon.
Companies paraded under Company Commanders, morning and afternoon now.
Khaki clothing received and issued, also advance of pay to all ranks.

26-11-1915
PORT SAID.
CANAL DEFENCES 3rd SECTION.

Fine day, strong breeze and dust storms appear to be hovering around which are the cause of this wind, and may be pretending rain.
Major General Sir Herbert Cox., K.C.M.G., accompanied by the C.O., inspected the SALT-WORKS this morning at 11.a.m., returning at 1.p.m.
Result of action by Mysore Lancers opposite Kantara very successful the bag including mential Seckh.
S.S.ARABIA with English mails arrived, and had on board several British officers of Indian Army returning India including Lieut.Col.Cassells and Lieut.Meclean, 2/8th G.R. and 2nd Lieut.RANA JODHA JANG BAHADUR, of Tehri Sappers attached to us, was going on 4 months leave.
Companies paraded as usual under Company Commanders.

www.ingramcontent.com/pod-product-compliance
Lightning Source LLC
Chambersburg PA
CBHW080805010526
44113CB00013B/2329